MW01012087

PROOF OF GUILT

PROOF

of GUILT

BARBARA GRAHAM *and the* POLITICS
of EXECUTING WOMEN *in* AMERICA

Kathleen A. Cairns

UNIVERSITY OF NEBRASKA PRESS | LINCOLN AND LONDON

Library of Congress
Cataloging-in-Publication Data
Cairns, Kathleen A., 1946–
Proof of guilt : Barbara Graham
and the politics of executing
women in America / Kathleen
A. Cairns. p. cm.
Includes bibliographical
references.
ISBN 978-0-8032-3009-5
(cloth: alk. paper)
1. Graham, Barbara, 1923–1955.
2. Women murderers — California — Case studies. 3. Women
death row inmates — United
States — Case studies. 4. Capital
punishment — United States.
I. Title.
HV8701.G73C35 2013
364.66092 — dc23   2012039747

Set in Sabon Next by
Laura Wellington.
Designed by Nathan Putens.

Contents

Illustrations

Author's Note

VERY FEW PEOPLE profess neutrality when it comes to the death penalty, and I am no exception. During my working life I've been on both sides of the issue. As a young newspaper reporter in the post-Watergate era, I was a staunch opponent of capital punishment, believing it to be a barbaric relic of a medieval past. Then I was assigned to the 1982 Los Angeles trial of "Freeway Killer" William Bonin. A thoroughly repulsive individual, he kidnapped and murdered at least a dozen teenage boys and young men, whose bodies he dumped along Southern California freeways. Every morning the victims' mothers sat huddled together inside the courtroom. Bonin looked like such an ordinary man—pale, pudgy, and nondescript—yet he had done horrific things to their young sons. Good riddance, I thought, as jurors sentenced him to death. I had switched sides and now favored the death penalty.

In 1983, still on the pro-capital-punishment side of the issue, I wrote a newspaper series about the death penalty in California. I traveled to San Quentin and peered into the gas chamber. I met face-to-face with a death-row inmate and solicited letters from condemned men, whose scrawled missives were filled with misspellings and mangled grammar and reeked of self-pity. Astoundingly—considering that I was an avowed feminist and later chose to research and write on condemned women—it never occurred to me to ponder whether women had been executed in California. I also never questioned whether innocent people had been executed. Virtually all of my condemned correspondents claimed they had been framed. Had any of them been?

Neither omission seems surprising in retrospect. In 1983 there were no women on death row, and no one had been executed in California for nearly two decades. With a state supreme court that consistently overturned death sentences, it seemed unlikely that an execution would occur anytime soon. In fact, it took another nine years and a conservative resurgence for the state to resume executions. By 1992, when Robert Alton Harris became the first person executed in California in twenty-five years, my support for capital punishment had begun to waver. Harris, like Bonin, had been thoroughly despicable. He had managed to live fourteen years longer than the two teenaged boys he had kidnapped and shot in the back. And yet something seemed wrong with a system in which dozens of journalists clamored for credentials to watch a man's death while a San Francisco television station—unsuccessfully, as it turned out—sought a court order enabling it to broadcast the event to an audience of millions.

For me, the death penalty existed largely as an abstraction until 2002, when I began research for a book on Nellie Madison, the first woman on death row in California. I knew by then that the state had executed four women. Madison was not among them. The fact that she had escaped the ultimate punishment seemed to border on miraculous. She had gone on trial in June 1934, charged with murdering her husband. Charles Fricke, the judge who later presided over the trials of Barbara Graham and Caryl Chessman, had presided in Madison's case as well.

Fricke had clearly favored the prosecution, going so far as to take the stand as a prosecution witness. Madison's attorney bordered on incompetent, yet appellate justices were willing to overlook egregious legal shenanigans in order to uphold her death sentence. Only a last-minute grassroots movement, fueled by revelations of extreme physical and psychological abuse on the part of Eric Madison, saved Nellie Madison's life. The governor reprieved her, literally days before her execution. This introduction to the bizarre and labyrinthine politics of capital punishment tipped me toward the abolitionists' side of the argument. I have remained there ever since.

By 2006 I was reading books on death-penalty cases and following debates on blogs and elsewhere about the capricious, arbitrary, and inequitable nature of capital trials. I decided to enter the discussion by choosing an executed woman and writing about her. Enter Barbara Graham, arguably California's most famous executed individual, male or female. Examining Graham's life, trial, appeal, and execution revealed just how easily police and prosecutors—with help from publicity-seeking judges and stool-pigeon conspirators promised immunity from prosecution—could rig the process. Graham's case also revealed the role of the media in shaping perceptions of guilt and innocence. Was she guilty? It is impossible to know with any degree of certainty. But she was condemned following a grossly unfair trial. That alone should have earned her a reprieve from death.

Graham's case also raised an issue that has been virtually ignored in all of the public hand wringing about capital punishment. Proponents argue that execution brings a sense of closure to the families and friends of victims. What about the families of the executed? I thought of this frequently while writing this book. Barbara Graham had three young sons when she died in 1955. She fervently hoped, she said just before her death, that they would never know what happened to her. She could not have foreseen just how long her story would remain in the public realm—in film, books, proposed legislation, even in song—making it all but impossible for her children to remain ignorant of her fate.

This book is dedicated to the children of America's executed men and women. They were victims too.

Introduction

HER GIVEN NAME was Barbara Elaine Ford, but her friends called her Bonnie right up to the end, when she walked into the gas chamber at San Quentin. It was 11:31 a.m. on June 3, 1955. By then the world knew her by another name: Barbara Graham. It knew that she was the third woman executed by the State of California, and by far the prettiest and the youngest. It knew that she dressed carefully for the occasion, wore a mask, and received two last-minute stays. The world also knew that it had taken her eight minutes to die.

Just shy of her thirty-second birthday, Graham had left behind a mess of a life. She had married four men. She had borne three sons. All of her sons lived with other people, and she had not seen the older two for several years. She had been in and out of trouble since her early teens, and her rap sheet spanned much of California. Most of her arrests were for misdemeanors, but she spent nearly a year in San Francisco County Jail for perjury.

The final arrest did her in. Los Angeles police picked up Graham and two men, Emmett Perkins and John Santo, on May 4, 1953, and charged them with murder in connection with a robbery gone wrong. Reporters and photographers quickly leapt on the story. They virtually ignored Perkins and Santo, both violent career criminals, but clamored for access to the woman they dubbed Bloody Babs and the Titian-Haired Murderer.

Her trial in Los Angeles Superior Court in August and September 1953 played to standing-room-only crowds hoping for a glimpse of a real-life femme fatale. Graham acted out the role as if born into it. Prosecutors accused her of trying to sway male jurors by "sitting there, looking pretty," and they worked diligently to squelch any possibility of empathy. They need not have worried. Graham proved to be her own worst enemy; she always had been.

If events had taken their normal course, Barbara Graham would have faded from public view shortly after her execution. She would have been merely a statistic, the thirty-seventh of forty-two women executed in the United States in the twentieth century. But history veered off center and Graham did not disappear. In fact, her story was being rewritten even before her death. As her appeal worked its way through higher courts, a handful of journalists visited her in prison. A few came away shaken, believing that she had been framed.

Following her death, one journalist, Edward S. Montgomery of the San Francisco *Examiner*, initiated a campaign to posthumously clear her name. In 1956 he contacted Hollywood producer Walter Wanger with a proposal for a movie. *I Want to Live!* was released in fall 1958 to nearly unanimous raves. Filmmakers kept the ending but altered the rest of the story in significant ways. Their Barbara Graham emerged as an innocent woman railroaded to her death by a punitive male bureaucracy that was heavily invested in making her pay for her easy sexuality, cocky attitude, and life of small-time crime. The film catapulted Graham onto the top rung in the hierarchy of executed American women, the only one with a Hollywood fan club.

Montgomery also helped to write a book about Graham's case. *I Want to Live! The Analysis of a Murder* leaned heavily on Graham's horrific childhood with a mother who abused and neglected her. In this version, Graham loved her children. She listened to jazz and tragic operas. She read and wrote poetry. She struggled to do right, to marry, to settle down and raise a family, but her past always caught up with her. The book became a best seller.

San Francisco Chronicle reporter Bernice Freeman also featured Graham in a book, *The Desperate and the Damned*, recounting her experiences writing about condemned inmates. Graham may have been "amoral" in many life choices, but, Freeman insisted, she had not been capable of murder.[1]

Police and prosecutors who had tried Graham might have simply ignored the movie, the books, and even the song, "The Ballad of Barbara Graham," by songwriter Val Norman. But they did not. Authorities feared, with some justification, that sympathy for Graham might help abolitionists in their quest to end the death penalty in California and thus play a role in a larger national effort.[2]

To thwart this possibility, law enforcement officials decried *I Want to Live!* as a fictional whitewash. One of Graham's two prosecutors insisted that she had confessed to the murder before her execution. He also recruited a newspaper reporter to write magazine articles and a book. *The Case of Barbara Graham* appeared in 1961, six years after Graham's execution. It cast her as a villain, only this time even worse than the femme fatale of her trial. The book sold a few copies and soon disappeared from view. It seemed that Graham finally was destined to disappear as well, moving out of the spotlight that kept her at the center of a relentless tug-of-war over her guilt or innocence.

Graham, in fact, did begin a slow fade-out, but her presence hovered over capital-punishment debates during much of the 1960s. She had put a human face on what seemed, to many people, to be a theoretical discussion about an abstract topic. Her story is riveting on its own, but her role as catalyst in facilitating dialogue about such an important topic makes her story relevant still, even though nearly sixty years have passed since her death.

Graham's case raised many thorny and troubling issues about the death penalty that remain relevant today, among them its arbitrary application, the power of police and prosecutors to engage in questionable tactics, the role of media in constructing images that shape public attitudes, and the execution of condemned inmates absent incontrovertible proof of guilt. Her case holds particular resonance because of her gender. Women account for less than 1 percent of executions in America, making Graham a valuable subject, both from a sociological and a historical perspective.

Media accounts of condemned women generally posit them as one-dimensional archetypes. Close examination of Graham's case offers a more complex and nuanced view, and it provides a window into an era when a female murder defendant's sexual persona could make or break her chance of escaping conviction, even condemnation.[3]

Any examination of Graham begs the question: Of all the women executed in the United States in the twentieth century, why was she the one who so captivated abolitionists, journalists, and filmmakers? Such sympathetic treatment seems particularly oxymoronic, given the timing of her case. The early Cold War period was not known for hand wringing over the guilt or innocence of condemned men and women. The public had not yet grown accustomed to the prospect of wrongful convictions and executions.

The executions that fueled debate centered on individuals condemned for crimes other than murder. Caryl Chessman, for example, was executed by the State of California for kidnapping, and New York housewife Ethel Rosenberg was executed by the federal government, alongside her husband Julius, for espionage.

In the 1950s most people, at least if they were white and middle class, generally trusted the police and courts. Few individuals believed or suggested that white men and women convicted of murder were victims of miscarried justice. The system was supposed to work for them. If they were executed, they were guilty, plain and simple.

And yet the system clearly had not always worked. In the years after World War II a few ambitious politicians rode roughshod over the lives of ordinary, law-abiding men and women. Opinion makers, journalists, and filmmakers viewed these political machinations from front-row seats—some uncomfortably close to the action. Barbara Graham's trial occurred at the height of the so-called McCarthy era. By the time of her execution, Wisconsin senator Joseph McCarthy had been brought down and no longer held the power to destroy lives and reputations. A few journalists and filmmakers might have felt emboldened to challenge other forms of authority, including courts and the justice system.

But, again, why Barbara Graham? If mainstream journalists and filmmakers felt compelled to turn their attention to controversial cases involving women, why not Ethel Rosenberg? Scant evidence existed to connect her with espionage activities. Civil rights groups, liberals, and abolitionists around the world protested the Rosenbergs' death sentences during their lifetimes, and serious scholars wrote of them afterward. But few mainstream journalists and no powerful filmmakers rushed into the breach to proclaim Ethel's innocence to the world.

Graham obviously possessed some attributes that Rosenberg lacked, namely her striking good looks and sexuality. It would be hard to overestimate the importance of these factors. Virtually every story focused on Graham's appearance. Reporters wrote about her hair, her clothes, her makeup, the way she walked, and even how she held her cigarettes. Graham also lived in Los Angeles, the setting for many popular noir films, and she had a riveting backstory.

Ethel Rosenberg had been a dutiful wife—possibly too dutiful. Graham had a much more interesting resume. She had been, according to one alliterative account, "a mother, a murderess, a mobster, and a moll."[4] The combination of "mother" and "moll" proved irresistible to journalists and filmmakers. Graham was also white. Historically, few mainstream journalists or members of the public in general have paid much attention to the executions of men and women of color. But other executed women had been beautiful, white, and possessed interesting life stories. Toni Jo Henry, for example, was electrocuted by Louisiana in 1942. Henry, like Graham, had been a prostitute. No one protested her execution.

There had to be something about Barbara Graham, and her case, that turned fascination and titillation into activism and outrage. In fact, there was. In addition to beauty and sexuality, Graham was one of only two white American women in the twentieth century executed with no conclusive proof that she committed the murder in question. Controversy also emerged in the case of Anna Antonio, who was executed in New York in August 1934 for hiring two men to kill her husband. Debate arose only toward the end of Antonio's appeals, when one of the killers changed his story.

The murder for which Graham was condemned had numerous problems from the beginning. Five people initially were named as suspects. One talked to police, got Graham's name wrong, was kidnapped, and was never seen or heard from again. A second talked to police and was granted immunity by prosecutors, but he changed his story between his police statement and trial testimony.[5]

Since no weapons, fingerprints, or any other physical evidence linked Graham to the killing, police set her up in a sting operation as she awaited trial and then surprised her in court with wiretapped conversations. From a distance of nearly sixty years, it is impossible to know why prosecutors were so desperate to condemn her. Perhaps their real targets were her codefendants, two violent recidivists suspected of murder in other jurisdictions as well as in Los Angeles. But they faced a quandary: Could they ask jurors to vote death sentences for the two male defendants, but vote something else for the female?

This strategy might send the wrong message: it would suggest that Graham's gender made her different. Or, possibly, her sordid past led prosecutors to use her in order to send a message to other marginal characters: this is what happens to reprobates who commit crimes and consort with hardened criminals.

Graham's court-appointed trial attorney vehemently protested many police and prosecution tactics, but he found no sympathetic ear in superior court judge Charles Fricke. Fricke's nickname revealed all that anyone needed to know about him. Defense attorneys called him San Quentin Charlie, and he boasted of sending more defendants to the gas chamber than any other judge in California.

Ironically, had Graham not been condemned but instead sentenced to a long prison term, abolitionists would have had a much slimmer peg on which to hang their arguments about injustice, and Hollywood would have had no incentive to feature her in a film. The notion that the system abused her provided activists with ammunition. "I felt if they could do those things to Barbara Graham and get away with it, they could do [them] to each one of us," her appellate attorney, Al Matthews, said after her execution.[6]

Continuing controversy over Graham and a few others enabled abolitionists to chip away at the death penalty in California and at the national level. On several occasions between 1955 and 1964 lawmakers seemed on the verge of abolition but fell short of the needed votes. The pendulum, nonetheless, was swinging in that direction. In 1957 California became the first state to mandate bifurcated trials, in which defendants convicted in capital cases were given the chance at second minitrials to present mitigating evidence. By the mid-1960s, executions across the country had dropped into the single digits and abolitionists had shifted to a new strategy — challenging the constitutionality of capital punishment.

In 1972 both the California Supreme Court and the United States Supreme Court abolished the death penalty as cruel and unusual punishment. The U.S. high court ordered states to rewrite their laws, specifying exactly what crimes committed under what circumstances qualified for the ultimate punishment. Good fortune for abolitionists proved fleeting, however. Many states, including California, soon implemented new laws.

By the end of the 1970s, thirty-five states had reinstated capital punishment. Death rows filled and executions resumed. Since 1977 more than 1,200 men and 12 women have been executed in the United States. California's death rows currently hold 700 men and 20 women. California has executed 13 men, but no women.

Few people today recall Graham's trial, appeal, and execution, though writers occasionally mention her in books and articles about post–World War II Los Angeles noir. Film devotees may watch *I Want to Live!* and ponder whether the Graham character was even a real person. Legal and criminal justice scholars are drawn to the film as a cultural artifact. A few use her case as a touchstone to analyze how the politics of execution have, or have not, changed.

In many ways, it seems that not much has changed at all. Despite the new laws, rules, and safeguards implemented since the 1950s, the politics of life and death remain a crapshoot. Prosecutors engage in underhanded tactics. Some trial attorneys are incompetent. Accomplices are given incentives to testify. Innocent people are condemned. On the other hand, though, DNA evidence and systemic safeguards can also exonerate the wrongly convicted.

A new generation of abolitionists again struggles to find a way to end the death penalty in America. Barbara Graham might seem irrelevant to this battle. To prominent men in 1950s Los Angeles she must have seemed irrelevant as well. Graham was a nobody. She had few resources and no friends in high places. She was the kind of person easily shipped off to prison, even the gas chamber, with no challenges, questions, or political ramifications.

And yet friends somehow had appeared—some of them men with powerful connections. Graham's newfound allies managed to craft a competing narrative in which she was the abused child, the sad and lonely young woman who longed for love, a prostitute but definitely not a killer. This new narrative trumped dire warnings about vicious criminals and victims and caused male authorities embarrassment, humiliation, and impotent rage. The judicial system has always been reluctant to execute women. Barbara Graham serves as a lingering reminder of the potential consequences of choosing the wrong ones.

This book is divided into ten chapters. The first three discuss the murder that set Graham on the path to execution, her life leading up to trial, and the trial itself. Chapters 4 and 5 examine her appeal, her execution, and some of the journalists who came to question her guilt. Chapter 6 places Graham's case in context alongside those of other women executed in the United States between 1900 and 1955.

Chapter 7 discusses the film *I Want to Live!* Chapters 8 and 9 shift the focus to the abolition movement of the 1950s and early 1960s and Graham's part in it. Graham disappears from the narrative through much of Chapter 9, but her absence does not mitigate her importance to the movement. Chapter 10 examines the cases of women now on death row in California and details the cases of the twelve women executed in the United States since 1984. The fact that California has not executed any women since 1962 can be attributed, in part, to the lingering consequences of Graham's execution.

PROOF OF GUILT

1

A Murder in Burbank

MABLE MONAHAN LIVED in a residential neighborhood of immaculately landscaped yards and spacious homes in Burbank, California, about a dozen miles north of Los Angeles. Her tidy white stucco house straddled the corner of West Parkside Avenue and Orchard Street. A sturdy row of decorative hedges hugged the house on three sides. A concrete walkway led from the street to the front door, which was partially obscured by a latticed trellis covered by climbing vines. Despite the area's low crime rate, Monahan took extraordinary precautions to ensure her safety.

A six-foot tall concrete wall separated her front and back yard, and the two areas connected via a gate that opened onto the driveway. Monahan always kept it locked. Every Wednesday morning her landscape gardener, Mitchell Truesdale, performed the same ritual at Monahan's home: he mowed the front lawn, knocked on the front door, retrieved the gate key, unlocked the gate, immediately relocked it from the inside, mowed, edged and clipped the backyard, locked up again, and returned the key.

Monahan also installed large floodlights under the eaves on the part of her home that could be seen from the street. She turned them on each night at sunset and turned them off when she rose in the morning. She kept her living room drapes tightly shut at night so that no one could see inside the house, and she installed safety latches on all the windows and double bolts on the doors. The front door held a small, unobtrusive peephole located at eye level.

Monahan never discussed the basis for her fears with friends or family members. But several factors may have enhanced her sense of vulnerability. Her daughter Iris had been married to Las Vegas gambler Luther "Tutor" Scherer, well-known for his high-rolling lifestyle and reputed mob connections; the Scherers had lived in the Burbank house before divorcing in the late 1940s.

Monahan was a widow in late middle age who lived alone, and she suffered from a slight disability as the result of a decades-earlier automobile crash. The accident had ended her somewhat colorful career as a professional roller skater and palm reader who toured with her late husband George on the national vaudeville circuit. At sixty-five she was still attractive, with a slender figure and short, curly, grayish hair, but she walked slowly and with a slight limp. Often she used a cane.[1]

As it turned out, Monahan's fears were justified. It seems, in retrospect, that she possessed a sixth sense about the disaster that would befall her. Inexplicably, her premonitions and many precautions did not prevent her from opening her front door to a stranger just after dark one cool evening in March 1953. That split-second decision cost Monahan her life and catapulted her into public view as part of a sensational murder case, the significance of which far outlasted its time and place in history.

Six months after Monahan's death, jurors in Los Angeles County convicted Barbara Graham, Jack Santo, and Emmett Perkins of her murder. Twenty months after that, Graham, Santo, and Perkins went to their own deaths in the gas chamber at San Quentin. All because friends of Santo's heard rumors that Tutor Scherer had stashed one hundred thousand dollars in a safe in his former home.[2]

On Monday, March 9, 1953, the last day of Mable Monahan's life, she awoke just after 11:00 a.m. She had spent the previous night playing her weekly poker game with a group of women friends. One of them, Merle Leslie, had driven her home after midnight. Leslie was tired and decided to stay over at Monahan's. Shortly after 2:00 p.m. on Monday, Leslie left for home, promising to check in with Monahan later. When she phoned shortly before 7:00 that night, Monahan said she had eaten dinner and was sitting in her den, reading *The Purple Pony Murder*, a mystery novel. She was tired and planned to turn in early, she said. It was the last time Leslie spoke to, or saw, her friend.[3]

About 11:15 a.m. on Wednesday March 11, the gardener, Truesdale, arrived for his weekly appointment. He noticed the curtains still closed and the floodlights still on. As he approached the house to retrieve the backyard key and notify Monahan about the floodlights, he saw that the front door stood slightly ajar. He knocked. When no one answered, he pushed open the door and peered into the house. The entryway led directly to a spacious living room and separate dining room. Truesdale saw that the house had been ransacked. Furniture in both rooms had been upended.

Further back, he noticed drawers hanging askew, their contents strewn across the floor. Carpeting had been ripped up, and the walls and baseboards looked as though they had been sprayed by pellet guns or gouged with sharp instruments. Truesdale stepped gingerly into the house. What he saw sent him reeling backward in horror. "There was blood all over a partition that protrudes into the living room," he said later. He ran from the house and called Carl Lane, a friend and officer on the Burbank police force.[4]

Lane arrived within minutes and Truesdale reluctantly followed him back inside. Toward the end of a long hallway that led to two bedrooms, they found Monahan, fully clothed in a print dress and lying face down, obviously dead, the bottom half of her body obscured by the open door to a linen closet. A bloody, torn pillowcase partially covered her head, held in place by a piece of cloth tied around her neck. Her hands were bound together behind her back with another strip of cloth. Lane quickly called for back up.

While his colleagues examined the body, Lane searched the house. In Monahan's bedroom closet he found a purse containing a wallet with nearly five hundred dollars in cash. An ornate carved box sat on top of her dressing table. It held several pieces of expensive jewelry: a Bulova watch encrusted with four diamonds, a horseshoe-shaped clasp covered in diamonds, and three rings, all embedded with jewels; their estimated value was ten thousand dollars. Lane concluded that robbery probably was not the motive for Monahan's murder, though the perpetrators obviously were looking for something.[5]

Police removed the pillowcase. Monahan's head bore several gaping wounds, accounting for most of the blood. It appeared that she had been struck with a blunt object, causing internal, as well as external, bleeding. But the blows did not kill her, an autopsy surgeon later concluded. The cloth tied around her neck had strangled her. The murder scene yielded few fingerprints and only two or three marks from shoes with waffle-weave soles, apparently left by a man standing behind the living room sofa, but too faint to be traced.[6]

Contacted by police, Monahan's daughter was stunned. She had just returned to New York the previous week after spending nearly a month visiting her mother. Nothing untoward had happened during her visit, she said. Her mother had no enemies. Quite the contrary, she "had a large and faithful circle of friends with whom she enjoyed an active social life."

Tutor Scherer, at seventy-three, was nearly a decade older than his former mother-in-law. He had only fond memories of Monahan, he told police. At one point she had taken care of him during a lengthy illness. Scherer had given his ex-wife the Burbank house as part of the divorce settlement. Monahan had always loved the place.

Rather than selling it when she moved East with her new husband, Iris deeded it to her mother. Scherer said he knew of no one who wanted to harm Monahan.[7]

The case remained cold for a brief period. Then, slightly more than a week after the murder, Burbank police chief Rex Andrews received a phone call from an informant known as Indian George. Fifteen months earlier, in December 1951, George told Andrews, he had overheard two men, Baxter Shorter and Willie Upshaw, plotting to burglarize Mable Monahan's home, which they believed held a hidden safe containing one hundred thousand dollars left behind by Scherer. Both Shorter and Upshaw were reputed to be henchmen for Los Angeles mobster Mickey Cohen, who made his living through "book-making, gambling, loan-sharking, slot machines, narcotics, union agitation, and a substantial portion of the city's other illicit pastimes."[8] Shorter reputedly was an expert safecracker, Upshaw a gambler and a bookie.[9]

It took several days to locate Shorter. He refused to talk until police threatened to hold him in the Los Angeles County Jail overnight. Shorter acknowledged helping to plan the burglary, even going so far as to case Monahan's house, but those plans eventually were scrapped, he said. Under pressure, Shorter acknowledged a second plan. The first week of March 1953 an acquaintance whom he refused to name had contacted him about again trying to retrieve the rumored one hundred thousand dollars. Was Shorter willing to participate? He needed the money and reluctantly agreed.

Shorter recalled meeting two men on Sunday, March 8, at a drive-in eatery in the town of El Monte, a dozen miles east of Los Angeles. One of the men was named John, he said. He claimed not to remember the other man's name, but together the three men came up with a second burglary plan. "No one was supposed to be at home," Shorter insisted to police: "They said the house was empty." Before dawn the morning of Monday, March 9, the men met up again and drove by

Monahan's house. All of the interior lights were off. The floodlights reinforced the notion, at least for Shorter, that the home was vacant. They scheduled the break-in for that night.

Just before 7:00 that evening, Shorter said, he went to the restaurant to wait for John. A short time later, John drove up in a late-model, dark-blue Oldsmobile. He was alone. Two other men and a woman pulled up in a second car. Shorter had never met any of the three people in the second car, he told police. The men were named Jack and Emmett, he recalled, and the woman was named Mary. At least he thought that's what they called her. The two men and the woman got out of their car and climbed into John's. Shorter joined them. Together they drove to Monahan's house.

"We'll send the woman up first," Shorter recalled Jack saying as they cruised to a stop and parked across the street. Jack ordered Shorter to stay in the car long enough to give the group time to find the safe. The woman led John, Jack, and Emmett to the house, according to Shorter, and the three men hung back as she approached the door. After a minute or so, Shorter heard a scream then saw the door close.

He waited about fifteen minutes. When no one came to get him, he left the car and entered the house. What he found horrified him, he said. Monahan was lying on the floor moaning. "There was blood all over the rug," Shorter recalled. He saw John holding Monahan's head, covered with the pillowcase, in his hands. Emmett hit Monahan, and the five fled the premises.

Back in the car, Shorter worried aloud: Did they think Monahan might die? Jack sneered at him, "You're not such a man, are you?" Shorter then glanced at Mary, sitting in the front seat next to Jack. "Who does she belong to?" he asked: "I never saw a woman anyone was crazy enough to work with." Emmett responded: "She can handle herself fine."

Shorter lived with his wife, Olivia, in a downtown Los Angeles apartment. After the others dropped him off, he told police that he walked the dark streets searching for a pay phone and finally locating one. He dialed for an ambulance and gave the dispatcher Monahan's address. But in his agitated state, he failed to mention the city. Ambulance drivers, assuming the address was in Los Angeles, therefore could not find the house and never arrived at the scene.

Two days later Shorter read that Monahan had died, and he panicked. He had nothing to do with the beating or murder, he insisted, but feared the wrath of Jack or Emmett if they learned that he had talked to police. "They'll kill me," he said. Officers asked if he knew where either man lived. He did not know, but had heard them talking about Northern California, he said. The police agreed to keep his cooperation secret and released him.[10]

Burbank lieutenant Robert Coveney had acquaintances in numerous Northern California police departments. By this point, however, the Monahan murder had outgrown the Burbank department. The Los Angeles Police Department, under the direction of deputy chief of patrol, Thad Brown, joined the investigation. Brown was the LAPD's highest-ranking detective. During his three decades on the force, he had become an expert at cultivating confidential sources throughout California and the rest of the country.

Additionally, LAPD chief William Parker had put together an intelligence unit whose members were proficient in the use of wiretaps. Therefore, when Coveney arrived in San Francisco with LAPD detective Dick Ruble to meet with officers from the San Francisco and Oakland Police Departments, both men had a wealth of information from which to draw.[11]

Together, all of the officers perused hundreds of arrest records, booking sheets, and court cases before finally coming up with a name: Emmett Perkins. Rail thin and jug-eared, with a sallow, pockmarked complexion and a receding hairline, forty-five-year-old Perkins had a long criminal record. As a juvenile, he had spent a year at the Preston State School for Boys in Whittier, California, on a grand theft charge.

He had served time at San Quentin for auto theft and robbery and additional time at Folsom Prison for first-degree robbery and parole violation.[12]

Detective Ruble knew Perkins, he said. Perkins currently lived in Southern California and operated a gambling parlor in El Monte where he employed a shapely twenty-nine-year-old woman named Barbara Graham as a shill. Using her considerable charms, she brought in potential "marks," then encouraged them to keep betting larger and larger sums of money. She also had a criminal record, though a minor one: none of her arrests had been for violent offenses.

Graham, also known as Barbara Kielhamer and Barbara Radcliff, had convictions for vagrancy, prostitution, bad checks, and perjury dating back to the early years of World War II. None of her convictions had resulted in prison time, though she did spend nearly a year in San Francisco County Jail for providing a fake alibi to a heroin addict convicted of robbing and beating San Francisco madam Sally Stanford in February 1947.[13]

Jack, detectives surmised, probably was forty-eight-year-old John Santo, a beefy man with dark, wavy hair, glasses, and a violent past that began in Portland, Oregon, in the 1920s. Santo had been arrested in San Francisco in 1930 for attempted murder, again in 1934 on suspicion of kidnapping, and again several years later for assault with a deadly weapon. He lived in Auburn, a small town centered on mining and ranching about forty miles northeast of Sacramento. Santo, in turn, was friendly with thirty-eight-year-old John True, who sometimes lived in the small mountain town of Grass Valley. True also stayed on a boat in Marin County, north of San Francisco and worked as a deep sea diver, scavenging scrap metal. He had no criminal record that police could immediately access.[14]

By early April 1953, police had learned from another informant that Perkins and True almost certainly had participated in Monahan's murder. The Burbank department sent a team of officers to

Grass Valley to locate True. Without a criminal record, he seemed the most likely bet to provide information. Police tracked him to Reno, then to the small mountain town of Paradise, and, finally, back to Grass Valley, where they picked him up on April 12, 1953. They flew him to Burbank for questioning. True acknowledged Santo as a "hunting and fishing companion" but insisted he knew nothing about any murder. Santo was, True told police, "as nice a guy as I've ever known."[15]

Baxter Shorter might have disagreed, but he was no longer available for comment. Shortly after the early morning "bulldog" edition of the *Los Angeles Examiner* announcing True's apprehension hit the streets on April 13, Shorter called district attorney Ernest Roll. He feared for his life, Shorter told Roll, who offered him protection. It did not come soon enough. The next day Shorter opened the door of his Los Angeles apartment to find a man standing there, holding a gun.

Shorter's wife, Olivia, screamed and grabbed a rifle. She ran to the door, but Shorter warned her off. As Olivia Shorter watched in horror, the man shoved her husband into a car and sped away. She later identified the abductor as Emmett Perkins and described the getaway car as a 1951 Plymouth or Dodge. "We'll sure as hell find this guy dead someplace," police predicted: "Those men didn't just take him out to talk."[16]

On April 15 police released True from custody. The department released a statement: "After thorough questioning, we have secured no further evidence in corroboration of the information already in our possession." True met with the media outside the county jail. He had never been to Burbank, he said, nor did he know anyone involved in the Mable Monahan murder. He told reporters that he planned to return to Grass Valley, pick up his diving gear, and resume his search for sunken logs in an Idaho River. True's attorney, Patrick Cooney, accused Los Angeles police of falsely arresting his client.[17]

For three weeks police remained silent about the case. When reporters asked about their progress, they had no comment. District Attorney Roll, whose office would oversee prosecution of the perpetrators, said curtly, "What I want is facts and evidence." In reality, police and prosecutors had enough evidence to arrest Graham, Perkins, and Santo on other charges, and to hold them until they could build a murder case. But they wanted to make the arrests only when they could capture all three at the same time.

Perkins and Santo had not been seen since Monahan's murder. Graham hid in plain sight, "walking freely about town." In late April four policewomen trailed her through a Los Angeles shopping district, but lost her in the crowd. The LAPD assigned them to remain in the area in case she returned. Ten days later, she did.

On May 4, 1953, policewoman Kay Sheldon managed to keep Graham in view long enough to trail her to an industrial section of Lynwood, a mostly working-class city south and east of Los Angeles. Eventually, Graham entered a "shabby Lynwood storefront" converted from an auto shop into a three-room apartment constructed out of pasteboard. Sheldon recognized this as the probable hideout and called for backup. Within minutes sixteen officers from several area police departments surrounded the building. As one team crashed through the back door, another broke down the front door. Perkins, officers told reporters, was found fully clothed in one bedroom. Santo was half-dressed and lying on a mattress in the living room.

Newspaper accounts offered different descriptions of Graham. The *Los Angeles Times* said "she was only partly clothed" and it "appeared that she had just given herself an intravenous injection from a hypodermic needle found in her purse." The *Los Angeles Examiner* said police surprised her "as she was changing clothes in another bedroom" and reported that her arms bore scars from needles, including a fresh puncture wound.

Police found no guns in the apartment and no evidence that Baxter

Shorter had ever been there. "We presume Shorter is dead," police told the *Examiner*. It appeared, they told reporters for the *Times*, that "the trio had lived [at the converted apartment] for about two weeks."[18]

All three suspects were taken to police headquarters at city hall, interrogated for seven hours, and then booked into the Los Angeles County Jail. Graham claimed to be suffering from a heart ailment and said the needle scars came from heart medicine she had injected into herself. She had only five months to live, she told police, who then took her to the Georgia Street Receiving Hospital. Doctors there checked her heart, found nothing wrong and examined her arms for needle tracks before sending her back to jail.

Newspaper accounts of the arrest offered the first hint that Graham soon would become the centerpiece of this particular story. She received top billing in all the publications that covered the arrests. A *Los Angeles Times* story noted that "a blonde woman and two men, sought for questioning since March in the Burbank slaying of Mrs. Mable Monahan . . . were taken into custody yesterday."

The paper's front-page photo depicted all three suspects. Emmett Perkins wore a suit, tie, and hat and cast his eyes downward. Incongruously, considering his predicament, he appeared to be smirking. Santo sat next to Perkins, wearing a sweater, slacks, hat, the same downcast eyes, and an inscrutable expression. Graham sat on the other side of Santo. Despite the story's reference to her as a blonde, Graham's hair appeared to be brown. She wore a form-fitting, light-colored jacket and skirt. Her interlaced fingers obscured the left side of her face from view, but as the photographer snapped the picture, she turned slightly, peering up at the camera and leaving her right eye and jawline exposed. Even with this limited view, newspaper readers could see that this was a very attractive woman.

An additional photo of Graham appeared on an inside page of the *Times*. She sat in a chair, leaning forward, with hands behind her back, possibly in handcuffs. Her hair was now swept up, pulled away from her heart-shaped face. This time she looked to the left of the photographer and appeared to be talking to someone. Her eyes were fringed with dark lashes and her lips were carefully made up in what appeared to be dark-red lipstick.[19]

The *Los Angeles Examiner*'s front page carried only one large photo, of Graham alone, dressed in a form-fitting suit jacket with the top two buttons undone. She looked skyward and to the left, with about three-quarters of her face in view. The accompanying story described her as a twenty-eight-year-old redhead.[20]

On May 5, 1953, District Attorney Roll filed criminal charges against all three suspects, but not for Monahan's murder. That case still had holes, it seemed. Baxter Shorter's wife had picked Perkins out of a lineup at police headquarters, and the suspected kidnapping getaway car had been found abandoned near the Lynwood apartment where the suspects had been arrested. Perkins was charged with kidnapping and assault with a deadly weapon and denied bail. Police also linked Santo to the kidnapping via the car, which turned out to belong to his former girlfriend.

Olivia Shorter had not named Santo as a kidnapper, so he was charged with forging a fictitious telegram. His bail was set at fifty thousand dollars. Graham was arraigned on seven counts of forgery, as the "result of a clothing-buying spree in March and April when she passed more than $200 in fictitious checks." Her bail was set at twenty-five thousand dollars. The bail amounts were extraordinarily high for such minor offenses, but officials aimed to ensure that all of the suspects remained in jail until murder charges could be filed. At that point all three would be held on no-bail warrants.[21]

For the first time, newspaper readers throughout Los Angeles learned that Graham was the mother of a son. The *Times* cited his age as fourteen months; the *Examiner* said he was two years old. None of the stories mentioned her son's whereabouts. "I haven't seen my husband or boy for two months," police quoted Graham.[22]

With the absence of physical evidence against the three suspects and only a short time before attorneys would surely demand their release, police cast a wider net. It brought in thirty-four-year-old William Upshaw, who had helped to plan the first, aborted break-in of Monahan's home. Newspapers reported that authorities wanted him for questioning.

A friend had notified Upshaw, who was in Mexico City. "I left down there as soon as I could and arrived here this morning," Upshaw told reporters on May 13. Police had hinted at his relationship with Los Angeles mobster Mickey Cohen, but Upshaw denied any connection to the underworld and described himself as "an airline parts procurer."

Upshaw claimed that he had met Shorter a decade earlier when Shorter owned a bar in Long Beach. "I didn't keep up the friendship, but every now and then I'd run into him." Police kept mum about any information Upshaw might have provided about the Monahan case, but within days John True was brought in by San Francisco police and sent back to Los Angeles. The district attorney set June 2, 1953, for a closed hearing before the Los Angeles County grand jury.[23]

Such a proceeding could accomplish two goals for prosecutors. Since no defense witnesses testified at grand jury hearings, subsequent indictments would establish at least the appearance of guilt. And prosecutors could use grand jury testimony to coach witnesses whose memories might have dimmed by the time criminal cases went to trial. Witnesses had strong motivation to stick to the script, since changed testimony could result in criminal charges.

Both Upshaw and John True offered testimony. Upshaw admitted helping to plan the aborted December 1951 burglary and refusing at the last minute to participate in the one that led to Monahan's death. He had been the unnamed person at the original meeting with Shorter when the second burglary was planned, Upshaw acknowledged. More important, Upshaw told grand jurors that he knew what had happened in the actual robbery-turned-murder. A shaken Baxter Shorter had contacted him the next day to express his concern that Monahan might die and to confide his fears of retribution by his male accomplices.[24]

True testified voluntarily, he said. Rumor had it that police were about to offer him immunity from prosecution if he testified against Graham, Perkins, and Santo. Rumors also had circulated claiming that police had first offered Graham immunity, but that she had refused, citing her innocence. In his grand jury testimony, True acknowledged being at Monahan's home the night she was murdered. He seemed to revel in what he depicted as his heroic role.[25]

The perpetrators believed the house to be unoccupied, True said. But just in case it was not, Santo concocted a story to convince Monahan to open her front door. He named Graham as the woman who accompanied the four men to the home. In Santo's plan, she was to go up first, claim to have car trouble, and ask to use the telephone.[26]

Monahan opened the door but began to scream as she saw the men standing behind Graham. They pushed their way inside and shut the door. True testified that Graham began hitting Monahan with a gun butt to quiet the terrified woman. "I ran my hand between the gun and the lady's face and I told Barbara, 'Don't hit her anymore,'" True told grand jurors. "The lady was bleeding. She fainted . . . she just collapsed. Everybody was running around."

After subduing Monahan, the group "shook the whole house down" looking for the hundred thousand dollars, even going as far as dismantling the floor furnace and the garbage disposal unit. As they prepared to leave, True said, Graham put a pillowcase over "the lady's head and Perkins tied the lady's hands." Perkins then "grabbed [Monahan] by the feet and said, 'Let's get her out of the door.' The lady's head was in my lap as we moved her. We put her in a closet. Santo came by with a piece of cloth. I don't know whether it was a sheet or what it was." Santo wrapped it around her neck. "The lady was moaning and I said, 'This lady is going to die.'" True testified that he slashed a hole in the pillowcase so that Monahan could breathe and told the others, "You'd better call an ambulance. Then I realized I had said the wrong thing."[27]

Neither Graham, Perkins, nor Santo attended the hearing. Grand jurors deliberated less than a half hour before issuing indictments against all three for conspiracy to commit burglary, robbery, and murder. Superior court judge William Neeley arraigned the suspects and denied them bail.[28]

Graham again earned top billing in all of the stories. The *Los Angeles Examiner* story of the indictment included four photos. Graham's was the biggest and it appeared just below the headline. On this occasion she obviously had aimed for a somewhat subdued look, with her thick, curly hair pulled back in a ponytail and her eyes largely obscured by black-rimmed glasses. Upshaw and True appeared only in small mug shots, less than a quarter the size of Graham's. The bottom of the page featured a photo of Perkins and Santo together as they sat outside the grand jury hearing room.

Graham also took star billing in the *Times* story, partly because of what occurred several hours after the indictment, when she collapsed in her jail cell, fell backward against her cot, and briefly lost consciousness. Authorities feared a blood clot in her brain and rushed her to Los Angeles General Hospital for tests. They turned out to be negative, but Graham "either could not or would not speak" for several hours afterward.[29]

The trial was still weeks away when Graham, Perkins, and Santo were arraigned in superior court. Judicial officials obviously recognized that the case would draw significant attention from the press and public, since district attorney Ernest Roll assigned J. Miller Leavy and Adolph Alexander, his two top deputies, to prosecute the trio. Presiding Los Angeles County Superior Court judge Charles Fricke always picked the highest-profile cases. True to form, he assigned the trial to himself.

None of the defendants had money, so Fricke appointed public defender S. Ward Sullivan to represent Perkins and Santo. Graham needed her own attorney, since she was deemed to have a conflict of interest with her codefendants, but she could not afford to pay a private lawyer. Under rules in place at that time, the trial judge could appoint a private attorney, who had to work for free unless he could convince the county to reimburse him. Jack W. Hardy, a well-respected criminal lawyer, was in Fricke's court on another matter when the judge tapped him to represent Graham. He had never represented a defendant in a capital murder case.[30]

Up until this point, the newspaper-reading public had seen only minor, though tantalizing glimpses of Barbara Graham. They would soon become riveted by the young woman whose life story might have sprung from the imaginations of any number of hard-boiled fiction writers specializing in stories depicting "a dark world below the placid surface, whose inhabitants" were "grasping, emotionally twisted creatures." Their common theme was murder and the perpetrators very often "busty and beautiful" women who were also willful, sexual temptresses. Such women always came to bad ends. Or, as writer Geoffrey O'Brien phrased it, the objects "of desire had a very slim chance of reaching the last page alive."[31]

2

A Life on the Lam

IF ANY LIFE could be squeezed into a one-dimensional archetype of the bad and beautiful female, it was that of Barbara Graham. She had been on the wrong side of the law since her early teens, using her good looks, shapely figure, and street smarts to survive. She spent nearly two years in a reform school. She prowled ports throughout California, drinking and partying with sailors. She worked in bars, brothels, and gambling joints. By May 1953 she had spent time in police stations and jails from San Diego to San Francisco, with arrests for disorderly conduct, vagrancy, prostitution, narcotics possession, bad-check writing, and forgery.[1]

Married four times, Graham had three sons ranging in age from almost thirteen years to fourteen months at the time of her arrest. She barely knew the older two, who had lived since infancy with relatives or friends. *Normal* seemed to be a concept that had eluded Graham for most of her life. But she never had a chance to find out how "regular" people lived; her hard-knock early years taught her little but how to survive.[2]

Barbara Elaine Ford was born in an Oakland, California, boarding house on June 26, 1923. Eight miles east and across the bay from San Francisco, Oakland possesses a much less storied history than its glamorous neighbor. Until the first decade of the twentieth century, Oakland was a bucolic small town, named for the trees that dotted its hills and best known for its port. But the massive April 1906 earthquake and fire that devastated San Francisco filled Oakland with nearly fifty thousand refugees.

The years surrounding World War I brought shipbuilders and manufacturing. By the 1920s Oakland held a diverse population that included artists and intellectuals, a large working class, and a rough element drawn to the port for work and for after-hours entertainment at the area's bars and saloons. The last category included characters that populated the stories of homegrown writer Jack London.

Hortense Ford, Barbara's mother, was born in San Francisco in June 1906, two months after the earthquake, and her family was among those relocating to Oakland. Nothing is known of Hortense's background, but she had just turned seventeen and was unmarried when she gave birth to Barbara. Given the overwhelming social stigma that accompanied illegitimacy during this period, Hortense's decision to keep her baby seems somewhat surprising, particularly because she appears to have had no further contact with Barbara's biological father.

Even more surprising was her refusal to let this circumstance hold her back. Instead, she seems to have treated Barbara's birth as little more than an irritating inconvenience. Her solution: leaving her daughter with relatives or friends while she resumed her high-flying social life. Hortense also refused to become emotionally attached to her daughter, at least if Barbara's later comments are to be believed: "My mother couldn't stand the sight of me. She hated and resented me."

In May 1924, when Barbara was not yet a year old, Hortense, still an unmarried teenager, became pregnant a second time. Claire Elizabeth Ford was born in February 1925. Like her older sister, she never knew her biological father. Several months after Claire's birth,

Alameda County authorities deemed Hortense to be "incorrigible" and made her a ward of the juvenile ourt. In September 1925 she was remanded to the California School for Girls at Ventura, an institution for wayward adolescents and young women about a hundred miles northwest of Los Angeles.

Ventura was a state reform school, established in the 1910s as part of a wide-ranging Progressive agenda in California. Politicians and reformers believed that young people who lacked strong moral values and a work ethic could be retrained to become solid citizens via facilities designed to correct bad behavior. They included Ventura, the Whittier School for Boys, city and county juvenile halls, and El Retiro, a halfway house for delinquent girls in Los Angeles. The inmates at Ventura included "defectives," "morons," criminals, and girls who were "over-sexed."[3] The facility generally served females between the ages of sixteen and twenty, though occasionally younger ones were sent there as well. Hortense was nineteen at the time of her incarceration.

It is unclear how long she actually remained at Ventura, but her "term expired" on June 12, 1927, her twenty-first birthday.[4] Authorities may have at least partially succeeded in scaring her straight, because it took three years before she revealed a third pregnancy. This time she decided to marry Joseph Wood, the baby's father. The wedding took place in October 1929, when Hortense was five months pregnant.

Both Barbara and Claire took Wood's last name, though he lived with them less than four months. He contracted appendicitis and died in January 1930, two months before the birth of his son, also named Joseph. Barbara was not yet seven when her stepfather died. Wood appears to have been the only father figure Barbara had during her childhood, and she recalled him as the singular stable force in her chaotic life.[5]

After her husband's death, Hortense Wood received a small widow's stipend from the State of California. It did not pay the bills, however, so she went to work at an Oakland laundry. Being a single parent with three small children in the face of limited financial resources and few job skills would be difficult for anyone, but Hortense seems to have been particularly ill-equipped for the task. As a result, Barbara and Claire spent much of their childhoods placed out with friends, acquaintances, and, on occasion, strangers. At some point Alameda County officials stepped in and provided the two girls with a social worker. They "were beginning to become problems, running around the streets until after dark," a caseworker noted.

Since the family was Catholic, officials decided to send both sisters to a convent school in San Jose, about thirty miles south of San Francisco. They arrived at Saint Mary's of the Palms in February 1935, when Barbara was eleven and Claire ten. The arrangement meant that Saint Mary's received much of the money Hortense had gotten from the state. Perhaps for that reason she decided to reclaim her daughters in October 1935.

Claire appears to have remained with Hortense and with her younger half-brother from that point on. Barbara, however, was soon sent to another Bay Area facility, The Home of the Good Shepherd, where she resided for several more months. In late 1936, at the age of thirteen, she finally moved back home and was enrolled in the eighth grade at a regular public school.[6]

This arrangement, unsurprisingly, did not last. Once an appealing, waiflike child with curly blonde hair, Barbara—called Bonnie by her friends—had developed into a curvaceous adolescent who seemed to know instinctively how to attract males. In fact, it was the one thing she could count on. If her life so far had taught her anything, it was that adults could not be trusted and that permanent, loving relationships were illusory. She had spent years drifting from one place to another and found rules difficult and confining.

Reunited with her mother, Barbara acted out by skipping school and running with a crowd of other wayward young people who smoked, drank, and begged money to ride the ferry from Oakland to San Francisco. Instead of trying to repair her fractured relationship with her daughter, Hortense, as she had done so many times before, sought to dump Barbara on someone else.[7] The best place for her oldest daughter, she determined, would be Ventura, at the same reform facility where she had been housed years earlier. Apparently missing the irony in her statement, she told police that her daughter had been "a very bad girl, unmanageable all her life."[8] Barbara pleaded with her mother and promised to reform, but her pleas fell on deaf ears.

From a modern-day perspective, Hortense Wood's casual, neglectful, and thoughtless parenting seems appalling. As the historian Linda Gordon has revealed, however, the practice of "placing out" one's children—particularly among working-class families headed by single mothers—was a relatively common and acceptable practice in America, even as late as the 1930s and 1940s. Nonetheless, Hortense's decision to keep Joseph and Claire and to send Barbara away seems to cross the boundary from normal to abusive, and it provides some evidence for Barbara's charge that her mother "hated" her.[9]

Barbara arrived at Ventura in July 1937, just after her fourteenth birthday. She was one of the youngest girls at the facility, which also housed burglars, forgers, bigamists, kidnappers, gang members, and teenage prostitutes. Mrs. J. D. Herndon, Ventura's superintendent, described two classes of girls at the institution: those who never had a chance because of family backgrounds, and a "criminal class."

Ventura administrators obviously took a dim view of their charges' intellectual capabilities, since they sought to train them only for "commercial" or "domestic" work upon release.[10] This task required the equivalent of an eighth-grade education. Barbara Wood had a spotty academic record at best, yet she excelled in English and spelling, having reached nearly a tenth-grade level of proficiency.

It was her battered psyche that most needed shoring up. Her

nomadic lifestyle and lack of sustained affection made her desperate for attention, bitterly resentful, and very angry. A psychologist might have helped her, but in the 1930s juvenile authorities did not view therapy as the preferred antidote to bad behavior. Instead, they promoted hard work and discipline, with days beginning at 5:30 a.m. and ending at 8:30 p.m.

This approach may have worked as a general principle for many, if not most, of Ventura's wards. It did not work for Barbara Wood. She remained at Ventura for twenty-one months and proved troublesome virtually the entire time, according to file notations made by staff members. Days after her arrival, she proved "impossible to supervise, need[ing] lots of attention and correcting." In early August 1937 she was "shirking work." On September 1, 1937, she "escaped through a basement window with Evelyn Jordan." On December 8, 1937, she "was noisy in her dorm room." Over the following year, Barbara was punished for "cutting pictures from books," "impudence and dark looks," and "writing on the wall."[11]

It is impossible to know what punishments she received for these infractions. The facility endured bouts of criticism throughout its nearly fifty-year history for its punitive approach to slackers and nonconformists. At various points, officials used the "water treatment," in which they pushed a hose down the throats of miscreants; "hydrotherapy," during which they applied heavy wet towels to the skin to calm down hysterics; and periods of long solitary confinement. After each period of adverse publicity, officials promised to heed critics, while also arguing for the validity of their approach.[12]

Since the facility had no fence—a holdover from the Progressive period and its belief in personal responsibility—runaways were common. Three times Barbara escaped and hitchhiked back to the Bay Area. She begged her mother to take her in and hide her, but Hortense refused and called police, who took her back to Ventura. Then in her early thirties, Hortense had pulled her life together and lived in San Francisco with her two younger children and possibly a second husband. For a period, Hortense used the last name Lopes, though she later reclaimed her first husband's surname. From time to time, Hortense also seems to have resided with her own mother.[13]

By April 18, 1939, Barbara had managed to frustrate and stymie even the most experienced professionals at Ventura, who agreed to release her on parole. She was not yet sixteen. Theoretically, she would be under state supervision until she turned eighteen in June 1941. Until then, she had to live under a strict set of guidelines. Authorities would find her suitable places to live, and she had to check in regularly to discuss her progress. Barbara failed to meet either of the conditions.[14]

In her first placement, she performed housework and other tasks for a Los Angeles couple who agreed to pay her fifteen dollars per day. The arrangement lasted for less than a month. Next, she went to work for another couple, but they soon left on vacation. Since by law Barbara could not stay in their home alone, she went to the Los Angeles County Juvenile Hall to await their return. Within days, she fled to the city of Long Beach, which, like Oakland, boasted a busy port where individuals fleeing their pasts or the authorities could quickly meld into the general population and become anonymous.

"I have notified her mother and also the Juvenile Bureau of Long Beach," a Ventura official with the initials L. S. wrote on June 18, 1939, "as the enclosed address book seems to indicate a fondness for sailors!!! Will you send a description of any identifying marks and also finger print code if available?" On July 1 authorities were still looking for her. She had moved north with another Ventura alumna, Peggy Caldwell. Both girls had been spotted at the ports of San Francisco and Oakland, where they appeared to be fraternizing with sailors. "It is felt they had known a good part of the fleet, at least by name and [Barbara] stated in a running comment that she was 'in circulation again,'" L.S. wrote. "It is felt that in view of her youth and her absolute disregard for any parole supervision, that a return to the school is indicated should she be apprehended."[15]

M. G. M., another Ventura official, saw the situation in slightly less dire terms on July 1. "My experience with these girls is that they write every man's name in [address] books that they meet. I wanted the names of the men Peggy Caldwell met at her married sister's home as I think they might be useful. In Peggy's letter to Beverly Parks she stated she had met sailors through her brother-in-law and they were very attentive. But again one can't believe much these girls say. I fear after 15 years I have lost faith in their truthfulness."[16]

In fact, forging relationships with sailors was a somewhat common practice for undersupervised adolescent girls and young women who lived near naval facilities in the years leading up to World War II. The military even had a name for them: "seagulls," after the hungry birds who scavenged for food on beaches and docks. Some relationships were sexual but others platonic, as lonely and adrift young people created a loose-knit community of sorts. For Barbara Wood, the sailors provided temporary companionship, but some seagulls would remain her life-long friends.[17]

Barbara's family proved unhelpful in the effort to find her. "Mrs. Mitchell went to home of Barbara's mother in S. F., no one at home," and "mother and grandmother of Barbara told Mrs. Mitchell that Barbara not there." Finally, in August, Peggy Caldwell's father "wired Mrs. Mitchell with the probable whereabouts of Barbara—74 Palm St., San Francisco." She was using the last name Radcliff, he said, but an address check showed "no one by the name Radcliff there—high class residence district—only way girl could be there would be as a servant. Not a district one could go around ringing bells."[18]

By the fall of 1939 Ventura authorities appeared to be making only desultory efforts to find Barbara, who proved an elusive target. In October she was "drifting around the Oakland or Bay region, and eventually she will probably turn up in some jail," an official predicted. In November she was back in Southern California. "I have it on excellent authority that she is hanging out at George's in Long Beach," wrote an unnamed staff member. "I am sure we could get her. However, except for her extreme youth I do not feel it would be advisable, as I think a return trip would probably do her very little if any good." By January 1940 she was back in Northern California, and apparently living in the East Bay town of Vallejo.

The next month she returned to Long Beach. When police there arrested her for disorderly conduct, she used the name Barbara Olivia Radcliffe. Ventura officials never mentioned this arrest in their next report, from April 1940, which placed her back in Oakland and five months pregnant. The pregnancy rumors were true.[19]

Barbara met Harry Kielhamer, a shipping clerk and mechanic, during the first of what would become several efforts to turn her life around. During one of her Bay Area sojourns she enrolled in a San Mateo business college. She spent some of her off-hours at local bars and that was where she met Kielhamer sometime in the fall of 1939. He was twenty-six and she was sixteen, though she claimed to be twenty-three. The couple became intimate; Barbara became pregnant and dropped out of school. She chose to marry, she said much later, because she did not want her child to live under the stigma of illegitimacy, as she had. Since she was not yet eighteen, she had to obtain Hortense's permission. She had virtually no relationship with her mother and disliked having to ask her, but reluctantly did so. On July 1, 1940, Barbara Kielhamer gave birth to her first son, William.[20]

The marriage did not last long. Not surprisingly, given her youth and her own lack of maternal nurturing, Barbara found motherhood frightening.[21] She also resented her new husband's "plodding and dull" outlook on life. He in turn may not have known of his wife's delinquent past. Less than a year after William's birth, Barbara fled the Bay Area for San Diego.

In early March 1941 San Diego police picked her up for vagrancy—a euphemistic word used when authorities suspected prostitution but could not prove it—and gave her a sixty-day suspended sentence. She briefly returned to the Bay Area to give birth to a second son, Michael, on December 5, 1941. The timing of his birth suggests that he may not have been Harry Kielhamer's child, but Kielhamer gave the boy his last name. Shortly after Michael's birth, Barbara returned to Southern California and Harry Kielhamer filed for divorce. He sought and received custody of both boys, though he did not keep them for long. Instead, his mother agreed to raise them. By the time of her divorce, Barbara had begun a dangerous dance—one step forward, two steps back—that would end in an arrest for murder a decade later.[22]

In San Diego she again took up a high-flying lifestyle. In March 1944 she married Aloyce Pueschel, a sailor who was preparing to ship out for overseas duty in World War II. Within weeks, both partners recognized their mistake and he filed for divorce. Barbara later recalled Pueschel as "a nice kid. I wouldn't recognize him today if I saw him on the street." Less than three months later, San Diego police again arrested her for vagrancy, but she denied being a prostitute and managed to avoid jail time.[23]

Her next vagrancy arrest came in June 1944 in San Francisco. The judge sent her to the probation department for evaluation. Officials there gave her a battery of intelligence and personality tests and discovered that she had an IQ of 114, but also "psychopathic tendencies that lead to delinquency." Despite this conclusion, the probation department released her on her own recognizance, provided that "no adverse reports" arrived within thirty days. None did and she returned to her vagabond life—moving from Reno, Nevada, to Stockton, California, to Los Angeles and even as far east as Chicago. Usually, she worked as a prostitute and as a dice girl at casinos. Occasionally she held traditional jobs. In Chicago, for example, she worked as a cocktail waitress. But she could not hold her life together for long.[24]

In January 1948 Barbara faced her first serious criminal charge. It resulted from her decision to lie for an acquaintance in a robbery case. As the victim of the robbery, San Francisco madam Sally Stanford, later described the terrifying experience, it was a cold and foggy morning in February 1947 when Mark Monroe and Thomas Sitler broke into her home. Armed with a .45 automatic and a .38 revolver, the two men beat Stanford's maid then attacked her. With blood pouring from her wounds, Stanford ran to the window, opened it, and began screaming. The two men fled, but were quickly apprehended. Monroe, who knew Barbara only casually, asked her to testify that she had been with him at the time of the attack. She agreed, though she had been two thousand miles away in Chicago. Another young woman lied for Sitler.

At the men's trial, the testimony of both women was easily refuted, and Monroe and Sitler were convicted of attempted murder. In April 1948 the women went to trial themselves and were convicted on perjury charges. Initially, Barbara was sentenced to serve a year at the California Institution for Women, Tehachapi—the state's prison for female felons—but the other woman's lawyer arranged for her client to serve her time at the San Francisco County Jail. Barbara challenged the court's unequal treatment, and she was allowed to serve her time there as well. She later sought out Stanford, who accepted her apology and described her as "a poor, broken-down hustling broad and tenderloin tramp . . . made to order for the role society decided she should play. It was obvious she had been a psychiatric problem, sick for years."[25]

When she left jail in January 1949, Barbara Wood Kielhamer Pueschel was twenty-five. The years were slipping away. She still had potential; even her probation officer acknowledged as much. He described her as "good natured, a pleasant and quiet girl."[26] She also enjoyed literature and music and had sophisticated tastes in both. Persian poet Omar Khayyam and British author Oscar Wilde were favorite authors, and she spent hours listening to classical music and jazz. Gerry Mulligan and his brand of West Coast cool jazz were particular favorites. Unfortunately, she had made so many poor choices in her life, and she seemed to lack the ability to make good decisions or resist temptation.

This time she boarded a bus for Reno. She had no money, few skills, and a thin resume, at least when it came to so-called legitimate work. Her criminal record provided an additional stumbling block, since many employers conducted background checks. In Reno she found work as a nurse's aide but disliked working with sick people. She waited tables in a coffee shop but soon quit that job as well. Ultimately, she fell back on what she knew best and found work as a casino dice girl. She met Charles Newman, who worked as a sales representative, and he became her third husband. She hoped the marriage would enable her to travel. It was strictly "a business arrangement" on her part, she later said, but Newman settled her in Tonopah, Nevada, an isolated desert town about two hundred miles northwest of Las Vegas. By early 1950 she had had enough of the desert and her husband. She also feared getting pregnant, so she filed for divorce and returned to California.[27]

En route, she stopped over in Seattle to visit her two sons. William was eleven and Michael nine. Though she kept in contact via letters, she had not seen the boys for several years. Hortense had kept in touch with her grandsons as well, and when she learned of Barbara's plans, she contacted Harry Kielhamer's mother and informed her of Barbara's criminal past, including her perjury conviction. In addition to being extraordinarily vengeful, Hortense's action seems particularly ironic, given her own maternal history. Hortense's actions spoiled Barbara's visit. She also sent a letter to Barbara's probation officer, declaring her to be an unfit mother.[28]

This experience represented a turning point for Barbara. She abandoned any effort to straighten out her life. Distraught, she fled

Seattle and stopped reporting to her probation officer. On September 18, 1950, her probation was revoked and San Francisco officials issued a bench warrant for her arrest.[29] By this time, however, she was back in Southern California. At twenty-seven years old and on the lam as a parole violator, she cut ties with all of her family. She did not know it, but her situation was about to get much worse.

In San Francisco she had briefly been acquainted with Emmett Perkins, a bottom-feeder in the hierarchy of local criminals. It is unclear how much Barbara knew about Perkins's criminal past or his time in prison. She met Perkins just after her release from county jail in early 1949 and before she left for Nevada. She was looking for work and friends informed her that Perkins planned to open a gambling parlor in the city.

In the years following World War II, the Bay Area was becoming the center for an edgy, alternative lifestyle that eventually came to be called beatnik, and Perkins's proposed club sounded to Barbara like an alluring opportunity. It would feature gambling, jazz, and, possibly, some low-level drugs. Barbara asked her friends to put her in touch with Perkins. The two met, but nothing came of the venture and Barbara moved to Reno.

When she arrived in Southern California in mid-1950, she learned that Perkins had relocated there himself. He lived with his family in a house in El Monte and rented a second house in the same town, where he operated a gambling parlor. It featured various poker games and some dice games. Barbara went to work for him. At some point that year, she also met Henry Graham. Graham was not conventionally good-looking: he was small and slender with a high forehead, dark, wavy hair, and a receding chin, but he had soulful eyes, a nice smile, and a wicked sense of humor.

Graham worked as a bartender in Los Angeles. He liked setting up attractive young women with male bar patrons who might want sex or just intimate conversation. The men were liberal with tips and drinks and sometimes gave him a little extra money for his trouble. To Graham, Barbara must have seemed perfect for the role of escort: still young and good-looking, sexy, and world-wise, but also charming and friendly. She agreed to work for him as well.[30]

The two jobs meshed nicely. Barbara picked up men at Graham's bar, among other places. When they suggested going someplace more intimate, she put them off, suggesting that they first try gambling at Perkins's establishment. There she acted as a shill, joining the games and urging her "dates" to bet ever higher amounts of money. At closing time she drifted away, usually leaving them with enough cash to keep them happy and to make it worth her time.

She forgot, or did not care by this point, that associating with gamblers was illegal for a woman on probation for perjury. Possibly, she believed that if she stayed below the police radar, she could avoid detection, or that, if she were to be arrested, she could talk her way out of any jam; it had happened so many times before. But she was also walked a tightrope of another kind. Gambling was tightly controlled in Los Angeles by the underworld, specifically by the mobster Mickey Cohen. Perkins seems by that point to have become a bit player in Cohen's organization. By going to work for Perkins, Barbara became tangentially involved in the underworld as well.[31]

At some point in 1950 she became sexually involved with Henry Graham, and they moved in together to a duplex on Ennis Street near downtown Los Angeles. He introduced her to a new vice: drugs. She may have dabbled in marijuana and other illegal substances previously, but never with serious drugs—at least her arrest reports do not mention them. Henry was a regular user of marijuana, heroin, opium, and amphetamines. Barbara joined him in drug use, though she later denied she was an addict.[32]

In November 1950 Barbara and Henry Graham traveled to Tijuana, Mexico, and got married. When they returned to Los Angeles, Henry continued working as a bartender. Barbara kept her job with Perkins, spending two or three nights a week at the El Monte gambling parlor to earn extra money. At least some of it went toward drugs. On May 3, 1951, the Los Angeles Police Department arrested both Henry and Barbara on narcotics charges, though the record does not specify the kind of drug or the disposition of the cases.

The LAPD apparently had no knowledge of her probation violation, because she was soon released, as was Henry. In her booking photo she wore a tailored suit jacket, but her eyes were half-closed, her face puffy, her hair carelessly brushed, and the area under her eyes held dark bruises. Soon after her arrest, Barbara became pregnant. Since she could no longer work at either of her jobs, she began to write checks on nonexistent bank accounts to pay bills. One of them went to pay the obstetrician who delivered her third son, Tommy, born in February 1952.

After Tommy's birth Barbara's patched-together life began quickly to unravel, and it became only a matter of time before the inevitable disaster struck. Henry stopped working and spent his unemployment checks on drugs. Barbara took care of Tommy by day and went back to working for Perkins at night. She nagged Henry to go back to work. The Grahams fought constantly.

Since they had no money, Barbara wrote more bad checks. Some days she dressed in revealing clothing and cased shopping districts, looking for items to steal. Wearing dark glasses and carrying a large purse, she flirted outrageously with male employees, hoping they would look the other way when she placed pilfered items in her handbag. She even asked one male employee of a grocery store to drive her home. That day, she wore a strapless, form-fitting sunsuit. Employees at all of the shops said it appeared as if she were casing their places as a prelude to theft.[33]

In early 1953 Jack Santo arrived in Southern California and began spending nights at the El Monte gambling parlor, which had an unused back bedroom.[34] Santo and Perkins were suspected of several vicious crimes, including murders, in Northern California. One involved the killing of a gold miner; another, the murder of a grocer and his family.

Barbara had not previously met Santo, but she soon got to know him well. With yet another marriage falling apart, she took Tommy and began staying over in El Monte some nights. It is possible that she began a sexual relationship with Santo during this period, though she later vehemently denied ever being involved with him.

The details of her living arrangements grow murky at this point. Sometime in early March 1953 Henry moved out. Rent had been paid through the end of the month, but Barbara decided to leave as well. Perkins came and moved her and Tommy into the gambling house full time, but that arrangement proved temporary. In early April Barbara left Tommy with Henry's mother and stepfather, Anne and Oscar Webb, in downtown Los Angeles.

Barbara, Perkins, and Santo moved several times over the next few weeks, finally ending up at a rundown, converted auto-parts store in Lynwood. There, police arrested them for the murder of Mable Monahan. Barbara Graham had been running virtually all of her life. She was twenty-nine and her years on the lam were finally at an end.[35]

3

A Femme Fatale On Trial

Buxom Barbara Graham is a woman of many sides, most of them lurid.

Name it and Barbara seems to have done it. . . . The record runs from charges of escape from reform school through prostitution, perjury, narcotics, and bad checks.

Barbara Wood Kielhammer Puchelle [*sic*] Newman Graham may become the third woman legally executed in California.

Though she got by "the hard way" since she was 13, Barbara is far from unattractive at 30. Her tinted titian blonde hair is drawn up in a school teacher's bun. Her complexion is good. . . . But her green eyes are cold.

> "Monahan Case Femme Fatale, Story of a Girl Who May Die
> for Killing," *San Francisco Chronicle*, September 20, 1955

BY THE TIME *San Francisco Chronicle* readers scanned these words on September 20, 1953, jurors four hundred miles away in Los Angeles were only days from determining the fates of Barbara Graham, Emmett Perkins, and John Santo. Readers might have been excused if they failed to immediately recall Perkins and Santo. Virtually the entire trial had centered on Graham, who captivated a large audience reaching to the Bay Area and beyond.

The public, in California and elsewhere, may have been fascinated by Graham, but not in a way that encouraged empathy. Throughout the month-long trial she had refused to adhere to the unwritten code covering female defendants in murder cases, namely, to forge an emotional bond with jurors and nudge them toward at least one "there but for the grace of God" moment.

This was a difficult proposition for any murder defendant in the early 1950s, but women were held to different standards. With the exception of female jurors, virtually all the major players in criminal trials were men who generally subscribed to a gender ideology that envisioned women as more nurturing and less prone to violence than men.

Since men controlled trial narratives, it behooved defense attorneys to cloak their female clients in traditional garb, or as close to traditional as they could get. Success in this endeavor not only encouraged juror identification, but also fueled empathetic coverage from journalists. Sympathetic stories created public sentiment in favor of defendants, which in turn could shape the way prosecutors and judges treated them.[1]

As a decidedly unconventional woman charged with bludgeoning a stranger, especially one always described as elderly and thus exceptionally sympathetic, Graham had a particularly strong incentive to heed these rules. She needed to project herself as submissive, as deferential to authority, and as an admittedly flawed individual who agonized over her many mistakes in judgment. She had to emphasize her role as a mother and suggest that she could never physically harm another human being. And she needed to dress the part of a modest supplicant, since female criminal defendants historically have faced journalistic and public scrutiny of their appearances to a degree not shared by their male counterparts.[2]

The success of this approach can be seen in cases of female murder defendants who did manage to prevail in death-penalty trials. In 1949, for example, a Los Angeles jury acquitted Elizabeth "Betty" Ferreri of murder, even though she had acknowledged hacking her husband Jerome to death via twenty-three blows with a meat cleaver. For her courtroom appearances, Ferreri was deathly pale, wore no makeup, dressed in black widow's weeds, wrung her hands, sobbed inconsolably, and claimed, through copious tears, that she had murdered Jerome to stop his abuse.[3]

Graham took the opposite tack. She was carefully made up with face powder, mascara, and dark lipstick. She dressed in tight clothing and strode into court on high-heeled pumps that showed off her trim ankles and shapely legs. She radiated anger and resentment as she sat, casually smoking, at the counsel table. Perkins and Santo, on the other hand, expressed little emotion throughout the trial. And they dressed conservatively in slacks, dress shirts, and jackets.

As a result of her appearance and demeanor, defense lawyer Jack Hardy had difficulty constructing her as anything other than a femme fatale. Graham might have faced condemnation no matter what her behavior. She had a criminal record. Her codefendants were hardened felons and suspects in other murders, and Graham's trial took place in Southern California, the setting for hard-boiled detective novels and noir films. These books and movies virtually always featured voluptuous women who brandished their seductive charms as lethal weapons.[4]

During ordinary times, fictional renderings of female characters as diabolical dames might be seen as harmless, designed only to entertain. But Graham's trial occurred in the early Cold War period. A cadre of powerful politicians used media to disseminate warnings about the dire threats that deviation from traditional norms posed to a society fighting for its life against godless Communism.

Tough and virile men guarded the gates of America in this narrative, but they could be rendered weak and helpless by forces outside their control. These forces included seductive females and homosexual males, whom hard-liners constructed as dangerous deviants, arguing that their flouting of traditional norms left America open to attack by foreign enemies. This authoritarian mindset made it easy "to brand [Graham] as a brazen freak, a negative example [of] women who lived beyond the boundaries that had been carefully set out in postwar popular culture."[5]

The power structure that tried Graham for capital murder consisted of individuals who subscribed completely to this masculine ideology. Hard-drinking Los Angeles police chief William Parker ran a tight ship. He brooked no criticism and expected his officers to do whatever it took—legal or illegal—to keep his city clean and his reputation burnished.[6]

Superior court judge Charles Fricke was a former prosecutor with a take-no-prisoners attitude toward criminal defendants. Defense lawyers called him San Quentin Charlie, reflecting the fact that he sent more men and women to prison than any other judge in California. Nearing the end of his career in 1953, Fricke had presided over many of the most sensational trials in Los Angeles dating from the early 1930s.[7]

The Los Angeles County district attorney's office boasted the highest death-penalty conviction rate in the state. Forty-four percent of San Quentin's death row inmates came from Los Angeles County in the 1950s. J. Miller Leavy and Adolph Alexander, prosecutors in Graham's case, were district attorney Ernest Roll's go-to men in the most high-profile capital trials."[8]

Even with these circumstances, Graham might have had several factors in her favor. The prosecution's case was entirely circumstantial. Only one witness, John True, could place her at the murder scene. He had an exceedingly strong incentive to do so, since prosecutors had offered him immunity for testifying. Additionally, none of Graham's arrests had involved violence. And, during jury selection, several potential panelists said they were uncomfortable sentencing a woman to death.

Their discomfort was not unusual. California had executed nearly five hundred men by the early 1950s and only two women. But Graham's tin ear when it came to gender politics made her a near perfect foil for sensational journalists anxious to sell papers, and a notch on the belts of prosecutors desperate to burnish their credentials by eliminating one sexual deviant and two very bad men.[9]

Graham's insistence on playing by her own rules became evident the first day of trial, August 18, 1953, when she entered the courtroom "looking ... like a showgirl."[10] On the second day, she stumbled and fell down the stairs en route from her jail cell to the courtroom. She cried out, loud enough to be heard inside the court. Prosecutors claimed that she "staged the fall to delay the trial" or to facilitate "a break for freedom." The trial, in fact, was postponed for several days as Graham recovered.[11]

The appearance of John True as the prosecution's star witness on August 25 gave Graham her first opportunity to signal how she intended to behave in court. She was understandably angry, since the district attorney had dismissed all the charges against True. Graham was not alone in her anger. Newspapers carried rumors of death threats aimed at True. The most bizarre rumor involved a plot to hurl "liquid fire" at him as he walked to the witness stand. Police apparently believed the rumors; eleven plain-clothed officers accompanied True to court.[12]

Graham "glared malevolently" at True throughout his testimony. He explained that John Santo had invited him to drive from Grass Valley to Southern California the first week of March 1953. It was Saturday, March 7, True told jurors, when Santo first discussed plans for robbing Mable Monahan during a meeting with Emmett Perkins and Graham.

Monahan's presence in the home forced the perpetrators to change plans in a hurry, with obviously disastrous consequences. True placed Graham front and center in his testimony: It was she who beat

Monahan about the head with a gun butt and was responsible for placing the pillowcase over her head. She also helped him wash blood out of his pants after the botched robbery, he said. True and Santo left Southern California shortly after midnight on March 10 and drove all night back to Auburn. "I told him if we got picked up it would go pretty rough," True testified. Santo warned him: "'If they catch you, you die; if you squeal, you die.'"

Graham was also the featured player in the testimony of three individuals who had conspired to trap her into a confession. Their actions were questionable and underhanded, if not illegal, yet they were just business as usual in 1950s Los Angeles. No physical evidence linked Graham to Mable Monahan's murder, so police and prosecutors decided to trick her into admitting involvement.

The plan had three parts. First, police planted Shirley Olson, one of the LAPD's few female officers, as an undercover inmate in the women's jail. Her job: to scout out a potential friend for Graham among the female inmates. Donna Prow filled that role. Prow was a young mother of two small children serving a year for vehicular manslaughter. She agreed to get close to Graham in order to discern whether she had an alibi for the night of the murder. If not, Prow would help Graham arrange for one by setting up a meeting with a "fixer." LAPD officer Sam Sirianni was to pose as the fixer, and, wearing a wire taped to his chest, he would arrange for an alibi. To guarantee the alibi, Graham had to confess.[13]

First to testify was Prow. She arranged to meet Graham, and the two women held several conversations before Prow raised the alibi question. Graham admitted that she could not remember where she had been on March 9 and easily fell into the trap when Prow offered up her alibi witness. Graham even arranged a code phrase, "I came like water, and like wind I go," from her favorite writer, Persian poet Omar Khayyam. Prow denied under cross-examination that prosecutors had given her inducements for her participation, but the day after her testimony she left jail, seven months before her scheduled release date.[14]

Graham reacted with barely concealed rage when Sirianni took the witness stand to discuss his part in the sting. He had used his real name, but she never suspected he was a police officer. Thad Brown, chief of detectives for the LAPD, had recruited him, Sirianni said. He had met with Graham four times. At the first meeting—less than two weeks before the trial started—he and Graham just exchanged preliminary information, Sirianni said. In the three later meetings, when he pushed her to confess and concocted an alibi, he wore a hidden wire taped to his stomach beneath his belt buckle and a microphone taped to his chest. Two recordings were unusable due to background noise in the jail. The third was only slightly better, Sirianni said.

Jurors could not hear the actual recordings, so prosecutors sought and received permission for Sirianni to read from a typewritten transcript. According to the transcript, Graham had agreed to pay Sirianni five hundred dollars for his testimony. He had continually pressed her to recall where she had been on March 9, 1953.[15]

"I don't know," she responded several times.

"Where were you from ten o'clock Monday morning until seven o'clock Tuesday morning?" he asked at one point.

"I was home most of the time."

Finally, after the sixth or seventh time Sirianni failed to get the answer he sought, he rephrased the question: "You were with those four guys on March 9 when everything took place—weren't you?"

"I was with them."

It is impossible to know whether Sirianni came up with the alibi on his own or whether he had help, but it also revealed Graham's cavalier attitude toward sex and adultery. The agreed-upon alibi had the pair trysting in a motel room in the San Fernando Valley town of Encino the night of Mable Monahan's murder.

Graham attorney, Jack Hardy, was outraged by Sirianni's revelations and asked to be taken off the case. His client had told him about Sirianni, Hardy said, but he never suspected the alibi was fraudulent. Judge Fricke denied Hardy's request, but he allowed Hardy to play the third—slightly more decipherable—recording in open court. Most of the words were muffled, but the words "I was with them" could be heard.[16]

Hardy had not planned to ask Graham to testify. Her anger, tendency toward histrionics, casual relationship with facts, and obvious distaste for authority made it a decided gamble. The sting operation forced his hand. On September 1, 1953, as the blazing-hot courtroom sat "in dead silence," Barbara Graham walked to the witness stand to begin "the unhappiest day of her life."[17]

Hardy's instinct about Graham as a witness quickly proved prophetic. She had difficulty recalling biographical details, such as her marriages and divorces. "I'm not good with dates," she explained. She also could not immediately bring to mind the number of children she had borne with first husband Harry Kielhamer.

"One, uh, two," she replied to Hardy's question.

"I beg your pardon?" Hardy asked.

"Two," Graham said.[18]

She admitted working for Emmett Perkins, but was somewhat vague about her job. "What did you do there?" Hardy asked.

"I knew a few people who liked to gamble and I took them out to El Monte."

"Did you receive compensation for this?"

"I would enter into the games myself."

"Did it work out that you would win money?"

"I would usually win some."

"Were you shilling for this game?" Hardy asked.

"Yes, you might say that," Graham replied

She met John Santo at Perkins's gambling parlor in March or

early April 1953, she said, but could not pinpoint the date. She did not know Mable Monahan, she insisted, and had never been to the dead woman's home. She agreed to meet Sirianni and concoct an alibi only after "I wracked my brain to remember where I'd been. I thought the neighbors could tell me and I could tell you what happened."

Hardy tried to take the blame for Graham's predicament: "Did I tell you if you could not remember where you were, you probably were headed for the gas chamber?"

"Yes," she said.

From the witness stand, Graham offered a new version of the events of March 9. That morning she had gone to the grocery store. When she returned home, Henry and their son, Tommy, were gone and she found herself locked out. "I was getting ready to take off my hose and climb in the window when a neighbor—the only name I know him by is Pitts" volunteered to help.

Pitts climbed through the window and let her in, then "used the phone and messed around awhile." Graham gave him some money "to buy something" for her, then admitted that the "something" was marijuana. Pitts took her money but never returned.[19]

Henry returned home and "we started yelling at each other. We fought and argued until about 11 [p.m.]. He started moving his things to the car." At one point Henry hurled a bottle of perfume at his wife. "It hit me on the knee and bruised and cut me," Barbara recalled. Tommy woke up crying, so she went in to soothe him. "Then we started fighting again and Hank was taking his clothes to the car." He left for good at around 4:00 a.m. on March 10, Graham said. She called Emmett Perkins, who took Barbara and Tommy to El Monte.

Jack Hardy wondered why Graham had gone with Perkins rather than remaining in the duplex, since her rent had been paid through the end of March. Graham said she had no money; besides, she feared arrest for writing bad checks—in the amount of $221.

"Were those checks written on accounts that you had in banks?"
Hardy asked.

"I didn't have a bank account."

"In other words, you wrote fictitious checks?"

"Yes."

He asked Graham about her relationship with Donna Prow. Graham said Prow began pursuing her from her first days in county jail and persisted in offering to help find an alibi. "I was frantic," she confessed.[20]

Graham needed only one juror on her side to avoid the gas chamber, but her testimony diminished, rather than enhanced, that prospect. One reporter described her "lolling back and displaying her buxom figure in a new blue blouse." Another insisted that Graham's testimony had not impressed "the ladies of the jury, particularly juror number 5, who goes in for white blouses and for a general appearance designed for comfort more than chic. Juror number 5 even looked down her nose at the woman who potentially could become the most beautiful victim the gas chamber ever has claimed." Illustrating the importance of small gestures, the same journalist noted that when Graham crossed her left hand over "a shapely thigh," there "was no wedding ring on the third finger."[21]

Prosecutor J. Miller Leavy had no way of knowing in the summer of 1953 how Barbara Graham's trial would come to define his career and reputation. His job on cross-examination was to demolish her already-tattered credibility. He also needed to ensure that no juror possessed even a shred of sympathy for Graham. During her time in jail, she had penned mash notes to fellow inmate Donna Prow, some of a sexual nature. For example, she referred to Prow as "doll," "baby," and "sweet candy pants."[22] In one note, Graham had written, "You are the sweetest girl I know and I wish we had met under different circumstances." In another, she penned: "Hi baby. Your note was so sweet, honey, but I want you to be very sure of your feelings, or I wouldn't want to start something we couldn't finish. You are a very lovely and desirable woman, honey, and I want you very much."

A third note referred to her effort to obtain an alibi: "Hi sweets. My attorney wrote me a letter. He told me I was facing the gas chamber because he couldn't locate two people. So I guess you could call it 'the short, happy life of B. G.' I have some terrific plans and you are included in all of them." Sometimes Graham signed off with her given name, or with "xoxo." Other times she used her nickname, Bonnie, including one missive that she ended with "Many kisses, and much love, Bonnie."[23]

"Did you write these?" Leavy asked her.

"It would seem that I did," Graham admitted. She insisted that Prow had initiated contact. Leavy did not introduce Prow's notes into evidence, though it was apparent from the tone of some that Graham was replying to Prow's missives.

Not all of her notes carried a light touch. "If we are given a chance to be together in the future there are a lot of things I want to do for you," Graham wrote. "On the other hand, if you are crossing me, you know what I would have to do."

Leavy asked, "What did you mean by that?" Graham replied, "I meant I would have to "break off the relationship."[24]

By this point in her testimony, Graham "seemed disconcerted," noted one journalist, "and she kept looking down at her neat little ankles while she regarded, also, the arms of the oaken chair that held her; just as the arms of another big chair will keep her confined, the prosecution hopes, while a pellet of poisonous gas is dropped into a little mug right behind the trim little ankles."[25]

Jack Hardy tried to repair his client's battered image on re-cross examination. "Who wrote the first note?" he asked. "Donna did," Graham replied: "She said that I was pretty." He also asked her to read aloud from a letter she had written to Henry Graham from jail. It contained the same terms of endearment, suggesting that she used similar phrasing in all of her correspondence. The letter also revealed Graham to be a caring mother.

"Hi, Hon," the letter began. "Would have written sooner but circumstances prevented it. Anyway, I'm as well as can be expected in here.... My bail is $25,000.00 on the checks, isn't that ridiculous? Also, my checks are paid off. I don't know if it will help or not because the state of California can prosecute on checks without a witness."

She went on to declare herself innocent of the Monahan murder. "You know that I ... could never commit the horrible atrocities." And she spoke of their son, living with Henry Graham's mother: "I was really happy to know that Mom is going to keep Tommy here. It makes me feel better. I was really worried about him. I told Mom I would see she got the money but she said she could manage all right." She ended by noting that "I can only write three pages, but I want to tell you not to worry about me. I'm all right and the only thing I have to worry about is the checks.... Take good care of Tommy baby. I miss him very much. Give him a big hug and kiss for me."[26]

On September 3, as Graham completed her third day on the witness stand, prosecutors sprung a surprise. Henry Graham, her "will-o-the-wisp estranged husband," walked into the courtroom looking somewhat dazed. Both sides had sought him as a witness and ordered him to appear. Graham testified for the defense, but it was a pyrrhic victory, since he contradicted his wife's story. Had he left home on March 9, as Barbara testified? Hardy asked. "No. I moved out the day after getting my last unemployment check," he said, "or the day after that—March 7 or 8."

Asked why had had not tried to help his wife fight the murder charge, Henry said, "I didn't want to get involved." He returned to court the next day to change his testimony. After thinking about it, Henry recalled that he had left his wife on March 9 after all.[27]

As the trial entered its final phase, observers might have wondered whether Emmett Perkins and Jack Santo would play any role in the proceeding. They had sat quietly through more than two weeks of testimony, seldom talking to their attorney, to each other, or to Graham. On September 4 attorney Ward Sullivan opened his defense of both men. He did not plan to call either of his clients to testify.

Sullivan believed he had witnesses who could place both Perkins and Santo somewhere other than Mable Monahan's house on March 9. Harriet Henson was Jack Santo's common-law wife. She testified that Santo had been at home in Northern California at the time of the murder. A number of people could verify her information, she added. She named Jack Ferneaux, a Modesto truck salesman.

As it turned out, Barbara Graham was not the only person lured into a trap. Ferneaux was working with law enforcement in an effort to link Santo and Perkins to a number of murders throughout California. When he learned that Henson sought an alibi for Santo, he offered his services and arranged to meet. He wore a wire to the meeting. "We both know Jack did the [Monahan] job," he said to Henson.

Henson had responded, "Yeah, but that's why I've got a girl who will say she was with him."

Ferneaux asked if Perkins had an alibi. Henson said, "He's going to say that his wife was with him."

Henson also implicated herself as the driver of a getaway car in the 1951 murder of a miner. Police had long suspected Santo and Perkins of committing the crime. Just after Henson finished testifying, police took her into custody. Sullivan called no other witnesses and abruptly rested his case.[28]

The trial had been a wild and chaotic ride. Both sides understood that Perkins and Santo undoubtedly would be convicted of first-degree murder and condemned to die. Graham was the only question mark. In his closing argument Graham's attorney, Jack Hardy, leaned heavily on the lack of evidence. "I don't care whether Barbara Graham was a shill for a gambling place, whether she was a prostitute, whether she had four husbands, or whether she was a liar at another time. She's not on trial for any of those things," he told jurors. Donna Prow and Sam Sirianni had been recruited to "befriend" his client, Hardy added. Both had motives for doing so: "He was a rookie cop and she wanted to get out of jail."[29]

Hardy also admonished jurors to disregard John True's testimony because of its self-serving nature. And he detailed inconsistencies, such as True's admission that he had not seen Graham with a gun during the ride to Mable Monahan's house and yet she had beaten Monahan with a gun minutes later. Graham's dissolute lifestyle did not make her a killer, he insisted. In fact, she abhorred violence.[30]

In spite of prosecutors' unstinting efforts to cast Graham as an unrepentant killer, they obviously worried that she would evade the state's ultimate penalty. Most of their closing statements, which began on September 16, 1953, centered on her.

Adolph Alexander conducted the closing argument. By law, the testimony of accomplices was not enough in itself for conviction, so he was compelled to tell jurors they should view John True's testimony "with caution." Nonetheless, a preponderance of evidence—primarily the effort to obtain a fake alibi—brought "the crime home to these three defendants," he argued.[31]

Turning to Graham, Alexander homed in on her calculating disregard for laws and rules. "March 9 was a very, very fatal and eventful day in the life of Mrs. Graham," he said. "She remembered it because of a fight with her husband. . . . And I was wondering where, when you heard that, you gathered the impression that . . . fighting was a continuous deal there . . . fights were very common, a very usual thing in the life of Mrs. Graham."

Alexander then began to pile on, reading entire letters from Graham to Prow into the record. In one letter, she spoke about the fake alibi: "It is pretty risky, but I'll take the chance. I only hope [Sirianni] doesn't breathe a word. I could be caught in an awful trap. No one is to know, but you, me, and the other party. Sometimes I get to wondering why you're doing this. Do you fully realize what it is?"[32]

The fake alibi may have afforded prosecutors their closest link to a smoking gun, but they were also bent on using the letters as their final weapon in the campaign to reinforce the image of Graham as a sexual deviant. In case jurors failed to grasp the implications of earlier letters, Alexander made certain that they got the point. In one letter, Graham had written to Prow: "Honey, do you take your bath early in the morning? If you do, why don't you take it in number four? Then I can see you. OK?" Alexander paused in the midst of reading. "Is that the mind of a woman desperate because of anything that had been said to her?"[33]

Jurors retired to deliberate and Graham braced for the worst. As she dressed and combed her hair in her cell on September 21, she spoke to a matron: "My stomach is all in knots. Life is so short. Is mine to be shorter?" The answer was not long in coming. After deliberating less than seven hours, the jury foreman rang to notify the court that panelists had reached a verdict.

Graham walked slowly to her seat at the counsel table, with her face "pale and taut, and her reddish-blonde hair drawn up into the familiar bun on the back of her head." She "nodded to an acquaintance. . . . All seats in the courtroom were filled and many spectators crowded around the door and jammed the hall, but there was no demonstration when the verdicts were announced."

Judge Fricke skimmed the verdicts before handing them to the court clerk. Graham "nervously blew her nose with a small handkerchief." The clerk read them one by one, starting with Graham. "Perhaps this was by design. She has been the star of this prolonged murder trial," a reporter noted. Graham sat rigidly still as the clerk intoned: "In the case of the People v. Barbara Graham, we the jury find the defendant guilty of murder, a felony, and find it to be murder in the first degree."

She stood quietly as the bailiff read identical verdicts for Perkins and Santo. Silence followed all of the verdicts. Jurors offered no recommendation on sentence. In the early 1950s, no jury recommendation meant only one thing: death in San Quentin's gas chamber. At first, "Mrs. Graham did not bat an eye." When the sentence finally sunk in, "tears welled in her eyes and she wiped them away with her handkerchief."[34]

As jurors left the courtroom, reporters and photographers surrounded them, but they initially refused to talk. "Our deliberations were our own and we voted as we saw fit," said foreman Robert Dodson of North Hollywood: "The job is done and we want to forget it." Another juror acknowledged that it had taken just five minutes to find the defendants guilty. It took several additional hours to agree on death sentences. The juror declined to say whether Graham's fate had been the most difficult to determine. With the trial ended, Perkins and Santo soon faded into the background. But Barbara Graham did not fade away. Her story, as journalists were fond of saying, had legs.[35]

4

Crime Doesn't Pay

ON NOVEMBER 16, 1953, author Stuart Palmer penned a letter to Richard McGee, director of the California Department of Corrections, asking for permission "to do, if possible a story or series of stories on the [Mable] Monahan murder case, concentrating on Barbara Graham. The aim of the articles is to emphasize the Crime Doesn't Pay angle; there will be no glorification of Barbara or her associates.... I believe that what I write, based on the inside of this mess, may have a deterrent effect on juvenile delinquency."

He concluded by noting that he had the full cooperation of Al Matthews, the attorney hired to handle Graham's appeal. Her trial lawyer, Jack Hardy, had resigned soon after the verdict. The case had cost him emotionally and financially, Hardy said, and he needed to get back to the paying customers in his private practice.[1]

Slightly more than two weeks after sending his letter, Palmer had not heard back from McGee, possibly because he had misspelled McGee's last name as McGeehee. So he wrote again. This time he got McGee's first name wrong, calling him Patrick. Palmer offered a few more details about himself, noting that he was "an author and newspaperman" who worked "occasionally for the Hearst newspapers on special assignments involving murders and murder trials." Palmer

49

informed McGee that a letter from former California attorney general Robert Kenny vouching for his veracity and his work would be arriving at the department of corrections shortly. He also complained that another reporter, a "woman from the *San Francisco Chronicle*" had already been granted permission to interview Graham: "I don't see the justice in excluding other reporters who have a legitimate purpose in mind."

Palmer reiterated his plan to focus on a "crime doesn't pay" angle and acknowledged that the Hearst Corporation had offered him two thousand dollars to pen a lengthy profile on Graham for *American Weekly* magazine, carried as a Sunday supplement in all of the company's nearly two dozen papers that spanned the country. Fearing that McGee might view the money—nearly four months' pay for the average American worker—as excessive and unwarranted, Palmer assured the corrections director that neither he nor Graham would benefit. Rather, the money would go to Henry Graham's mother, Anne Webb, "for help in support of the baby."[2]

McGee eventually approved Palmer's request. His decision was not surprising, since, as Palmer noted, he had already granted another reporter permission to talk to Graham. Additionally, in the early 1950s journalists enjoyed relatively easy access to notable—and notorious—individuals, since the emphasis on arms-length relationships and objectivity was not yet embedded in the profession. Reporters did, however, have to tread carefully and appear to be deferential to high-level officials who had the power to pick and choose interviewers.

As Palmer's letter suggests, Graham was a sought-after interviewee, and understandably so. She was the country's most glamorous death-row inmate, and she obviously possessed a fascinating, if not yet fully revealed, backstory. Reporters, titillated with tidbits of information during her trial, had been waiting to delve more deeply into her life and psyche, and to bask in the presence of such a beautiful, sexual woman.

Their first chance to speak directly with Graham came on September 24, 1953, just two days after the trial verdict, when "more than 25 newsmen—reporters and photographers, television newsreel cameramen, sound technicians, and announcers" crowded into a small anteroom next to the county jail for a press conference. Graham shared media attention that day with actor Rita Hayworth, who married singer Dick Haymes after a stormy marriage to and divorce from Pakistani Prince Aly Khan. Both Graham and Hayworth offered the public respite from drearier news, such as the stalled Korean War peace negotiations, NATO's plan to drop imaginary bombs on Germany, and Wisconsin senator Joseph McCarthy's campaign to withhold United States aid to Britain until that country stopped shipping consumer goods to "Red China."

Adding to Graham's celebrity image was the presence of "several motion picture cameras on tripods, batteries of floodlights, sound equipment, and a maze of electric wires. Shouted directions even provided the noise typical of a movie set." For her initial posttrial appearance Graham exhibited "all the aplomb of a movie queen starring in a colossal production—which, indeed, it appeared to be."[3]

She did not look like a film star though. Possibly at the behest of her new lawyer, she had jettisoned the femme fatale and gun moll personae and now wore jail attire: a loose, dark-blue denim dress that featured a square neck, short capped sleeves, and pockets in the front. Her hair hung limply in a ponytail and, except for lipstick, her face had been scrubbed free of makeup. If reporters hoped to obtain personal information, they came away disappointed. Instead, she again insisted on her innocence and declared that "if the appeal or anything else doesn't go through, I would rather die than spend the rest of my life in prison."

Asked how she felt about the stool pigeon John True, she replied: "I don't know the man. I don't know how he could say the things he did. I only met him once." She also said she had never met the missing Baxter Shorter. One reporter asked her if she believed she might be insane, opening a possible avenue for appeal. "No, I don't," she replied.[4]

Reporters got very little additional information at their second meeting with Graham, more than two weeks later, after she received her formal death sentence from judge Charles Fricke. They waited outside the county jail late on the afternoon of October 14, 1953, to watch her depart Los Angeles for the California Institution for Women, Corona, in a two-car procession. As she walked toward a "light sedan, flanked by two women deputy sheriffs" who would accompany her on the sixty-mile trip, she "paused for television newsreels and answered questions quietly. 'I am innocent of this crime. I swear to God I am innocent. I hope my baby drops dead if I did it.'"

Earlier that day, journalists learned, she had visited with her twenty-month-old son, Tommy. "The boy was wheeled into the room in a stroller, carrying a toy stuffed horse. Tears came to Mrs. Graham's eyes at the sight of her baby. She rushed over to him and clasped him tightly. 'Tommy, Tommy, oh my baby,' she sobbed."[5]

Graham arrived at Corona with an eclectic array of personal items: cash in the amount of $20.63, a gold watch and bracelet, the gold wedding band she had neglected to wear during her trial, thirty record albums, makeup, magazines, matches, a mirror, several blouses and skirts, yellow wool socks, and playing cards. It would take a few more weeks for reporters to wangle personal interviews, but officials at Corona sat down with Graham on October 16, 1953, to put together a formal social history that would become part of her prison file.

The report listed her height at five feet three inches and her weight at 121. She was in excellent health except for her teeth, which had many cavities. Graham acknowledged that both she and her half-sister Claire were illegitimate, with different fathers who were unknown to them. Both girls had been wards of the Alameda County Court until their mother married Joseph Wood on October 10, 1929. After Wood's death in January 1930, Hortense received state aid for them, even though Barbara lived with her mother infrequently. She had "not kept up with her sister and brother," she told prison authorities. The report listed Graham's criminal offenses, but it also included her explanations for some of them. For example, Graham insisted that her June 1944 San Diego arrest for vagrancy did not mean she was a prostitute. And, despite her May 3, 1951, arrest for narcotics, she claimed she was "not a user" and that she had "never used drugs except on a doctor's prescription." She did acknowledge smoking between a half- and full pack of cigarettes daily and drinking socially.

Graham's self-description revealed a hint of grandiosity and a glimpse of the kind of person she might have become, given different life circumstances. Under hobbies, she listed reading, traveling, horseback riding and poetry writing. She claimed to have "had some verses published." The prison's Catholic chaplain noted that she "has a sense of religious values and is definitely aware of the relationship that exists between God and herself. . . . Her early religious training has been neglected with the resultant loss of spiritual values."

The report also included a brief letter from the San Francisco probation officer who oversaw Graham's case following her perjury conviction. He wrote, "I stated to a newspaper reporter when questioned after her arrest that I did not believe Barbara was the violent type, and I could never believe that she would pistol-beat any elderly woman to death."[6]

When Palmer wrote his first letter to McGee, Graham had just settled into the women's prison at Corona to await the state supreme court ruling on the automatic appeal of her death sentence. By the time he wrote the second letter, she had been transferred "under heavy guard" from the women's prison to San Quentin.

Alleged death threats from the underworld led corrections officials, in November 1953, to make the transfer. Rumor had it that Graham would talk to save her life and that the mob feared any information she might divulge.[7] During her years in the San Francisco Bay Area, Graham had many opportunities to glimpse San Quentin, set on a majestic cliff in the Marin County town of San Rafael, just across the San Francisco Bay. Now she lived there, in a cell specially constructed to keep her, as the prison's only female inmate, apart from the approximately 4,800 male prisoners.[8]

The inmates included Caryl Chessman, condemned to die for kidnapping and rape in 1948 but still appealing his verdict and sentence. The time from sentencing to execution ranged from a few months to slightly more than two years in the early postwar period. Judge Charles Fricke had presided over Chessman's case as well as Graham's. His refusal to order a new trial for Chessman following the death of his court reporter and incomprehensible trial transcripts kept the appeal process, and Chessman, very much alive, though five years had elapsed. Chessman was also famous, having smuggled a soon-to-be-published manuscript out of San Quentin. *Cell 2455, Death Row* detailed his life and his prison experiences.[9]

Emmett Perkins and Jack Santo stayed at San Quentin only briefly after their death sentences. They arrived in early October 1953 by armored convoy, accompanied by thirty-six "heavily armed deputies and police" carrying "riot guns, Tommy guns, and sawed-off shotguns." The protection was deemed necessary because police had been tipped that Santo and "Perk" would "never make Quentin alive."[10]

Less than a week later, the men were taken, again under heavy guard, to Nevada City to stand trial for the murder of Edmund Hansen, a gold-mine operator. During the trial, Perkins and Santo tried unsuccessfully to escape from jail via hacksaws. When questioned about how they happened to come by the tools, both men refused to answer. The county sheriff called the escape attempt "just one of those screwball things." Perkins and Santo received life sentences for the killing.[11]

Asked about their trial, Graham said: "I haven't thought about it. I'm busy fighting for my life." Both Perkins and Santo were returned to San Quentin following the Nevada City trial, though they still faced charges in Plumas County for another murder spree, this one involving a grocer and his family. Each earned a second death sentence in this case. Graham would never see either man again.

Graham insisted that her transfer to San Quentin had been unnecessary. "I am positive in my own mind that no one would come in to hurt me and I certainly have no desire to escape," she said. Besides, she was "almost positive that I'll get a new trial and that's the way I want to go free. I want to clear my name. I don't want to run away." In preparation for Graham's arrival, San Quentin had hired four matrons to guard her around the clock. Workmen converted small rooms in what was called the psychopathic hospital into her living quarters. They removed a door leading into the corridor and put up bars, and they installed a small shower and clothes dryer to enable Graham to do her laundry.

Asked by reporters to estimate the annual cost to taxpayers for Graham's unique housing, corrections officials pegged it at fifteen to twenty thousand dollars. This additional expense enraged some lawmakers, who decried what they deemed her "luxurious" living quarters. "I don't think she's worth it," declared Republican assemblyman Caspar Weinberger of San Francisco. Other legislators pressured San Quentin warden Harley O. Teets to deny her any special items, such as the television set she requested.[12]

Teets acceded to the lawmakers' request on the television, an action that led Graham to pen a letter to governor Goodwin Knight asking, instead, for a radio. Knight had just become governor a month earlier. He had been lieutenant governor when Earl Warren resigned to become chief justice of the United States Supreme Court. If, or when, the time came for Graham's execution, California's governor ultimately had the power to commute her sentence to life. Her willingness to approach Knight about a radio can be viewed from several possible angles: perhaps she wanted to establish a personal relationship with Knight, perhaps she felt unfairly singled out for criticism, or perhaps she simply wanted a radio. In addition to revealing Graham's assertiveness, the television incident suggests how closely the press—and the public—still watched her case.

"When I first came here to San Quentin," her letter began: "Mr. Teets, the warden, said I could have a T.V. set, so my attorney made the arrangements to bring me one. Well somehow it got to the press, then the public took it up and I guess they gave Mr. Teets a hard time and people wanted to know why I should have a personally owned set, as none of the other inmates were allowed same. Well, it seems to me that the public should have enough intelligence to know that I cannot sit with 4,800 men, some of whom haven't seen a woman in years, and watch T.V. Do you agree with me there?" She needed the radio, she added, because "every other inmate in this institution has someone to talk to. I do not. I am locked in this tiny cell day and night (22½ hours) except for one hour a day and ½ hour for my shower.

"Even with things as they are, I do not complain and if you should care to inquire I think you will find that I am a model prisoner. So please, please, Gov. Knight, will you give Mr. Teets permission to let me have a radio? I hope I have made myself clear, and that you understand how I feel, it is terrible, in fact, plain hell, just sitting here day after day with nothing to do." Knight authorized the radio.[13]

Graham may have been a public pariah, but some individuals sympathized with her, or at least viewed her predicament as an opportunity to save her soul. She received hundreds of letters, verses from scripture, and numerous Bibles.[14] In late November 1953 Graham received her first prison visits from members of the press. Dilys Jones of the San Francisco *Examiner* reported the obvious: "Her fight to escape execution apparently obsesses Barbara. She chain-smoked and drank coffee while she discussed it yesterday. 'All I want to do is to be a housewife, just like I always have been,'" she told Jones. Graham also wanted to put to rest rumors that Henry Graham had left her. "My husband is still with me," she insisted.[15]

To Carolyn Anspacher of the *San Francisco Chronicle*, Graham revealed that she was unable to eat and had lost weight. "I don't sleep either," she said: "I keep having dreams about going to the gas chamber." As she spoke, she fingered four religious medals knotted on a piece of string around her neck. "If I get out of this, it will be because of Saint Jude. He is the saint of the impossible and I sure need his help." Anspacher also spoke with Al Matthews, Graham's appellate attorney, who said he was convinced that she did not kill Monahan. A psychiatrist had examined his client, he added, and found that "despite mild depression, she gave no indication of psychopathy."[16]

Graham had perked up somewhat by the time Bernice Freeman, the *San Francisco Chronicle* reporter mentioned by Stuart Palmer, sat down with her. Freeman was destined to become closest to Graham of all the female reporters covering her story, possibly because she strongly opposed the death penalty. Freeman came to abhor capital punishment, she later wrote, after witnessing several executions, including that of Eithel Spinelli, the first woman executed in California. Freeman described Spinelli's demeanor during a press conference just before her November 1941 death: "She spoke in a rasping, gravelly voice, muttering, 'lies—lies—all lies.'" As she turned to leave, Spinelli had pointed a finger at reporters as she muttered a curse.[17]

Freeman met Graham in her cell at "the end of a corridor on the third floor of the prison hospital. Heavy, dark curtains concealed ugly steel bars separating her from male hospital patients." She was taken aback by how little prison had affected Graham's appearance, and how much care she still took to make herself up, despite her limited contact with outsiders. Freeman described Graham as "a small brunette with huge brown eyes fringed with long, dark lashes and soft olive skin. She wore her floor-length navy blue housecoat like an evening gown and around her slender neck was a narrow band of black velvet ribbon. . . . The girl was a little beauty."[18]

Graham refused to discuss her trial and death sentence, but opened up regarding other aspects of her life. About her mother, Graham said, "She never cared whether I lived or died as long as I didn't bother her." For the first time, she admitted to being a prostitute: "At least I am what I am, and not a damned hypocrite. Why do people make so much of sex? It's part of our natural makeup. . . . I love clothes and jewels and furs. I'd do a lot of things to get them. But not murder. I'm no killer."

After the interview, Freeman sought out John True, who was repairing boats in the Marin County town of Sausalito. True called Graham "the meanest, coldest little bitch I ever come across, and I come across some beauts." Freeman quickly came to doubt True and to discount his depiction of Graham, however. She questioned him about other events and individuals as well, and after checking out his stories, she declared that True was "extremely untruthful, a liar." Four months later, Freeman returned to San Quentin. She found Graham much changed from the previous visit. She was pale and nervous and "smoked incessantly." Her hands shook. Whenever she wanted to emphasize a point to Freeman, "she swore it on Tommy's head."[19]

Stuart Palmer finally sat down to talk with Barbara Graham in March 1954, about the same time as Freeman's second visit. The interviews gave him everything he aimed for in terms of a good—perhaps too good—story. Palmer went into the assignment promising a "crime doesn't pay" angle, but he emerged believing that Graham "is not exactly guilty as charged." In fact, Palmer seems to have become somewhat smitten with her and convinced that jurors had wrongly sentenced her to die.

He discussed his change of heart soon after interviewing Graham, when he wrote again to corrections director Richard McGee. His articles had not yet appeared in print, and to McGee he wrote: "I have tried to be objective and will not express my private opinion as to her possible innocence though I think she is not exactly 'guilty as charged.' My private investigation of the angles of the whole mess impel me to the conviction that it is not all out in the open yet." Palmer then made what he acknowledged was "perhaps an impertinent suggestion"—to allow Graham to take a lie detector examination. "We both know that lie-detector tests are fallible, but something useful might come out of it. . . . The thing could be handled quietly, with competent state medical men in charge."[20]

No record exists of McGee's response. It appears that he passed on the lie detector request to Los Angeles County authorities, who declined to schedule one. District attorney Ernest Roll acknowledged that such procedures could be "useful during the investigative phases" of criminal cases, but were "inadmissible in court."[21]

Palmer's stories appeared in *American Weekly* in two separate installments, on April 4 and April 11, 1954. Taking a page from *True Detective* and other pulp magazines, they carried Graham's byline accompanied by the phrase, "as told to Stuart Palmer." The first-person account made Graham sound like a hard-boiled dame in a Mickey Spillane novel, though one with a soft side.[22] Palmer apparently hoped to achieve several objectives: to entertain and elicit sympathy from readers, while at the same time at least taking a stab at presenting his "crime doesn't pay" angle. Not all of the details exactly squared with earlier information, though, including that from official sources.

"The testimony of a thief, a safe-cracker, and a stool pigeon put me here in the death cell," the story began. "And my own foolish attempts to fake an alibi, when I found myself trapped, were chalked up as a sure confession of guilt. Maybe some psychologist could dig back into my past and point out the tragic milestone where my feet first strayed onto the path that has led me, in a devious way, to the death cell. As I sit here waiting, I've tried to find that first misstep too—for my own peace of mind and, perhaps, in the hope of softening the blow for my three little boys when someday they know all about what happened to their mommie."

She began her tale with Hortense, the mother who "hated me from the day I was born in an Oakland, California, slum back in 1923." When Graham was a toddler, "Hortense dumped me with relatives and disappeared." When she returned home, "she put me out to board with a woman named Kennedy who punished me by making me stand in a corner for hours, holding a raw onion up to my face."

Graham's stepfather, Joseph Wood, came to retrieve her when she was six years old, and life went smoothly for a few months. Then he died "and things really got tough. Hortense was young and pretty and had lots of boyfriends of one kind or another and didn't hesitate to let me know I was in the way. One day when Hortense got really mad, she took me to an orphanage, St. Mary's of the Palms in San Jose."

Graham was prepared to hate the place, but the Catholic sisters treated her kindly. "It's funny; almost the only happy memory of my childhood is that of the few months I spent in the orphan asylum."[23] She described being taken home after only eight months, being sent to another facility and, finally, moving back with Hortense and enrolling in the eighth grade, where she fell in love with poetry. "I've always been a pushover for poetry," Graham declared: "It speaks to me like nothing else."

The always-tenuous relationship between Graham and her mother soured quickly upon her return home. "I was big and mature for my age and a little interested in the opposite sex." Hortense refused to allow her to attend extracurricular activities of any kind, her daughter claimed, "so I ran away to San Francisco and tried to get a job as a waitress." There she met a man who took her home to his mother. "It was wonderful to have someone like me. I wasn't promiscuous."

Hortense came to get her and deposited her at the Ventura reform school. "The matrons there took pains to tell me I was traveling in my mother's footsteps," Graham recalled. "'A chip off the old block,' that's what they called me. I learned for the first time that her strange disappearance, when I was two, was an enforced one."

Graham cast her behavior at Ventura and on probation in a much more positive light than her official records indicate. "Somehow I stuck out my two years at the reform school and was paroled." Afterward, she went to work as "a domestic servant for a few measly dollars a week washing piles of greasy dishes and scrubbing miles of dirty floors with no nights off, no fun, no radio, and no books to read. All the while I could feel unseen eyes on me, watching to see if the criminal girl from the reformatory would steal the silverware." She claimed to have stayed with this job for "a whole eight months." Then she worked "at one job or another" until she met and married Harry Kielhamer, a "nice dull mechanic."

The couple met in a bar, she said, "a place where the men you meet take it for granted you'll say yes to the only question they have on their minds." They "teamed up about as well as a plow horse and a wild mustang, and the birth of our first son Billy didn't make the yoke any easier." They stayed together through the birth of Michael, whom Graham consistently referred to as Darryl Michael, contradicting the official birth record. Then, in 1942, Kielhamer divorced her. According to Graham, he did not want the boys and she could not support them, so they went to live with her former mother-in-law in Seattle.

After her divorce, she drifted up and down California, "trying to find some place I'd fit, somebody who'd want me." She briefly tried and mostly failed at getting legitimate jobs and found herself in San Diego. "I was pretty and knew I could trade on my looks, so I guess

I became what they call a 'sea gull,' following the fleet. When you're broke . . . that line of least resistance sometimes looks like the only answer. But there is no percentage in playing at the oldest profession in the world."

She described her brief second marriage, her few attempts to put her life right, and her decision in 1947 to lie for Mark Monroe, who was convicted of trying to murder madam Sally Stanford. "I'd always gone all out for my friends," Graham said. She received a light sentence "because the other girl who swore to the fake alibi made some deal to talk and my lawyer pointed out that it would look funny if she got off and I did the whole [sentence]. I've never sung in my life and I never will."[24]

The second *American Weekly* installment began with her introduction to Henry Graham in 1950. "He certainly was no movie star Adonis type, and I can't explain why I fell in love for the first time in my somewhat spotty young life, unless it was his ready grin and nice sense of humor. . . . I was mad for Hank and I guess I still am. He had a good job at that time as a bartender and so we made it legal.

"For a little while I was happier than I've ever been since I left the kind sisters at Saint Mary's orphanage," Graham said. "I even thought of getting Billy and Darryl Michael, my two little boys back from Seattle. I'd had that plan set up once before when I had a regular job as a dice girl in Reno, but Hortense queered it all by going to see Min Kielhamer and telling her I spent a year in the penitentiary on a perjury rap. A nice mother, Hortense!"

Eventually, Graham learned that her fourth husband had a drug problem. He lost his job and so she went to work for Emmett Perkins, "a sporty little guy with a face like a weasel. There'd be a nice split for me if I'd work as a come-on girl for the place. Wise little me! I'd doll up in my best, one or two nights a week" and cruise the big hotels. "A pretty girl alone in a bar means just one thing to men. I'd let them buy me a couple of drinks and then when they asked the $20 question, I'd hint 'maybe.' But I'd let on that I was just dying to do a little gambling first and that I knew a swell place. Then I'd steer them to Emmett's, where I won't say the games were exactly crooked, but the odds were slanted in favor of the house." She insisted that her relationship with Perkins was "strictly business."[25]

After the birth of their son, Tommy, Henry Graham drifted deeper into drugs and the couple began to argue and fight constantly. Nonetheless, "things went along pretty well until early March 1953," Barbara Graham recalled: I'm positive it was the 9th of March [that] Hank and I had an all-day and all-night knock-down, drag-out fight." Barbara was furious at Henry's refusal to get a job, and Henry was angry that Barbara, after a hiatus that began with Tommy's birth, went back to work for Perkins in his gambling establishment.

"I just had to keep on because somebody had to keep the family together. Nobody can say I wasn't a good mother either. I kept Tommy spic and span. Anyway, after that all-day, all-night fight, Hank walked out on us. When I called his mother a couple of days later, she said he'd gone to Mexico." Graham admitted writing bad checks to pay for groceries but "always aimed to make them good." Then came the crux of the tale: the Monahan murder and its aftermath. Some of the details of Graham's living arrangements during this period differed from those presented earlier in newspaper accounts. It is impossible to know which version, if any, is accurate. Graham said she did not read or hear about the murder until Henry left her and she "drifted over to Emmett's. The place was closed up," but Perkins and Santo were there, Graham recounted:

I hardly knew Santo. Emmett didn't waste any time breaking the news to me that all three of us were wanted for murder. That was the first time I heard of the crazy killing of a helpless old woman, Mrs. Mabel Monahan.

Maybe if I'd gone to the police right then I wouldn't be here now. But that wasn't my way. All I could think of was the five years of probation hanging over my head in San Francisco and the checks I hadn't had time to cover. I grabbed Tommy and off we went. It was Jack Santo's idea to hole up in a series of auto courts until the whole thing blew over. The whole thing was a nightmare and it was no life for Tommy. Finally, I drove him to his grandmother's and that's where he is today.

True lied to police, and then to jurors, about her participation, Graham insisted: "Does it sound reasonable—that four men would stand by while a girl does the strong-arm stuff? He swore that he saw me hold Mrs. Monahan with my left hand and beat her across the head and face with a pistol held in my right hand—me, that's left-handed."

American Weekly readers might have wondered why Graham's defense attorney never raised the issue of her right- or left-handedness at trial, since it might have enabled him to poke holes in True's story. But Graham had a history of misstatements, if not outright lies. This may have been another: Photographs show Graham smoking with her left hand, but she wore her watch on her left wrist, suggesting that she was right-handed. A police booking sheet from one of her arrests provided to the press after her execution notes her right-handedness, but it may have been altered, as prosecutors had a strong incentive to justify their actions in her case. Attorney Al Matthews could not include the question of handedness in the appeal because the information had been available during the trial, though it is unclear whether Graham realized this. In reality, she may have been ambidextrous.

Graham blamed attorney Jack Hardy for her decision to attain a false alibi; it was Hardy who had warned her repeatedly about the need for an alibi. "I knew I had to do something. I talked it over with another prisoner, a pretty little girl named Donna Prow. Donna said she knew a small-time operator named Sam Sirianni. He would swear, for a price, that he'd spent the night with me in an auto-court. I was so desperate I would have leapt at any chance to save myself. ... I talked pretty freely to Sirianni because he spoke my language. I was determined to gain his confidence and said a lot of things that weren't true so he'd think I wouldn't double-cross him. I broke Rule A—never lie to your lawyer. I didn't kill Mrs. Monahan. I never saw her in my life."[26] The story ended with Graham's declaration that "I'd rather die in the gas chamber than spend the rest of my life in prison. Life imprisonment without hope is a thousand times worse than a swift and sure death that will guarantee that I'll never need to run and hide again."[27]

The *American Weekly* series on Graham sold extra copies of many Hearst newspapers, but they did not please corrections chief Richard McGee. In early June 1954 continuing outcry from lawmakers over Graham's special accommodations led authorities to move her back to the women's institution at Corona. McGee wasted little time before writing to Corona prison superintendent Alma Holzschuh demanding that she cut off Palmer's access to Graham: "He has not been cleared ... as one of her regular correspondents, and I see no reason why he should be." McGee was most displeased by the use of Graham's byline over the articles, which appeared at a particularly delicate time. Caryl Chessman's autobiography had just been released, becoming an overnight bestseller.

"Please advise Mrs. Graham," McGee wrote, "that the rules and regulations of the Department require that if any inmate ... wishes to write for publication, they shall first submit the manuscript to this office for review and approval.... The sensational publicity that accompanies this type of thing interferes unnecessarily and improperly with the orderly administration of justice. It is probable that a mistake in judgment was made in permitting Chessman to offer his materials for publication until after his execution. Because one mistake was made is no basis for assuming that we should continue to make the same one over and over."[28]

McGee won his battle, at least with regard to Graham. After the *American Weekly* series, her byline never again appeared in print and Stuart Palmer never scored another interview. As her case wound toward its conclusion, however, other reporters stepped into the breach as Graham's regular correspondents. Bernice Freeman of the *San Francisco Chronicle* journeyed on more than one occasion to Corona. Some new journalists made the trek as well. They included Edward S. Montgomery of Hearst's San Francisco *Examiner*. Montgomery, like Palmer, initially had believed, strongly, in Graham's guilt and death sentence. Also like Palmer, he had changed his mind.

5

An Execution in California

EDWARD S. MONTGOMERY "covered everything from doll shows to executions" in his forty-year career as a newspaper reporter. He reveled in his job and in the power it gave him to shape public opinion and to hold public officials' feet to the fire. Originally from Colorado, he began his career in Reno, Nevada, before World War II, but spent most of his working life at the San Francisco *Examiner*. Part of the nationwide Hearst chain, the *Examiner* competed fiercely with other San Francisco dailies, but its most important rival was the *San Francisco Chronicle*.[1]

By the early 1950s, Montgomery was his newspaper's ace reporter and could be counted on to garner major scoops and prizes. One competitor described him as "a serious, bespectacled journalist—a loner."[2] Montgomery liked working alone and loved digging to find stories. In 1950 he spent weeks wading through records and interviewing dozens of people—including mobsters and a San Francisco abortionist—for a series detailing how Internal Revenue Service personnel extorted money from individuals facing scrutiny for income tax evasion. The series resulted in prison time for the conspirators and forced the IRS to acknowledge lax enforcement of professional standards. It won Montgomery the 1951 Pulitzer Prize for Local Reporting.

Several years later the *Examiner* assigned Montgomery to cover the disappearance of Stephanie Bryan, a Berkeley teenager. After Bryan's purse turned up in the home of University of California accounting student Burton Abbott, Montgomery went the extra mile—literally—chartering a plane to remote Alpine County, where Abbott and his family had a cabin. Accompanied by a photographer, Montgomery rented the services of a dog handler and, with two canines, combed the rugged mountain terrain. About four hundred yards from the cabin, in a heavily forested area, one of the dogs began to paw at the ground.

Montgomery moved in closer and spied a saddle shoe protruding through the earth. He called local police, who unearthed Bryan's body. His diligence and enterprise earned Montgomery approximately twelve thousand dollars per year. This represented more than twice the average male salary in the 1950s, and in a field that was notoriously low paying.[3]

Montgomery was forty-two and had been at the *Examiner* for eight years when the trial of Barbara Graham, Emmett Perkins, and John Santo began in August 1953. Though Los Angeles was four hundred miles south of San Francisco, *Examiner* editors assigned him to the story because Graham was from the Bay Area, John True was originally questioned by San Francisco police, and Perkins and Santo were suspects in Northern California murders. Montgomery attended the trial only sporadically. Nonetheless, he believed his journalistic experience enabled him to quickly and accurately size up the players and the narrative thread of the courtroom drama.[4]

Like many high-profile journalists of his era, Montgomery saw himself as a participant in the stories he covered, an advocate for the forces of good. He did not posit himself as an impartial observer, a status to which the next generation of reporters would aspire. As Graham's trial unfolded, he stood squarely on the side of prosecutors, believing that they possessed "a perfect case.... The evidence of murder was there. Conclusive evidence gilted [*sic*] by the confession of one of the participants—a third man who elected to 'sing' as State's witness to escape the gas chamber." Public outrage over Mable Monahan's murder made death sentences for the three defendants a foregone conclusion to newshounds, including Montgomery, who hungrily lapped up each crumb of information tossed by police and prosecutors.[5]

Montgomery believed Graham to be guilty of murder, but she also intrigued him. As he sat through the trial's closing arguments, he attempted "to evaluate the personalities of the three defendants seated before me." Knowing that Santo and Perkins already had been linked to other killings, "I found myself observing them with a jaundiced eye." He recalled later that Graham seemed different, less tough and hard than he had expected.

After her death verdict, Montgomery stood in the hallway outside the courtroom with dozens of other reporters clamoring for a comment from Graham. He asked her, cavalierly: "How about it Babs: Just a short statement?" She offered a terse response: "You're all invited to the execution. It's only fair." Turning to Montgomery, she added: "Bring your wife. She'll enjoy it."[6]

Her bitter comment stayed with Montgomery as he returned to San Francisco. He moved on to other stories, but could not get Graham out of his head. At some point in 1954, he found himself between assignments and decided to spend some time revisiting her case. Initially, he sought only to satisfy his reportorial curiosity. He started with the San Francisco Police Department, where John True had confessed before testifying to the Los Angeles County grand jury and receiving immunity from prosecution. Montgomery had many police sources and managed to gain access to True's confession.

What he found troubled him, he recalled later. True had given police a different version of events than the one he recounted in court. In San Francisco, True acknowledged that he and Santo had discussed retrieving the one hundred thousand dollars from Monahan's safe long before the actual event. They planned to use the money to finance a logging operation in Idaho. Santo recruited Perkins because he was an expert safecracker—a "box cutter" in criminal argot. Perkins planned to burn the safe open with a blowtorch. He told police that he had washed Monahan's blood off his pants before leaving Los Angeles for Northern California. At the trial True said he knew nothing of Santo's robbery plan until it was already under way; that Perkins planned to use nitroglycerine to "blow the safe," and that Graham had helped him wash blood out of his pants after the murder.

These discrepancies and others concerned Montgomery, who decided to dig deeper. He arranged to interview "a mobster whose underworld tips I had always found accurate." His source "insisted that Barbara had been framed, that it was John Santo's idea to implicate her if they got caught." Since she worked for Perkins, she was the logical choice. Both men "figured Barbara was certain to beat the gas chamber. She was a young, attractive woman, a mother. . . . That was why the men had put the murder weapon in her hand."[7] Montgomery never explained why he believed this particular source might possess valid information on the case. Nor did he question the story's authenticity, since it reinforced his growing conviction that Graham was innocent of first-degree murder.

Next, Montgomery sought out Al Matthews, Graham's appellate attorney. Matthews suggested that Montgomery talk to psychiatrist Carl Palmberg. Matthews had recruited Palmberg, who specialized in analyzing criminals, to give Graham a series of word-association tests preparatory to filing his appeal. Palmberg told Montgomery of his conclusion that Graham was a compulsive liar, with a "sick sense of humor and imagination." She was, however, "repulsed by violence," Palmberg said.[8]

Armed with this information, Montgomery contacted the California Department of Corrections to request an interview with Graham herself. At their first meeting she was understandably skeptical. "It's too late," she informed him. He shook her off: "I'm going to try to help you by writing a series of stories about your tragic childhood." In his recollection, she responded: "Do that, and point up a moral. Point out that I'm a bastard and never should have been born."

Montgomery also visited Santo and Perkins at San Quentin. He described Santo as "deliberate, yet impatient and quick tempered ... always motivated by his insatiable quest for a fast buck." Santo also was "a cowardly man who wanted a shoulder to cry on; a man who moped in self-pity." Perkins, on the other hand, was a "cool, methodical killer ... the gambler who, knowing something had gone awry, was willing to pay off when the cards totaled 22 in a 21 game."[9]

Montgomery wrote a few stories on Graham, but mostly used them to castigate journalists—himself included—for sensational, slanted, tabloid-style coverage of Graham's trial. Reporters had portrayed her as "the hop-head, the gun-moll, the ice blonde, the brazen femme fatale. . . . Here were the sparks, once kindled, that mushroomed into the all encompassing flames of public prejudice and bias. . . . The public was given no respite from the constant indoctrination that here was a girl every bit as rotten and as vicious as the two men seated to the right of her at the counsel table."[10]

By early 1955 Montgomery had become obsessed with Graham's case, viewing her death sentence as a gross miscarriage of justice. He had covered other stories about condemned criminals, so it is not entirely clear why this particular one grabbed him so fiercely. Perhaps, like other reporters, he had fallen prey to her beauty and sexuality. Additionally, Graham was a near-perfect human-interest subject; this kind of story sold papers. What made Montgomery's obsession unique was his decision to abandon his role as a journalist—he virtually stopped writing stories about her—and to take up the role of advocate.

Montgomery embarked on an intensive campaign to derail the

execution. Even with his credentials and access to authority figures, it was very much a long shot. Few condemned men or women had their sentences commuted in the 1950s. Moreover, the legal system and politicians in general comprised a closed fraternity whose members held firm against attempts by outsiders to challenge their authority. As a journalist, Montgomery had access to insiders, but in Graham's case, he was acting as a private citizen, without a powerful newspaper mogul behind him.

Montgomery believed that his best chance for action lay with California's top law enforcement official, California attorney general Edmund G. "Pat" Brown, who must have seemed a likely ally. Brown personally opposed the death penalty, and he held the power to authorize a lie detector test for Graham. If she took it and passed, Montgomery hoped the resulting publicity might lead to a new trial. Los Angeles officials had turned down an earlier request by writer Stuart Palmer for a polygraph examination, and Montgomery hinted that they feared the results might embarrass them and exonerate her.

Brown initially agreed to Montgomery's request and authorized two experts—one from the Berkeley Police Department and the other from the University of California—to administer an exam using sodium amytal, the so-called truth serum. But Brown's chief investigator soon intervened. He did not want to antagonize law-and-order forces in Southern California, did he? Brown did not. He planned to run for governor and needed the support of law enforcement. Reluctantly, he rescinded the request.[11]

Meanwhile, state and federal courts had begun ruling on Graham's case and those of her two codefendants. In his effort to win Graham a new trial, appellate attorney Matthews had cited "adverse newspaper coverage" and "entrapment, coerced admissions, and illegal search and seizure when a police undercover agent recorded conversations with her in the County Jail." These arguments failed to sway judges in California.

Matthews and appellate attorneys for Perkins and Santo then requested that the United States Supreme Court review all court documents in the case. Graham recognized that her chances for a new trial were slim. "Here I am again. Not anxious or anything you know," she wrote Al Matthews in October 1954. A few weeks later, she wrote again: "I am in a deplorable frame of mind. At my lowest ebb, I might say. Nothing seems to have any meaning."

On November 26, 1954, however, the U.S. high court ordered a stay of execution. This action extended the lives of all three Monahan defendants past the scheduled December 3 execution date.[12] Graham was in better spirits when she wrote to Matthews early in December: "I do the same thing every day. Never a change. Instead of just talking to myself, I'll soon be answering. I hear that is a bad sign."

Then in February 1955 she lost an important ally when psychiatrist Carl Palmberg died of cancer in Los Angeles. Graham was distraught. "Carl's death is a terrible shock to me," she wrote to Matthews: "We have lost a very loyal friend."[13]

In March the U.S. Supreme Court denied Graham's petition, along with those of Perkins and Santo. The justices' action lifted the stay, enabling Los Angeles Superior Court judge Charles Fricke to set a new execution date. He chose June 3, 1955, for all three condemned inmates.[14] Graham wrote to Matthews: "I feel as though the bottom of everything has given way in me. Now the enormity of it has fallen full force on me. Life is such an odd game. The suspense is almost over. At times it is still hard to realize that I am the main figure in all this. Insignificant Barbara Graham. If it wasn't all so serious, it would be funny, but my sense of humor has failed me at this point." She still held a spark of hope though: "Life does seem very dear to me. I do want to live."[15]

She refused to see or correspond with her two oldest sons. William was almost fifteen and still lived in Washington. Michael was thirteen and lived with friends somewhere in California; both his first and last names had been changed. Tommy was three and lived with his father in Los Angeles. Henry Graham and his mother occasionally brought Tommy to Corona for brief visits. Graham sought to shield all of her sons from the publicity and trauma associated with her pending execution and hoped they would never learn what happened to her. "I just want them to forget me," she told Bernice Freeman of the *San Francisco Chronicle*. Freeman asked Graham if her estranged mother Hortense Wood had contacted her. "No, Berni, but I wish she would," Graham replied.[16]

Freeman continued to visit Graham in prison and she reported that the condemned woman "had great, dark circles beneath her eyes." Graham herself commented on the toll the pending execution had taken on her health. "You should see my poor feet," she wrote to Al Matthews at one point. From the ankle down, "I look like an Egyptian Mummy. As I told you yesterday, my nerves are so bad, I have my feet in shreds, don't know why I picked on them. The Dr. is now giving me medicine to see if he can't get me calmed down." In another letter, she wrote, "I weighed today and have lost 15 pounds. 115 pounds. What is it they say about a hank of hair and a bone?"[17]

To keep her sanity, Graham listened to music, including Verdi's *Rigoletto* and Bizet's *Carmen*. "For the past two hours I've been listening to Carmen," she wrote Matthews. "It sure has some frantic music in it. I especially like where she does the Gypsy song and dance. For the most part it is the music that moves me."[18]

Though she was almost certainly headed to the gas chamber, Graham's partisans continued their efforts to save her life. In addition to Matthews and Montgomery, they included former San Quentin chief medical officer Dr. William Graves. After many conversations with Graham during her time at that prison, Graves concluded that she was eminently redeemable. Despite her "many unsavory relationships, there remains in her a capacity for growth and I feel confident in her eventual rehabilitation."[19]

San Francisco madam Sally Stanford, the victim of the attempted robbery that led to Graham's jail sentence for perjury in 1948, also pled her case. "I feel sorry for the girl," Stanford said. "I know she's not lily white, but I also know she's not capable of murder."[20] And Graham still had loyal friends. Sherry Keyes was a fellow seagull who had straightened out her life, married, and become a homemaker. Keyes visited Graham in prison, sent photos of Tommy, and wrote letters. "Dear little Bonnie," she wrote in one missive: "We are still hoping and praying. All our love, Sherry and Kevin."[21]

Keyes seemed to be the only person to whom Graham let down her guard. "The other day I was feeling so badly, and I had no shoulder on which to weep," Graham wrote her attorney, "so I sat down and wrote poor Sherry the longest, saddest, most morbid letter I have ever written. She said it took her hours to read it, because she had to cry every few lines."[22]

With days ticking away and hope diminishing for a new trial, Ed Montgomery turned to Graham's last remaining hope: California governor Goodwin Knight. At least once a week, starting in early May 1955, he drove two hundred miles round-trip between San Francisco and Sacramento. On several occasions, he met with Knight's clemency secretary, Joseph Babich, whose job entailed reading voluminous files in death-penalty cases and making recommendations to the governor. If Montgomery could convince Babich to recommend clemency, Knight would most likely commute Graham's death sentence to life in prison. So far, Babich had found no discernable grounds for commutation, he informed Montgomery.

As a last resort, Montgomery wrote to Emmett Perkins. He previously had met with Perkins and John Santo at San Quentin. "I have interceded with the governor on behalf of Barbara Graham," he began.

I have just returned from Sacramento, and while the Governor still has my request for a commutation of sentence under advisement, I must in all frankness advise you that I came away with the feeling there is little hope that my request will be granted.

It occurs to me that the one thing that might spare Barbara's life is a complete statement from you as to the events that transpired the night Mrs. Monahan met her death. While neither you nor Santo have ever acknowledged to me any complicity in the Burbank case, the fact remains you stand convicted and under sentence of death.

To take with you any personal knowledge you may have of the Monahan murder, especially with the realization that you might have provided the means of commutation for Mrs. Graham, would at best be a very hollow attainment.

Should you at this late hour be inclined to talk, and even though what you might have to say constitutes an admission, please convey such desires to Warden [Harley] Teets, who in turn, if he will, can convey your message to me. I shall be available regardless of the hour.

Perkins did not respond.[23]

By the time Montgomery wrote to Perkins, San Quentin officials had begun preparations for June 3. For the first time in California history, three condemned inmates would die on the same day. Graham was scheduled to go first, alone, at 10:00 a.m.; Perkins and Santo were scheduled to die together at 1:00 p.m., giving guards nearly three hours to clear the poisonous gas out of the death chamber. The two men were already housed on death row; Graham had to be brought to the prison from the women's institution at Corona.

On Tuesday, May 31, two officers with the California Corrections Department departed Northern California for the first leg of the journey. From San Quentin, they drove down Highway 101 to San Luis Obispo, where they spent the night. About 2:00 p.m. June 1, they arrived at Corona and made arrangements for departure early the next morning. Later that same afternoon they drove to San Bernardino, where they met two California Highway Patrol officers who were scheduled to accompany them on the trip north.

State officials sought extra protection to avoid slip-ups, such as a last-minute effort to rescue Graham. The guards spent the night of June 1 at the California Institution for Men in Chino, a few miles from the women's prison. Shortly before 5:00 a.m. on June 2, the corrections officers drove over to Corona to meet their highway patrol counterparts and to pick up Graham.

"We finished breakfast at approximately 5:15 a.m.," wrote one unnamed officer, "and were informed that Mrs. Graham was dressing, therefore not yet ready to depart. At 5:45 a.m., Mrs. Graham emerged from her quarters ready to leave on the trip. She was cuffed with regulation handcuffs and a leather belt, placed in the rear seat of our automobile, and was accompanied by Mrs. M. F. Dutro, Corona supervisor assigned to the detail." Dutro sat in the backseat with Graham and the two men occupied the front-seat. As the cars approached Corona's main gate shortly before 6:00 a.m., "we were met by a great many reporters and photographers. Many pictures were taken. No interviews were granted. The car proceeded slowly and made no stops."[24]

Graham had spent her final days at Corona listening to music and reading. "I listen to classical music and I'm reading a book about Socrates," she told one interviewer. "You always hope, but if it is the will of God that I die, then I'll die. I'm at peace with God and with myself."[25] In preparation for her last night, Graham packed a pair of red pajamas, cold cream, bath powder, a copy of *The Rubaiyat* by Omar Khayyam, a change of underwear, toilet articles, and a pair of pendant earrings. She wore the same tailored suit and shoes she had worn during her trial, as well as her wedding ring and a wristwatch.[26]

As the caravan made its way north, San Quentin warden Harley O. Teets announced that prison nurse Barbara Cates had volunteered to stay with Graham. Teets also notified guards who patrolled the prison's perimeter that when Henry Graham arrived to pick up his deceased wife's belongings the following day, "he is to be kept at the East Gate. I will talk to Mr. Graham on the phone." Keaton's Mortuary in the Marin County town of San Rafael "will arrive at 11:00 a.m. to take the remains."[27]

Meanwhile, Teets made preparations to receive Graham at San Quentin. He worried about her reaction upon first glimpsing the squat, green gas chamber and ordered prison personnel to cover it with a tarp. The steel structure stood in the basement of North Seg, the building that housed death-row inmates. The back of the chamber was windowless, but the front four sides, which faced a circular railing, held large windows with blinds that could be opened and closed. Execution witnesses stood behind the railing to watch the proceedings. Forty people would witness Graham's execution, including journalists, police officers, and prison guards. At her request, no family or friends would be there.

The chamber held two chairs. Both had holes in their seats and in the wrap-around metal siding that extended from the seats to the floor. The holes allowed gas—created when egg-sized cyanide pellets wrapped in cheesecloth were dropped into a bucket containing sulfuric acid—to permeate the chamber. The combination of chemicals caused death within minutes. The chair contained thick straps that guards affixed to the upper and lower legs, arms, thighs, and chests of condemned inmates. Graham, like all of her predecessors both male and female, would spend her last night in one of two holding cells fifteen feet away and around a corner from the chamber. The holding area also contained a black phone with a long cord, used to communicate last-minute stays of execution.[28]

By the time Graham's car drove through the gates at about 4:00 p.m. on June 2, dozens of reporters and photographers had gathered at the prison entrance. "No one seemed to care much about Santo and

Perkins," one reporter noted, "but there was a good deal of interest in Mrs. Graham."[29] Eleven reporters had signed up to witness her execution. Ed Montgomery would not be among them, though he would be at San Quentin. He would spend the night the warden's office, still hoping to convince Emmett Perkins, at the last minute, to exonerate Graham.

Gene Blake of the *Los Angeles Times* described Graham upon her arrival as "pale and hopeless." Bernice Freeman of the *San Francisco Chronicle* declared her to be "sick, tired and suffering from a toothache. . . . Her eyes were sunken and her jaw was red and swollen from the aching tooth." Gale Cook of the San Francisco *Examiner* described her as "dazed."[30]

Photographs reinforced these images. Graham stared into the middle distance, so slender that her head seemed too large for her body. This image was enhanced by her hair, pulled back into a French twist, which made her face seem more angular and her eyes more prominent. Out of pride, or the bittersweet recognition that she needed to look at least somewhat attractive for her last public appearance, she had carefully applied eyebrow pencil and lipstick. She managed a "weak smile" as the car snaked through the throng and onto prison grounds.[31]

Warden Teets met Graham just outside North Seg and led her to her cell. It was sparely furnished with a cot and toilet—both bolted to the floor—and a wall shelf, which held a radio. Teets offered her food; she could order anything she wanted, he said. She declined, though she had eaten nothing but a milkshake on the ten-hour drive from Corona. He introduced her to nurse Barbara Cates, explained the preparations for execution, and summoned the prison dentist to provide her relief from the toothache.[32]

Perkins and Santo also were moved into holding cells. Since Graham occupied the basement, they took up temporary residency in two cells on the floor above her. Teets offered them a special menu as well. Both men declined, insisting that "the regular bill of fare would do." Both also asked for magazines.[33]

Teets met with reporters after settling Graham into her cell. "The poor gal, she's dead beat," Teets told journalists: "But I finally got a smile out of her when I asked her for a cigarette." He admitted that preparing for Graham's highly anticipated execution had left him "drawn and weary" as well. His emotional turmoil undoubtedly was heightened by the swarms of media, the possibility of last-minute stays, and the fact that he had to oversee three executions on the same day.[34]

In the holding cell, Graham changed into her red silk pajamas. The Reverend Dan McAllister, Catholic chaplain at San Quentin during Graham's earlier stay, remained with her throughout the evening and offered her spiritual counseling and communion. Attorney Al Matthews arrived shortly after 10:00 p.m. with bad news. The California Supreme Court had denied a last-minute appeal, offering a terse statement: "This order is final and forthwith." Governor Knight also refused to step in, declaring that he had "reviewed the entire file in the case, including all reports, recommendations, and communications. I have also studied and analyzed the applications for habeas corpus. I find no basis in any of these proceedings for the exercise of executive clemency."[35]

But the rulings were not final, and Governor Knight remained at his desk, waiting for the inevitable onslaught of last-minute petitions to the state's high court, common in most death penalty cases, but particularly prevalent in high-profile cases, where emotions ride at a fever pitch. At 2:00 a.m. on June 3, Knight was still dressed in "a gray double-breasted suit," with "his face the same color." A dozen reporters stood outside his office.

Knight was not particularly comfortable sending condemned men and women to their deaths, since it contradicted the image he sought to project. He was a moderate Republican, an affable man who liked to be called Goodie and who "loved to shake hands, tell jokes, even occasionally dance or sing or juggle." Prior to becoming governor, he had little experience with criminal matters.

In a previous career, he had been a superior court judge in Los Angeles, where he mostly handled high-profile divorce cases. He knew, however, that a majority of Californians favored the death penalty. An anti-capital-punishment movement had begun to make inroads in the state and elsewhere, but older people—the demographic that voted in the highest numbers—believed in executing criminals. Knight had just been elected to his own first term as governor in 1954. If he wanted to win reelection in 1958, he needed to accede to the public's wishes.[36]

Nonetheless, as former Knight staff member Douglas Barrett recalled years later, "The whole question of executive clemency and the cases involved there caused a great deal of trauma in the governor's office. . . . Strange thing, he was not opposed to capital punishment . . . yet the diligence with which he attacked the files prior to making decisions on this would leave him limp, both him and his clemency secretary."[37]

Graham remained awake throughout the night as well, chain-smoking, talking with nurse Barbara Cates, and listening to classical music on her radio. At one point, she sat down and wrote letters to Matthews and Ed Montgomery, thanking them for their work on her behalf. During one newsbreak, an announcer took note of the pending executions and declared that four different couples had offered to adopt Graham's son Tommy. This information—untrue, as it turned out—threw her into a tailspin, and Cates tried to calm her by turning the radio to a different channel. Close to daybreak, Graham agreed to eat a hot fudge sundae, but put it aside after only a few bites.[38]

Shortly after 9:00 a.m. on June 3, she began preparing for the end. Still dressed in her pajamas, she began to comb her hair. The jarring phone broke the silence. Warden Teets informed Graham that the governor had ordered a stay. "Does this mean I'm going to live?" she asked. "No," he said, but the state high court had agreed to hear a petition by Al Matthews. This decision meant the execution had been rescheduled for 10:45 a.m.

Matthews's last-minute petition covered the same ground that he had previously trod, but with a new twist. The state upreme court had turned down his earlier claims that illegal wiretapping had resulted in an unfair trial, but just weeks earlier, in late April 1955, the same court had ruled in another case, *People v. Cahan*, that evidence seized illegally could not be used against criminal defendants. Plaintiff Charles Cahan was "the largest, most successful bookmaker in Los Angeles." When police caught him via illegal wiretaps, he sued and after the state high court ruling his conviction was overturned.

Now, just an hour before Graham's scheduled execution, Matthews argued that the *Cahan* ruling should apply to Graham as well. Knight told reporters that "one sentence particularly impressed me when we looked up the case." It read, "The contention that unreasonable searches and seizures are justified by the necessity of bringing criminals to justice cannot be accepted."[39]

At 10:25 a.m. the court turned down Matthews's appeal. Graham's case predated the *Cahan* ruling and it could not be applied retroactively. Governor Knight announced the denial two minutes later at a news conference. The execution was back on, he told reporters.

Graham began to dress. She combed her hair and carefully applied makeup, including lipstick. Her hands shook too violently to affix her earrings, so Cates gently attached them for her. Warden Teets and two guards approached the cell, carrying a white mesh harness. "What is that for?" Graham asked nervously. "It's a stethoscope," Teets replied. He explained that the harness, to be worn under her jacket, connected to a rubber tube that extended to the outside of the gas chamber. It enabled a doctor who, for obvious reasons, could not enter the chamber itself, to determine her exact moment of death.

Teets also held a mask, which Graham had requested, declaring that "I don't want to look at people." The mask was a holdover from the era before the gas chamber, when California hanged its condemned prisoners. Teets asked Graham to remove her shoes, but she refused with a wan smile: "I look better with my shoes on." He acceded to her request. Two priests arrived to give Graham communion and last rites. They gave her a chain necklace bearing the likeness of Saint Jude. She offered another pale attempt at humor: "Thanks, it's a lovely going away present."[40]

With witnesses in the viewing area and Graham preparing to leave the holding cell for the last time at 10:41 a.m., the telephone rang a second time. Governor Knight had agreed to another stay. This time Matthews's petition to the state high court argued that John True had perjured himself. The timing for this appeal seems unusual, since Matthews had long argued this point. He was grasping at straws, hoping for any sliver of mercy for his client.

At this point, Graham just wanted it to be over. As she returned to her cell, she paced in the tiny space. "Why do they torture me?" she wailed: "I was prepared to go at 10." At 11:15 a.m. came the final word. The court had denied Matthews's appeal. There would be no more.[41]

The execution was rescheduled for 11:30 a.m. At that precise moment, Graham, wearing the mask and harness, left the cell accompanied by Rev. Dan McAllister on one side and Warden Harley Teets on the other. At the door of the chamber, Teets patted her arm. "Goodbye, and God bless you," he said. A guard led her to the chair, strapped her in, patted her arm, and urged her to take deep breaths once the pellets dropped. Asked to make a last statement, Graham reportedly said, "Good people are always so sure they're right." Witnesses, who included three police officers instrumental in her case, said that Graham appeared to be silently reciting Hail Marys as she waited for the cyanide pellets to drop.

At 11:34 a.m., with the door closed and Graham sealed inside the chamber, the executioner pulled a lever and released the pellets. Her "breathing became labored and she tilted her head back slightly. Suddenly, it slumped forward and she appeared to lose consciousness." But death did not come easily or quickly. Several times her head flung backward and she gasped. "Again and again she gasped, until her head pitched forward for the last time at 11:41 a.m." A minute later the chief medical officer for San Quentin pronounced her dead. Teets called the execution "routine."[42]

Gale Cook of the San Francisco *Examiner* offered a more detailed account.

Barbara Graham was put to death by the sovereign state of California yesterday. She died with great dignity at 11:42 a.m., eight minutes after the cyanide pellets dropped in the lethal gas chamber at San Quentin prison. That was her last and final death.

She died a thousand times before that during the agony of two stays which delayed her execution from its scheduled time of 10:00 a.m. till 11:30 a.m.

Barbara achieved a strange beauty in her last moments. Her soft brown hair was perfectly in place. Her face was an ivory cameo accented by the mask and her rouged crimson lips.

Her lips moved constantly, apparently in prayer, as the guards adjusted the straps across each arm, her chest, and legs. One of the guards asked whether the straps were too tight, and she nodded slightly and seemed to speak. He patted her on the shoulder and stepped out of the chamber.

Barbara Graham was dead at the age of 31, bringing to an end a life of rebellion and conflict with the law which began when she was a 13-year-old in Oakland.[43]

Little confusion or emotion accompanied the executions of Perkins and Santo. The pair spent their last evening playing cards, watching television, and talking, mostly about cars. They also ate heartily: fried chicken, avocado and tomato salad, pie and coffee. Santo entered the gas chamber at 2:31 p.m. and was strapped into the same chair that Graham vacated just hours earlier. Perkins entered a minute later and was strapped into the other chair.

Both men wore white shirts open at the neck and blue jeans. As they waited for pellets to drop, they stared at witnesses and "chatted amiably with each other." When the pellets were released, "Santo inhaled deeply" and his head pitched forward. Perkins sat "impassively, with his head thrown back." Both died quietly, within a minute of each other.[44]

In life, as reporters had noted, few people had cared about Perkins and Santo. This sentiment accompanied their deaths as well. Both men were quickly cremated and forgotten. Only a few friends and Henry Graham attended Graham's funeral and burial at Mount Olivet cemetery in San Rafael on June 6. The sparse attendance was by design. Graham had requested that it be kept small and private. None of her sons attended. Three-year-old Tommy, in fact, had already forgotten her, Henry Graham told a reporter.

Barbara Graham began her last day objectified as a vicious criminal, but she ended it as something less: not exactly a victim, but no longer a public pariah either. Matthews and Knight later justified the petitions and stays as necessary to ensure a fair and thorough process.[45] But others deemed their actions cruel. Montgomery called the execution delays "horrendous."[46]

To police and prosecutors, Graham's execution represented a necessary evil. Prosecutors could not afford to be sentimental or regretful about sending defendants to the gas chamber. For the rest of his life, prosecutor J. Miller Leavy justified his actions in Graham's case. In June 1955 few people, including Leavy, could have predicted that he would need to do so, over and over again.

6

Executing Women in America

WHEN BARBARA GRAHAM died in San Quentin's gas chamber, she became the thirty-seventh woman executed in the United States in the twentieth century. Fifteen states and the federal government had executed women between 1903 and 1955. New York held the distinction of having sent the largest number of women to die: seven. California had executed three women, including Graham. By comparison, more than six thousand men had been hanged, gassed, and electrocuted in America during that same period.[1]

With such small numbers, it seems natural to wonder how these particular women earned the ultimate penalty while others were convicted but not condemned, or tried but acquitted. As death-penalty scholar Victor Streib noted, "Probably several times this many women were sentenced to death but never executed ... presumably hundreds, perhaps thousands of women committed capital crimes but were never sentenced to death." Thus it might be tempting to view all of the executed women through the same lens, to envision them as sharing a unique set of characteristics and similar circumstances.[2]

In fact, Graham and her female counterparts did share many common life threads. One was the crimes required for execution. Men could be executed for a variety of felonies, including murder, rape, kidnapping, robbery, even burglary, particularly if they were African American.[3] All but one executed woman had been condemned for first-degree murder. Only Ethel Rosenberg, electrocuted in 1953 by the federal government along with her husband, Julius, had been executed for another crime: conspiring to commit espionage.[4]

Graham, like many other executed women, had been condemned for committing murder in partnership with men. Other prominent cases included those of Ruth Snyder, electrocuted by New York in 1928 for murdering her husband, Albert. Judd Gray, Snyder's lover and partner in crime, also was executed. In 1929 Louisiana hanged Ada LeBoeuf and Thomas Dreher for killing LeBoeuf's husband. After shooting him, they hired a trapper to slit open the dead man's body, fill it with lead, and drop it into a swamp. The trapper earned a life sentence.[5]

New York electrocuted Anna Antonio in 1934 for hiring two men to kill her husband. Then in 1951 New York executed Martha Beck and Raymond Fernandez for duping and killing women involved in lonely hearts clubs—a post–World War II phenomenon wherein individuals looking for love paid money to meet up with potential mates. Beck also killed a child of one of the adult victims.[6] One of the most coldly calculating and brutal partner murders occurred in Missouri when Bonnie Heady and Carl Hall kidnapped six-year-old Bobby Greenlease from his private school, took him across state lines into Kansas, and then demanded a six-hundred-thousand-dollar ransom from his distraught family. The family paid, but Bobby was already dead, having been shot and killed by Hall and buried in a backyard. The federal government executed both Heady and Hall in 1953.[7]

Virtually all of the murders attributed to executed women—at least if they were white—can be considered predatory. They involved sex, money, or revenge. None of the executed white killers seem to have committed their crimes out of fear, jealousy, or passion, motives ordinarily ascribed to females who murder. Perhaps that offers a partial explanation for the disparity between the percentage of women initially charged with murder—about 10 percent of all such charges—and those eventually executed for the crime.

Ruth Snyder's decision to murder her husband can be deemed a sexual slaying with financial overtones. So can Martha Beck's, since she seems to have been in thrall to Raymond Fernandez and fearful of losing him. Other slayings with sex as a component included those of Mary Rogers, who helped a man murder her husband to cover up an illegitimate pregnancy and who was executed by Vermont in 1905; Frances Creighton, electrocuted by New York in 1936 for poisoning her lover's wife; and Toni Jo Henry, electrocuted by Louisiana in 1942 for killing a man who offered her a ride while she was en route to Texas. She hoped to spring her husband from the prison where he had been incarcerated for murder.[8]

Graham had been executed for murder involving financial gain. So had Mary Farmer, electrocuted by New York in 1909 for hacking her landlady to death and stuffing the body pieces into a trunk. Farmer subsequently moved into the landlady's home, where police arrested her.[9] Pennsylvania electrocuted Irene Schroder in 1931 for killing a police officer following a robbery spree. She also partnered with a man—a Sunday school teacher, no less. The pair took authorities on a cross-country chase before their arrest in Arizona.[10] Anna Marie Hahn was perhaps the most diabolical of this coterie, since she was a serial killer. In the early 1930s Hahn moved to the United States from Germany and began befriending a series of wealthy older men who lent or gave her money. All of them died under mysterious and painful circumstances. As it turned out, Hahn had poisoned her victims. She was executed by Ohio in 1938.[11]

Louise Peete killed two victims twenty-five years apart. She served two decades in prison for the 1920 murder of her wealthy Los Angeles landlord, Jacob Denton. After shooting him to death, Peete buried the body in the basement of his home and began spending his money.

In December 1944, five years after her release on parole, she killed again; this time her victim was a woman for whom she worked as a caretaker. Again, she spent her victim's money. California executed Peete in 1947.[12]

Several of the money-fueled murders were accomplished with life insurance as the motive. Eva Dugan was hanged by Arizona in 1930 for murdering her rancher neighbor to collect his insurance.[13] Anna Antonio's New York execution was based on prosecution allegations that she had sought her husband's insurance. Eva Coo was electrocuted by New York in 1935 for beating an acquaintance to death. On her deathbed, the man's mother had asked Coo to look after her son. Two women—May Carey and Marie Porter—killed their brothers. Carey was hanged by Delaware in 1935, and Porter was electrocuted by Illinois in 1938. Earle Dennison was electrocuted by Alabama in 1953 for poisoning her niece, and Ohio electrocuted Dovie Dean in 1954 for poisoning her second husband.[14]

Revenge cases included that of Sue Logue, electrocuted in 1943 by South Carolina for hiring a man to kill her neighbor. Earlier, the victim had shot and killed Logue's husband, claimed self-defense, and was acquitted of murder, a circumstance that enraged Logue. Rhonda Martin killed several members of her family. Alabama executed her in 1957. Eithel Spinelli ordered the murder of a young member of her gang because she feared the man talked too much and might give away secrets. In November 1941 she became the first woman executed by California.

Media attention is another factor most white executed women shared. Like Barbara Graham, they often had trials saturated with sensational press coverage, which was understandable given the small number of women charged with capital offenses and the public's demand for titillation, as well as the lurid and tantalizing details of the women's crimes. Reporters zeroed in on—and sometimes exaggerated—the unconventionality of capital defendants and their risk-taking personalities. Stories laden with sexual overtones provided the best opportunities; the defendants could be cast as deadly, diabolical femme fatales.

Journalists, most of whom were men, hoped no doubt that these stories would result in sufficient public attention to ensure them prominent play on front pages of the nation's newspapers. The reading public's continued fascination with female defendants might result in increased circulation and ad revenue, and hopefully it would help to garner the reporters even higher salaries and better jobs on bigger newspapers. Some reporters successfully used their early success in trial reporting to catapult themselves to prominence and fame in other media ventures.

Ruth Snyder's 1927 trial provides one example. Snyder drew intense coverage for a variety of reasons, including the timing, locale, brutality, and sexual underpinnings of her crime. In 1926 journalist Maurine Watkins had written *Chicago*, a play based on her newspaper stories about female jazz babies tried for murder in that city. The following year *Chicago* became a hit in New York.

Snyder, who lived on Long Island, New York, could easily be constructed to resemble Watkins's fictional protagonist, Roxie Hart, a bored housewife lured from home and toward murder by the prospect of a more exciting life. Hart kills a lover out of rage at his betrayal, then reverts to being a stereotypically virtuous woman during her trial and wins an acquittal. Thus, for Hart, crime does seem to pay.[15]

It certainly did not pay for Snyder, however, who did not try to hide her disdain for traditional life. She had been a wife and mother who loved the urban jazz scene, who "gambled a little, was fond of Prohibition booze, and liked staying out late."[16] In 1925 she took a lover, Judd Gray, and bought a fifty-thousand-dollar double-indemnity insurance policy on her husband, Alfred. In March 1927 Snyder and Gray bludgeoned Alfred with a sash weight, strangled him, and then, for good measure, stuffed chloroform rags in his mouth.

At Snyder's January 1928 execution a photographer for the New York tabloid *Daily News* smuggled a tiny camera into her execution chamber. The photo depicted Snyder at the moment of death. The four-letter headline, which spanned the paper's front page read simply, "DEAD!" Interestingly, neither the photographer nor the newspaper seems to have cared much about Gray, who was executed on the same day.[17]

James M. Cain covered Snyder's trial as a reporter. Afterward, he turned to fiction, penning novels with female protagonists who, not coincidentally, resembled Ruth Snyder. In 1934 Snyder morphed into Cora Smith Papadakis, the murderous, unfaithful housewife at the center of *The Postman Always Rings Twice*. The next year she became Phyllis Nirdlinger, the diabolical, greedy wife who pushed her insurance agent to help her commit murder in *Double Indemnity*. Both books later became noir films.[18]

Journalists often coined two- or three-word nicknames to help readers quickly identify the more high-profile female capital-murder defendants. Headline writers splashed these labels, in large type, across front pages of newspapers to direct audiences to the stories that nearly always appeared above the fold. The stories reflected both public fascination with the criminals in question and revulsion for the women's behavior and crimes.

Barbara Graham was Bloody Babs or the Iceberg Blonde. Ada Le Boeuf was Louisiana's Love Pirate; Irene Schroeder was known as the Blonde Tiger and the Gun Girl. Eva Coo was the Blonde Backwoods Innkeeper. Frances Creighton became Black-Eyed Borgia; Anna Hahn was dubbed Arsenic Anna. Sue Logue was Wanton Woman, a sobriquet that winked at her reputed sexual relationship with one of South Carolina's most prominent politicians, Strom Thurmond, then a county judge and later a segregationist senator and presidential candidate.[19]

Many journalistic tags suggested their subjects—Barbara Graham among them—possessed an enticing, if unacceptably bold sexual persona. This sexual image often proved detrimental at trial, but afterward it might lead some male journalists to shift their narratives and soften their depictions of the condemned women. Such a softening obviously occurred in Graham's case in articles by writers such as Stuart Palmer, Bernice Freeman, and Edward S. Montgomery. Some defendants were not reconstructed to make them seem more attractive. Writing about newspaper coverage of female executions, Marlin Shipman argues that a lack of physical attractiveness made it difficult for journalists to label these particular defendants. But the absence of stereotypical beauty or sexuality actually gave writers different opportunities—to brand these women as repulsive and thus extra deserving of punitive treatment by judicial powers-that-be and by the public in general.[20]

Martha Beck is one example. Beck weighed between two hundred and three hundred pounds, according to various journalistic accounts of her trial and execution. Hence reporters often referred to her as Fat Martha. This label was particularly significant in her case because the murder charges were enhanced by the role sex had played in the charges against her. Prosecutors claimed that Beck helped Raymond Fernandez murder at least three people because she was obsessed with him and addicted to the sexual gratification he provided. Journalists reveled in their ability to detail lurid testimony about the pair's romantic couplings. And they could not resist contrasting Beck's frumpiness with the slim suavity of her crime partner.[21]

Eithel Spinelli and Dovie Dean, both in their fifties at the time or their trials, were squeezed into the "repulsive" journalistic stereotype as well, though from the other end of the weight spectrum. At her 1941 trial journalists dubbed Spinelli the Scarecrow and described her as the "head of an underworld gang, an ex-wrestler, and a knife-thrower who could pin a poker chip at 15 paces."

Dean was similarly small in stature, but it was her unusual behavior that drew reporters' attention during her 1952 Ohio trial for the poisoning death of her husband. Dean apparently was unable to cry at "appropriate" moments. Journalists declared her composure to be "uncanny" and they dubbed her the "murderess without tears." Her attorney explained that a medical problem made Dean unable to produce tears, but her stoicism—and journalists' continual discussion of it—proved a distinct disadvantage.[22]

For all of their similarities, executed women also differed from each other in significant ways, one of which was age. The youngest, Virginia Christian, was barely seventeen when the state of Virginia electrocuted her in 1912 for murdering her employer. The oldest was Louise Peete. She began shaving years off her age even before her first prison term in 1920, which led journalists and prison officials to give her age at death as fifty-eight. She was really sixty-six. Nearly half of the executed women, including Barbara Graham, were in their twenties or thirties at the time of their deaths. Another third or so were in their forties and fifties. Two were teenagers, and one—Louise Peete—in her sixties. Ages are unavailable for several of the women, all of them non-Anglo.

Choice of crime victims and criminal backgrounds represented two other areas of difference. Only four of the executed white murderers—Barbara Graham, Irene Schroeder, Toni Jo Henry, and Bonnie Heady—had been condemned for killing people previously unknown to them. Two women—Anna Marie Hahn and Martha Beck—killed individuals who had been strangers until they were selected as marks for financial purposes. Ten of the white women were executed for murdering family members and the remainder for killing acquaintances, including neighbors, employers, a caretaker, and a fellow gang member.

The offenses for which they were executed might suggest that the women shared backgrounds in which violent crime had played a prominent role, but this was not the case. Before their arrests and capital trials, most of the women had no criminal records. This is true of many high-profile women: Martha Beck, Anna Hahn, Bonnie Heady, Sue Logue, Ethel Rosenberg, Ruth Snyder, and Irene Schroeder. In fact, only slightly more than a handful, including Barbara Graham, had prior criminal records.

Like Graham, Elizabeth Duncan and Toni Jo Henry had been arrested for prostitution. Only three women—Frances Creighton, Louise Peete, and Eithel Spinelli—had been charged with prior violent felonies. Creighton had been tried and acquitted twice for the poisoning deaths of her in-laws before her execution for poisoning her lover's wife. Spinelli's gang had been arrested for various crimes, and Peete had served twenty years for murder.

The methods of murder also differed. Poisoning has often been deemed the female method of killing, since it requires a passive approach rather than direct confrontation with the victim. In fact, nearly a dozen executed women poisoned their victims. But more shot or beat them to death with hatchets, brooms, and sash weights, among other weapons. One, Eva Coo, beat her victim with a mallet—hence an additional label used by trial reporters to describe her: the Mallet-Murderer. Coo then paid a friend to drive over the victim with a car. The friend earned a life sentence.

Race represented possibly the most significant factor differentiating executed the women from one another. At least a third of the thirty-seven women executed between 1903 and 1955 were non-Anglo. White women received press coverage and public attention during their trials and executions, but the same cannot be said of women of color. A sizeable segment of the white population was predisposed to view people of color in negative terms as hypersexual and as potential criminals. Thus white journalists had no particular reason to cover the trials of African American female capital defendants because they could not promote such women as unusual in their behavior or sexuality. Besides, such stories were unlikely to garner attention, since white readers cared little about women of color and advertisers cared even less.

African American newspapers might have covered some of these trials and executions, but many were published on a weekly, rather than a daily, basis. Their owners often operated with shoestring budgets, as most advertisers in the black community had little money and could not pay much for ad space. These newspapers had few reporters and had to carefully pick and choose their stories, selecting many from wire services and syndicates. Furthermore, African American journalists often proved reluctant to reinforce negative racial stereotypes and thus downplayed crime coverage in favor of more uplifting stories about the professional or educational accomplishments of community members.[23]

The dearth of court records and newspaper coverage means that modern-day death-penalty sources possess limited information on the backgrounds, crimes, or execution data for many non-Anglos. Both the Death Penalty Information Center (DPIC) website and Kathleen O'Shea, author of *Women and the Death Penalty in the United States, 1900–1998*, list fourteen executed women of color. Only eleven, however, are listed by both sources specifically as executed women of color.

For example, O'Shea includes Ann Knight among her entries, but lists her as having "no known race." Knight was executed in Mississippi in 1947. The DPIC does not mention Knight at all. This lack of information suggests that Knight probably was not white. Shellie McKeithen appears on the DPIC website but not in O'Shea's book. The DPIC lists McKeithen as an "Oriental" woman. As it happens, a mainstream Pennsylvania newspaper did cover McKeithen's 1945 trial for the robbery and murder of a "money-lender" because it seems to have been part of a bigger story involving political corruption. The *Pittsburgh Post-Gazette* identified McKeithen as a male "Negro."[24]

Both O'Shea and the DPIC include Rosa Marie Stinette. The DPIC lists her as a black woman executed by South Carolina in 1947. O'Shea lists her as a white woman executed by South Carolina for arranging to have her husband murdered for his insurance. Other websites and print sources identify Stinette as black, but they note that little is known about her. "Little is known about her" could be the phrase used to describe many of the nonwhite women. Southern states executed more than three-quarters of them. Julia Moore was hanged in Louisiana in 1935. Her victim was Elliot Wilson, but no additional information is available. Mississippi executed Carrie McCarty sometime in the 1920s for an unknown crime, and the exact date of her execution "is unconfirmed." Nor are there details relating to the execution of Pattie Perdue, hanged by Mississippi in 1922.[25] Betty Butler was executed by Ohio in 1954 for drowning a woman who may have been her lover in an abusive relationship. She was twenty-four, but other than her age and the victim's name, Victor Streib noted, "very little is known" about her.[26]

All of the non-Anglo women were executed for murder, a factor that might seem to link them to their white counterparts, but here again many of the circumstances differed. None of the nonwhite women killed members of their own families, and none poisoned their victims. They may have been convicted of premeditated murder, but many of the killings seem to have been the result of explosive rage or impulse, after what can be described as ill-treatment—or at least the perception of such.[27]

Selena Gilmore's crime was premeditated. She became drunk and disorderly at a restaurant, was asked to leave, came back with a shotgun, and killed the waiter who had been rude to her. Alabama executed her in 1930. Mary Holmes worked as a plantation cook when she beat her employer to death. Mississippi executed her in 1937. The same state executed Mildred Johnson in 1944 for beating her landlady to death. North Carolina gassed Rosanna Phillips in 1943 for killing her employer with an axe.

African American women, it seems, did not even have to commit the murders in question in order to be executed. North Carolina executed eighteen-year-old Bessie Williams in 1944 for killing a taxi driver after she discovered she did not have enough money to pay him. Williams hit the man on the back of a head with a brick, then stole one dollar from him. Two male acquaintances subsequently stabbed the driver to death. Williams's execution came despite the fact that she had not participated in the actual killing of the driver.

Corinne Sykes may or may not have been guilty of stealing from and then murdering her Pennsylvania employer in 1946. She herself had been cut and bloodied by a butcher knife when police arrested her. Because she was seriously mentally handicapped, Sykes had difficulty defending herself and could not explain the circumstances of her employer's death. An accomplice who stole two thousand dollars from the victim may have been the real murderer. He received a seven-year prison sentence.[28]

Helen Fowler also may or may not have committed murder, even though New York executed her in 1944. Kathleen O'Shea describes Fowler as a prostitute condemned for killing a man who may have been a client.[29] In an unusual editorial decision, the *New York Times* carried a brief item on Fowler's pending execution. The paper made no mention of prostitution, but noted that she had been condemned for the robbery and murder of a white gas station owner. According to the *Times*, Fowler's male partner, George Knight—who was also African American—actually committed the crime, and her participation consisted of helping him dump the dead man's corpse in the Niagara River. Prosecutors nonetheless charged both Fowler and her partner with first-degree murder, jurors convicted them, and both were electrocuted.[30]

Some of the executed African American women might have faced lesser charges had they been white. Georgia executed Lena Baker in 1945 for murdering her white employer, a man who had threatened to kill her if she left him. She took to carrying a gun for protection, and one day when the man went for his gun, Baker shot him. An all-white jury condemned her for premeditated first-degree murder. In 2001 Baker's family successfully petitioned the Georgia Board of Pardons and Paroles for an unconditional pardon. In 2005 the board agreed, noting that manslaughter would have been the appropriate charge for Baker.[31]

It took fifty-five years for Baker's case to come to wider public attention. The few white women whose trials and executions raised issues of questionable prosecution or lack of due process found partisans immediately willing to cry foul and plead their causes in the press and at public protests. Three women fell into this category. One was Barbara Graham; the others were Anna Antonio and Ethel Rosenberg.

In 1932 Anna Antonio's husband, Sal, was found shot to death on the side of a road near Albany, New York. No physical evidence linked her to the crime. Yet, at trial, prosecutors relied on the testimony of two men who claimed she had solicited them to kill Sal for his insurance policy. Anna vehemently denied the allegations, but jurors sentenced her to death, along with her accusers.

Shortly before the scheduled execution date, one of the men changed his story, now claiming that Anna had had nothing to do with her husband's death; instead, the murder was related to a drug deal gone wrong. This revelation drew swift attention from prominent liberals, including famed attorney Clarence Darrow, who pleaded with New York governor Ernest Lehman to reprieve Antonio. Ernest Whitehouse Cortis, a playwright who ran a shoestring anti-death-penalty organization, the Men's League of Mercy of the United States, also pled Antonio's cause.[32]

Women such as Antonio, Cortis argued, were "helpless, trapped by scheming men—male beasts who are simply parasites living off women."[33] Lehman heeded the activists' pleas and issued a temporary execution stay for Antonio and the two male conspirators. Ultimately, however, he let the trial verdict stand. All three were executed in August 1934. Despite complaints of judicial unfairness, Antonio soon disappeared as a subject of interest.

Ethel Rosenberg was a Communist. In 1951 she lived quietly in New York with her husband, Julius, and their two young sons. Several years earlier Elizabeth Bentley, an American who had spied for the Soviet Union, turned herself in to the FBI and named Julius Rosenberg, among many others, as fellow Communists. With anti-Communist hysteria running at a fever pitch in the early 1950s, the federal government homed in on Julius and on Ethel's brother, David Greenglass. To save himself Greenglass named Ethel as a coconspirator. Ethel vehemently denied spying, and scant evidence linked her to espionage. Government officials sought to use Ethel to elicit information on Julius and others, but she refused to cooperate. Following a sensational trial, both Rosenbergs were sentenced to death.[34]

A firestorm of protest around the world accompanied the announcement of the Rosenbergs' death sentences. Critics decried the rush to judgment, given the lack of clear-cut evidence against both Rosenbergs, but particularly against Ethel. It took two years to exhaust all appeals, and in June 1953 the Rosenbergs were put to death at New York's Sing Sing prison. They remain the only convicted spies ever executed by the United States.[35]

The fact that questions emerged in the cases of Antonio and Rosenberg rendered them different from other executed white women and similar to their non-Anglo counterparts. Their cases, like Barbara Graham's, had potentially serious evidentiary issues, yet the judicial and political systems—ordinarily very cautious when it came to executing white women—refused to acknowledge potential wrongdoing. And their advocates were unable to stop their executions.

The timing of both women's trials was significant. Neither the

1930s nor the early 1950s—as Barbara Graham's experience illustrates as well—were particularly hospitable eras for those who could be accused of challenging the status quo. Additionally, Antonio and Rosenberg were the daughters of immigrant parents. Antonio was Italian, not an auspicious heritage during a period when Italians, to many people, represented the face of organized crime. Both of Antonio's male codefendants were also Italian Americans.

Antonio was not physically attractive, which minimized journalists' incentive to soften her image following her death sentence. In photographs she appears gaunt, haggard, grim, and much older than her twenty-eight years. Even as her execution loomed, reporters generally depicted Antonio as pathetic and hysterical rather than as the victim of a possibly arbitrary and unfair justice system. A *New York Times* story on her fight for life, for example, quoted Antonio as being "discouraged, ill, heartbroken, yet hoping something will save me." A reporter noted that she appeared to have "aged ten years since she was brought to Sing Sing." At the time of the interview, she wore a homemade pink dress that she had sewn in prison.[36]

Ethel Rosenberg's parents were of Russian Jewish descent. The combination of Communism and Judaism turned out to be a lethal mix in her case, particularly since Irving Kaufman, the judge presiding in her case, was himself Jewish and politically ambitious. He feared showing the Rosenbergs any mercy, lest those in power question his own loyalty to American values.[37]

In spite of her politics, Ethel Rosenberg's execution drew condemnation from liberals throughout America and the world. Others, who might have been willing to plead her case at another time, undoubtedly remained silent out of fear of government reprisal. In the decades following the 1950s, writers and scholars—including the couple's two sons—have continued to debate the Rosenberg case. Most recently, Ethel made an appearance as a character in the play and television miniseries *Angels in America*. Her ghost tormented an AIDS-stricken Roy Cohn as he lay dying. Cohn was the government lawyer deemed largely responsible for her prosecution and execution.[38]

When state and national movements against the death penalty began to gain steam toward the end of the 1950s, abolitionists homed in on a few problematic cases they viewed as symptomatic of widespread judicial inequities. Only one executed woman made the list: Barbara Graham. In that regard, she stood alone, different than all the other executed women, Anglo and non-Anglo alike.

Few people reading about Graham's execution in June 1955 could have predicted her case would strike such a chord. What made her so special? Certainly she was shapely, attractive, and a mother; also, prosecutors may have crossed the line in their efforts to trap her into a confession. Such behavior was not uncommon, however, in the tough-on-crime 1950s. Graham was also a recidivist criminal—a prostitute, thief, perjurer and quite possibly a killer as well.

But she had partisans who worked for major news outlets. San Francisco *Examiner* reporter Ed Montgomery had struggled diligently to save her from the gas chamber. Following her death, he turned his attention to other stories but could not get Graham out of his mind. He plotted revenge against a judicial system that, he fervently believed, had unfairly and cavalierly convicted and executed an innocent woman. Montgomery needed assistance from more powerful individuals to accomplish this task. He decided to turn to Hollywood.

7

I Want to Live!

IN THE FALL of 1957 Hollywood producer Walter Wanger invited director Robert Wise to lunch at the famed Brown Derby restaurant in Los Angeles to discuss making a movie about Barbara Graham. The lunch capped off a year that began when Ed Montgomery wrote to Wanger, asking if he might be interested in the Graham story. Montgomery had put together an outline to familiarize Wanger with the case.

Wanger responded enthusiastically. He had been searching for an anti-death-penalty film, he wrote Montgomery in December 1956: "There is a very exciting and important picture in the Graham material."[1] Within weeks Wanger flew to meet Montgomery in San Francisco. He emerged from the meeting as a passionate Graham partisan, convinced that she had been the victim of a colossal frame-up. He "determined that Barbara's shabby treatment be thoroughly dramatized," Wise wrote later.

Wanger arranged the Brown Derby lunch to convince Wise to direct the as-yet untitled film. He gave Wise a three-page synopsis and told him that Don Mankiewicz was rewriting his first screenplay draft with his uncle Joseph. Actor Susan Hayward had signed on to play Graham. Wise read the synopsis and declared it "horrifying and fascinating. . . . This is a real-life horror story if I ever saw one. Let's go."[2]

Wanger, Wise, and Hayward were not minor players in Hollywood. All three were major leaguers, A-list talents. Walter Wanger was a pioneering, prolific producer whose films included *Stagecoach*, *Foreign Correspondent*, and *Invasion of the Body Snatchers*. He was well-respected for his ability to pull together all of the elements that went into successful films: scripts, talent, money, studio, and technical support. Robert Wise had started his career in the early 1940s with Orson Welles. He worked as an editor on *Citizen Kane* and as an assistant director on *The Magnificent Ambersons*. He directed the science-fiction thriller *The Day the Earth Stood Still* and would go on to direct the Oscar-winning films *West Side Story* and *The Sound of Music*.

Susan Hayward came to Hollywood in 1937 to screen test for the role of Scarlett O'Hara in *Gone With the Wind*—a coveted part that eventually went to Vivien Leigh. Wanger had rescued Hayward from B-level films and prodded her toward roles as tough, but tragic characters. In *Smash-Up: The Story of a Woman* she played a successful singer turned alcoholic. In *With a Song in My Heart* she played singer Jane Froman, who was disabled in a plane crash. In *I'll Cry Tomorrow* she played Lillian Roth, another ravaged, alcoholic singer. By 1957 she had garnered four Oscar nominations but no wins.[3]

Though Don Mankiewicz mostly wrote for magazines and television in the 1950s, he held a sterling pedigree as the son and nephew of famous screenwriters. His father, Herman Mankiewicz, wrote *Citizen Kane*, *Dinner at Eight*, and *Pride of the Yankees*, and was an uncredited writer on *The Wizard of Oz*. His uncle, Joseph Mankiewicz, one of Wanger's oldest friends, wrote *All About Eve*. In 1956 Joseph Mankiewicz began a partnership with Wanger in Figaro Productions, an independent company that produced films for United Artists, the studio that would distribute the Barbara Graham movie.[4]

Coincidentally, Don Mankiewicz had been loosely acquainted with Mable Monahan, a fact that had enhanced his interest in the film. The media depicted her as an infirm, elderly woman, but that was not how Mankiewicz recalled her: "She might have been sweet in other configurations, but I knew her in Gardena and she was a mean poker player." The infirm characterization, he said, "didn't fit."[5]

Walter Wanger's personal and professional experiences would seem to render him ill-suited for a film challenging the same system that afforded him wealth and fame. He came from a well-off, close-knit family. He spent part of his childhood in Europe and from an early age steeped himself in the arts—especially museums, symphonies, and plays. He attended Dartmouth College and during World War I made newsreels for the Committee on Public Information, a propaganda agency of the U.S. government created by President Woodrow Wilson to promote the war. He entered the Hollywood film industry in the 1920s, and over the next forty years he worked both independently and with top studios. For a time, he headed the Academy of Motion Picture Arts and Sciences.

But Wanger had experienced down times as well. Film projects fell apart, stars turned temperamental, and his movies lost money. His liberal political bent led red-baiters briefly to question his patriotism. Wanger's lowest point came in 1951, when he discovered that his film-star wife, Joan Bennett, was having an affair with her agent, Jennings Lang.

One December afternoon, he spotted Bennett's car in the parking lot of Lang's agency, went home, and returned with a gun. After a brief confrontation, he shot Lang twice in the groin, sending him to the hospital, though with non-life-threatening injuries. Wanger was initially charged with felony assault, but celebrity attorney Jerry Geisler convinced a judge to let his client plead guilty due to temporary insanity. Wanger's punishment: four months in a minimum-security California prison.[6]

His combined misfortunes left Wanger depressed, angry, and briefly unemployable. Circus-like press coverage of the shooting's aftermath led him to castigate the media's destructive power. Despite his light sentence, Wanger felt victimized by the judicial system, since, in Los Angeles, "influential people quietly escaped punishment."[7]

His cynicism and anger pushed him toward socially significant message films that challenged power structures and questioned conformity and the herd mentality. His first film after release from prison took on the penal system: *Riot in Cellblock 11* was based on the true story of a Michigan prison uprising. His second film, the cult classic *Invasion of the Body Snatchers*, illustrated how powerful forces could push susceptible individuals toward paranoia and conspiracy theories.

Wanger envisioned "The Barbara Graham Story" as a worthy addition to his message films, enabling him to target his favorite villains: the media and the judicial system. The timing was propitious in other ways as well. Most people, at least in California, still remembered Graham in 1957, but her image had softened with the passage of time. Stories by Stuart Palmer, Ed Montgomery, and others had facilitated this process.

As a longtime observer of human nature, Wanger undoubtedly possessed a shrewd sense of the box-office potential of Barbara Graham's story. It had all the elements of a winner: drama, conflict, tragedy, unresolved issues, police shenanigans, and a beautiful and sexual protagonist with a sad life story. Moreover, it centered on murder, a staple of theater and literature as far back as ancient Greece. As scholar Wendy Lesser wrote: "One of art's functions" is "to allow people to identify with something they are not, imaginatively experiencing other kinds of lives. The murder plots we remain most attracted to . . . are those which assume at least a partial identification with the murderer."[8]

With its questionable ethics, Graham's case made such identification

1. Barbara Graham listens to evidence during her 1953 Los Angeles murder trial. Journalists consistently focused on her sexual allure and her unconventional lifestyle, which they cast as abhorrent and antithetical to proper American values and traditional female gender roles. Los Angeles Public Library Photo Collection.

2. (*above*) Barbara Graham sits at the counsel table with her two codefendants: Jack Santo, left; and Emmett Perkins, center. Though the two men possessed much lengthier and more brutal criminal backgrounds, members of the media largely ignored them. Los Angeles Public Library Photo Collection.

3. (*right*) Barbara Graham visits with her husband, Henry, and her toddler son, Tommy, in a Los Angeles County Jail holding cell as she prepares to leave Los Angeles for the California Institution for Women, Corona, to await the outcome of the appeal of her death sentence. Los Angeles Public Library Photo Collection.

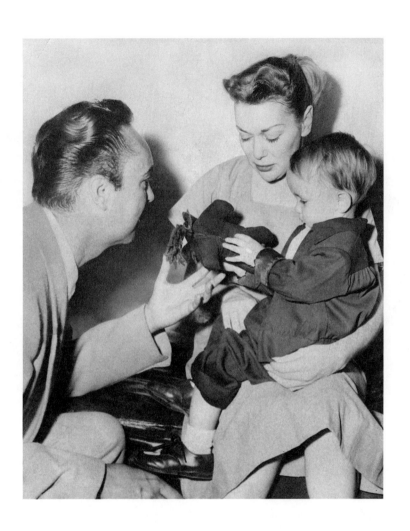

4. (*above*) Journalists clamor for Graham's attention following her September 1953 conviction and death sentence. Though they had dubbed her Bloody Babs, within a few months some reporters would lobby for a gubernatorial reprieve. Los Angeles Public Library Photo Collection.

5. (*right*) Mug shot of Barbara Graham upon her arrival at the California Institution for Women, Corona, in October 1953. It was here that she first began to tell her sad and sordid life story. California Department of Corrections and Rehabilitation.

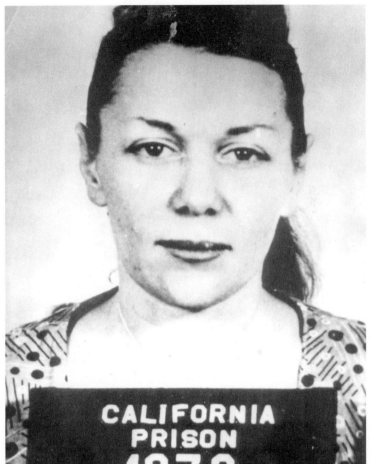

6. San Francisco *Examiner* reporter Edward S. Montgomery favored the prosecution during Barbara Graham's Los Angeles trial. Afterward he became convinced of her innocence, fought unsuccessfully to save her life, and then turned to Hollywood to plead his case via the 1958 film *I Want to Live!* The Bancroft Library, Berkeley CA.

7. Barbara Graham sits in the backseat of a police car as she begins the ten-hour journey from Southern California to San Quentin and the gas chamber. Susan Hayward, who played Graham in the film *I Want to Live!*, described the transport requirements as "barbaric." Los Angeles Public Library Photo Collection.

8. Built in the 1850s, San Quentin sits on a stunning spit of land in pricey Marin County, across the bay from San Francisco. Barbara Graham spent most of her youth in the Bay Area and was well acquainted with the prison that would claim her life. California Department of Corrections and Rehabilitation.

9. Before their executions, condemned inmates spent their last nights in a holding cell near the gas chamber and close to a telephone kept open for last-minute reprieves. Barbara Graham experienced two last-minute stays. California Department of Corrections and Rehabilitation.

10. More than five hundred people—including four women—were executed by lethal gas in San Quentin's gas chamber from the 1930s until the late 1990s. Since then, the chamber has been used for eleven executions by lethal injection. California Department of Corrections and Rehabilitation.

possible. As her appellate attorney, Al Matthews, said following her execution: "I felt if they could do those things to Barbara Graham and get away with it, they could do it to each one of us. I felt that justice was being abandoned."[9]

The 1950s was a decade replete with movies about murders and criminal trials. At a time when so much else seemed in flux, these stories had a sense of finality to them: the killer was almost always caught and punished. Many of the movies boasted tightly woven plots and top-rank performers. They included *Niagara*, starring Marilyn Monroe; *Dial M for Murder*, starring Grace Kelly and Ray Milland; and *Rear Window*, with Grace Kelly and James Stewart. Henry Fonda starred in two films in the genre: *Twelve Angry Men* and *The Wrong Man*. Both of Fonda's films depicted the flip side of guilty killers—innocent defendants. *The Wrong Man* told the true story of Manny Balestro, a New York man mistakenly identified as the robber of an insurance company. Balestro ultimately was exonerated, both in real life and on film.

Barbara Graham's story came to be called *I Want to Live!* and it differed from other films in the genre. Its downbeat ending refuted the notion that the system always worked and thus "bucked the trend toward adulation of the law" that was reflected in most midcentury films about murder.[10] Additionally, most movie murderers were men, and the few female movie murderers were guilty. Marilyn Monroe, for example, plotted her husband's murder in *Niagara*. In *The Bad Seed* the female killer was ten-year-old sociopath Rhoda Penmark. Chillingly portrayed by Patty McCormick, Penmark murdered a male classmate and the janitor at her New York apartment.

I Want to Live! proffered the vision of an innocent woman sent to her death by arrogant, uncaring men. "In sympathetically telling the story of a woman many felt was railroaded to the gas chamber, the film lines up against systems of male discourse, in this case, the media and the law, by which patriarchy speaks of and for women," wrote film scholar Dennis Bingham.[11] Walter Wanger not only chose to take on the male establishment, he allowed his protagonist to take center stage in her own story, beginning with the first-person title. *I Want to Live!* was based on comments Graham made in letters to her attorney and others. It reflected a sense of urgency and immediacy.

The film's ending may not have been an upbeat one, but such a denouement accomplished much more for filmmakers and opponents of capital punishment than a more traditional resolution could have. It exposed the Barbara Graham case to a national audience and inserted her, and the film, into an ongoing debate about capital punishment. And it gave anti-death-penalty activists exactly the symbol they needed in their campaign to end state-sanctioned executions in America.

Wanger midwifed *I Want to Live!* but the project was spawned by journalist Ed Montgomery. In the months after Graham's execution, he had gone back to work, covering other high-profile cases, including that of Burton Abbott, convicted and condemned for the murder of a fourteen-year-old Berkeley student, Stephanie Bryan. In his spare time, Montgomery wrote the outline that he sent to Wanger.

It is unclear why he sent the material to Wanger rather than to any number of other Hollywood producers. Whatever his reasons, he chose wisely. By February 1957 Montgomery had a contract for $10,000. He was to receive $2,000 up front, 20 percent when the film went into production, and the rest upon the film's release by United Artists, which ultimately set a budget of slightly more than $1 million. Montgomery's job was to cull all of the information from trial transcripts, stories, and interviews; contact sources for additional interviews; and write an extensive outline.[12]

Wanger and Montgomery kept in constant contact over the next two years, throughout the production and release of *I Want to Live!* Their letters illustrate the strong commitment that both men had to making a powerful film, but their correspondence also reveals their individual personalities. Wanger had a reputation for taking a laid-back, hands-off approach to his film projects. With Montgomery, he proved an unfailingly supportive sounding board, only reminding him occasionally about deadlines or unfinished tasks.

He also stroked the journalist's not-inconsequential ego. Graham had been Montgomery's story and he labored to keep it that way. For example, it appears that he initially envisioned writing the screenplay for *I Want to Live!* but Wanger gently discouraged him. He was interested in "the first outline of a story," he told Montgomery: "It does not have to be a screenplay; this I would rather leave to a screen writer."[13]

The initial draft of the outline carried a first-person narrative, suggesting that Montgomery envisioned a role—and not a small one—for a character bearing his name. At one point, he asked to play himself in the film. Wanger turned down his request, and actor Simon Oakland played the role of Montgomery. In a nod to authenticity, Oakland wore a bulky hearing aid in one ear; Montgomery was hard of hearing.

Wanger also kept Montgomery in the loop during filming, taking his advice on details both large and small. In one scene, for example, Susan Hayward and Wesley Lau, who played Henry Graham, fought over Graham's demand for money to buy drugs. The script called for Hayward to throw five dollars at Lau in disgust. Montgomery suggested that the sum be raised to ten dollars or even twenty, since "no one could get a fix for $5." He also objected to depictions of Graham using poor grammar. "She would never have used a double negative," Montgomery insisted: "She used good grammar."[14]

And he suggested a jazz score for the film, since that was Graham's favorite music. Wanger agreed and hired Johnny Mandel to compose the score. Wise dubbed it "anxiety jazz, pre–Beat Generation jazz, but with a beat, nevertheless." Graham's "downward slide . . . was paced by the sort of music that came out of San Francisco's Tenderloin district," Wise said. Wanger hired "an all-star quintet" to make the soundtrack. It included Shelly Manne on drums, Red Mitchell on bass, and Gerry Mulligan on saxophone.[15]

Except for a few weeks of leave, Montgomery continued to hold down a full-time job at the San Francisco *Examiner*, while spending dozens of hours each week retracing all his steps and reinterviewing dozens of people originally involved in the case. At one point he wrote Wanger: "I have been extremely busy, what with a narcotics scandal and a stock swindle. There is an outside chance I may fly to Mexico City within the next few days to return with a fugitive."[16] On another occasion, he explained to Wanger that he was "working about three hours each evening, finishing up the Barbara Graham story."[17]

The details Montgomery contributed lent the film authenticity and emotional impact. Before Graham's execution, for example, he had perused John True's original confession at the San Francisco Police Department headquarters, compared it with the trial transcript, and discovered discrepancies. Sometime early in 1957, he visited the department again and walked out with the only copy of the confession. He did so to prove to Wanger that True had lied. Otherwise, Montgomery said, Wanger would have "only my word" as evidence. He mailed the confession to Wanger, and several weeks later, he nervously pleaded for its return. He needed to take it back before police missed it. Wanger made two copies of True's statement and mailed back the original and one copy. "To get the fullest impact out of the execution ... every fact at our command pointing up her innocence should be portrayed," Montgomery wrote in May 1957. "The L.A. crowd knew of [True's] original confession. They knew of the contradictions and yet were willing to have True take the stand and perjure himself blind."[18]

Montgomery approached individuals whose characters might appear in the film and asked them to sign release forms. Henry Graham signed a release netting five thousand dollars for himself and his son, Tommy, by then five years old. Barbara Cates, the nurse who sat with Graham throughout her last night, expressed concern about the kind of film being made. "If they are just going to do a Hollywood thriller based on that poor girl's last few hours and minutes of life," she told Montgomery, "I'm not interested in even talking about it. She was quite a gal. She certainly had something about her and she left me with terrific respect for her." Montgomery apparently convinced Cates of the filmmakers' honorable intent, since her character appears in *I Want to Live!*[19]

Hortense Wood, Barbara's mother, proved the most difficult. Montgomery had never met Hortense and was prepared to dislike her on sight. He was not disappointed. Rather than signing a release, she tried to negotiate a higher, undisclosed price. "I have an idea she'll lower her sights considerably if she has reason to believe you can go without her," Montgomery wrote Wanger in June 1957.[20]

Montgomery identified so closely with Graham that he feared the filmmakers might fail to understand the depths of resentment the executed woman had felt for her mother and thereby depict Hortense in sympathetic terms. He typed up an affidavit, had it notarized, and sent it to Wanger. Graham "never once referred to Hortense as 'Mother,'" Montgomery wrote: "She held Hortense personally to blame for her own inability to regain custody of, and to establish a home for, her two oldest sons prior to her marriage to Henry Graham, contending that Hortense had maliciously interfered with pending arrangements to accomplish such an objective."

Further, "Hortense concealed from [Barbara] the fact that she was born an illegitimate child; that upon the belated discovery . . . she was advised by her mother that she was not certain who Barbara's father was; that while holding up Barbara to scorn and ridicule as an 'unfit' mother, Hortense was, herself, arrested in San Francisco for shoplifting." Barbara's mother does not appear as a character in *I Want to Live!*[21]

By early 1958 Don and Joseph Mankewicz had cut the original screenplay in half, but it still lacked focus. Screenwriter Nelson Giddings ultimately helped rewrite and tighten the story, earning screen credit for his work. The final script omitted Graham's childhood, her first three husbands, and her two older sons. It scrapped scenes showing Mable Monahan's murder and Graham's months at San Quentin during her appeal. The filmmakers also changed the names of many characters. Tommy Graham became "Bobby," possibly to spare Barbara's youngest son future embarrassment. The stool pigeon John True became "Bruce King." Donna Prow was called "Rita," and the alibi fixer, Sam Sirianni, became "Ben Miranda." The most significant decision by Giddings and Wise was to dedicate the last forty minutes of the film to the events surrounding Graham's execution.[22]

Shooting began in early April 1958. To ensure authenticity in the execution scene, Robert Wise traveled to San Quentin to witness the February 14 execution of James Reese, an African American man condemned for rape and murder. Susan Hayward requested photos of Graham for inspiration, and Montgomery mailed a half dozen, calling Hayward's attention specifically to "the AP Wirephoto profile showing her seated in the car en route to Quentin. It gives a good shot of the earrings which she wore the morning of her execution."[23]

Reporters queried Hayward about her decision to portray such a controversial character. She told one that she found Graham fascinating. "I just had to play her," Hayward explained. To critics, she replied: "If I hadn't thought they should make it, I wouldn't have played the part." Besides, she continued: "What do people know of capital punishment? When I was transported . . . to San Quentin, I was appalled when a leather strap was made tight around my waist and my hands were put through cuffs cut into it. This is medieval! Yet people assured me this was just the way it was."[24]

Wanger planned a late-fall opening for *I Want to Live!* He tapped

Montgomery to go on the lecture circuit, appear on television programs, and write articles for national magazines. In a foreshadowing of future controversy, though, Montgomery found publishers reluctant to print potentially inflammatory material about a dead prostitute and an alleged miscarriage of justice.

The Production Code Administration (PCA) still had censorship authority over film content in 1958. PCA officials previewed the movie and expressed concern about reaction from law enforcement in Los Angeles, but they suggested only minor changes. They sought, for example, to eliminate a scene hinting at a lesbian relationship between Graham and Donna Prow in the Los Angeles County Jail. Wanger and Wise removed the scene.[25]

Montgomery also completed a lengthy outline for a paperback book version of *I Want to Live!* to be published by Signet and coincide with the film's opening. Irving "Budd" Schulberg, a screenwriter and author of the novel *What Makes Sammy Run?* agreed to write the book, but not under his own name. Instead, he used the alias Tabor Rawson, possibly out of his own recognition of the incendiary nature of the story. Signet obviously anticipated a blockbuster film; it ordered an initial press run of one million copies.

Wise completed shooting *I Want to Live!* in late June. The film had a sneak preview in San Francisco in late September 1958 and opened on the East Coast in late October. Wanger hoped to build strong word-of-mouth momentum and garner favorable reviews before it reached Los Angeles, where he accurately anticipated a hostile reception from law-enforcement groups that were angry with the film's sympathetic treatment of Graham.

Wanger envisioned *I Want to Live!* as "the greatest film ever shot to end capital punishment." The film may or may not have attained that status, but it definitely promoted a strong anti-death-penalty message. It did not explicitly posit Graham as innocent, but every scene pushed viewers in that direction. One example pertained to

Graham's insistence that she was left-handed and therefore unable to beat Mable Monahan with her right hand.

In one scene *I Want to Live!* depicts Graham writing with her left hand as she sits on her prison cell cot. A crucifix hangs on the wall at the head of her bed and crayon drawings from Bobby take up the remaining wall space. Filmgoers who followed Graham's trial and execution might have recalled the unresolved issue of her right- or left-handedness, but viewers unfamiliar with the case might be drawn to conclude that she had been wrongly convicted, since the film showed her as left-handed.

Ultimately, *I Want to Live!* implied that Graham's guilt or innocence was largely irrelevant, that the real crime was committed by a justice system that framed her and a media that abetted that effort.[26] The film's power and significance lay in the fact that it claimed to be true. Before the opening scene, moviegoers read the following on-screen message from Ed Montgomery: "You are about to see a <u>factual story</u> based on articles I wrote, other newspaper and magazine articles, court records, legal and private correspondence, investigative reports, personal interviews, and the letters of Barbara Graham." It carried Montgomery's signature under the statement.[27]

In reality, the film took liberty with many facts of the case. The arrest scene in *I Want to Live!* for example, resembled a movie premiere, replete with searchlights, photographers, and crowds. Police with bullhorns demanded that Graham, Perkins, and Santo exit their hideout. The scene takes place at night as each member of the trio emerges individually to face the music. Graham emerges last, clutching a toy tiger belonging to her toddler son. Ed Montgomery is one of the reporters on the scene. The real arrest took place in the daytime, with no onlookers or media of any kind and no toy tiger to reflect Graham's maternal instincts, and Ed Montgomery was in San Francisco, not Los Angeles.

In another example of the film's artistic liberties, Graham sits in jail following her arrest when someone hands her a grand-jury indictment for murder. Graham is stunned; she has no idea she has been charged with a capital offense. In actuality, Graham and her codefendants were prepared for the ensuing indictment.

I Want to Live! did not flinch from depicting Graham's sordid lifestyle. In fact, it was reflected in virtually every aspect of the film, which was shot in black and white and carried a noir ambience throughout. The landscape is unrelentingly bleak, with sharp angles. The jazz score is jarring and often atonal. The photography is slightly off center. Viewers first glimpse Graham in silhouette as she languishes in bed with a man. It is late at night, and her lit cigarette and the neon signs outside the seedy hotel room provide the only light.

Filmgoers also witness Graham in her seagull days—in a jazz club dancing frantically to a frenzied bongo beat, in a hotel room casually agreeing to perjure herself for two acquaintances, at a bar trying to pass a bad check to a vice cop, and at Emmett Perkins's smoky card parlor where she works as a shill. She is obviously a prostitute, a small-time criminal, and a woman with no respect for laws, rules, or authority of any kind. In the film, each time Graham gets busted, she goes back for more; her antiauthoritarian tendencies seem to know no bounds.

Since the film takes Graham's point of view, however, it strongly suggests that she is self-destructive, rather than sociopathic, as a result of her barren, loveless childhood. "I don't like my mother and I never knew my father," she explains in an early scene. As she leaves jail after completing her sentence for perjury, the matron chides her about her lifestyle and reminds her that she spent time at a reform school in Ventura. "My mother was in Ventura before me; that should be worth extra points," she deadpans.

The Barbara Graham of *I Want to Live!* is also pathetic rather than pathological. She uses wisecracks and tough talk to conceal a desperate sadness. She longs for marriage and motherhood but is doomed to fail at these pursuits, a fact to which the audience already has been alerted. As she tells Emmett Perkins about plans to marry Henry Graham, he builds a flimsy house of cards. "I envy the housewives going to market. Wait until you taste my cooking," she says. Perkins is highly skeptical. Graham leaves and he knocks over the cards.

Henry Graham inevitably turns out to be a drug addict who cares only about his next fix, leaving his wife and son with nothing. No mention is made of Graham's own drug use. The real Henry Graham must have wondered at the wisdom of accepting only five thousand dollars from the filmmakers, since *I Want to Live!* depicted him in such an unrelentingly negative light. It is Henry's refusal to take care of his family, in fact, that sets the scene for Barbara's arrest for the murder of Mable Monahan. This part of the story is told through headlines from newspapers piled up on Graham's front porch and through commentary from television newscaster George Putnam.

By this point, the film has led all but the most oblivious moviegoer away from the notion that Graham had anything to do with the murder. Days afterward, for example, viewers see that she still lives in the duplex she shared with Henry and Bobby. She takes Bobby to Henry's mother and moves in with Perkins and Santo only because she is desperate and broke, not because she is evading police. She is stunned when Perkins informs her that Bruce King has fingered them for the Monahan murder.

At the police station, Graham masks her terror with sarcastic bravado. An officer puts his face inches from hers, then spits out accusations. Mable Monahan "was murdered." She responds, "Yeah, well so was Julius Caesar and I didn't know him either." Police eventually offer her the opportunity to testify against Perkins, Santo, and King. She refuses, ever the good friend who won't rat out" anyone. Besides, she insists, she "never knew the dame."

To this point, Graham has been victimized by virtually everyone in her life. Her only friend is Peg, a former seagull who has turned her life around, something Graham might have done as well. The movie does make this much clear. *I Want to Live!* shows the beginning of Peg's transformation when Graham agrees to perjure herself on behalf of her friends, who express their gratitude: "One thing about you Bonnie, you never let your friends down." Peg is asked as well, but she demurs. By the time she visits Graham in jail, Peg is married and a mother. Her husband knows about her past, she says. Graham appears to take some responsibility for her predicament: "I'm a little ball, bouncing around a roulette wheel. All the stuff I read and I couldn't read the handwriting on the wall."

But she is about to be victimized again. And this time the consequences are fatal. Her attorney pushes her toward a fake alibi by holding the gas chamber over her head. Her fellow inmate Rita sets her up with Ben Miranda, who drags a confession from her by threatening to pull out of the arrangement. Browbeaten into a corner, Graham finally relents. "Have it your way," she finally says: "All right, all right, I was with them."

The trial scenes reflected Graham's authentic shock when she discovers that she has been duped yet again. By this time she is a pariah, hated by everyone except her loyal friend, Peg. Prosecutors, reporters, jurors, the public at large, and even her attorney have abandoned her. No one believes her claim that she was at home the night of Mable Monahan's murder. Ed Montgomery, who has made few appearances in *I Want to Live!* to this point, proclaims her "guilty as hell." Newspapers prepare two different headlines: "Babs Guilty" and "Babs Innocent." As in real life, her codefendants, Perkins and Santo exist below the fold, footnotes in the larger saga of Barbara Graham.

The last forty minutes of the film cover Graham's appeal and execution. The real impact of *I Want to Live!* lay in its ability to counterpose the impersonal machinery of death with a flesh and blood human being, no matter how flawed. The film's implicit argument for Graham's innocence rendered the methodical preparations and dry court rulings even more horrific, particularly because *I Want to Live!* also depicts Graham's belated acceptance of her own responsibility for her misbegotten life. Earlier scenes may have taken liberties with the truth, but filmmakers did not need to dramatize or fictionalize the execution.

The denouement begins with Ed Montgomery's change of heart, which occurs when Graham's appellate attorney and a psychiatrist both suggest that Perkins and Santo framed her in a desperate ploy to evade the gas chamber themselves. From this point on, Montgomery becomes her most fervent supporter. He writes stories under such headlines as, "Barbara Graham's Childhood Enough to Make a Tiger Out of Any Girl." He contacts the governor's clemency secretary, then the governor himself. He tries to convince Emmett Perkins to exonerate her. The night before Graham's execution, he refuses to leave the office of San Quentin warden Harley Teets, hoping Perkins will have a last-minute change of heart; he wants to be available should Perkins decide to talk.

Graham arrives at San Quentin to a shrieking mob of journalists and photographers. She is shown to her cell and meets nurse Barbara Cates who will spend the night with her. As she slips into her red pajamas, Graham tells Cates that reporters "always call them scarlet when I wear them." Then time slows down, like water dripping from a clogged and rusted drainpipe.

Cates periodically looks at her watch. The camera pans upward to a large, menacing clock on the wall, ticking away the remaining moments of Graham's life. She and Cates talk through the night. Life goes on as the prison prepares for death. While the two women compare notes about their husbands and children, male prison guards pour sulfuric acid into a beaker and wrap egg-sized pellets in cheesecloth. They check the locks on the gas chamber door, the straps on the seat, and the lever that will release the pellets. Near morning, guards carry a heavy black phone past the holding cell.

The warden notifies the prison switchboard operator to hold all outgoing calls in case the governor phones.

The execution is scheduled for 10:00 a.m. A priest is with Graham at 9:15 a.m. as she prepares to dress. Then the shrill ringing of the phone breaks the silence. "Does this mean I'm going to live?" Graham asks Warden Teets when he informs her of the governor's stay. "No," he explains, the execution has simply been rescheduled for 10:45 a.m.

At 10:25, she begins dressing as witnesses file into the viewing area. The warden lays a carpet from her cell to the gas chamber. "The floor is cold," he tells her, and she needs to take off her shoes. She refuses. Just before she steps onto the carpet, another shrill ring pierces the air. Another stay. This one lasts thirty minutes. There will be no more. At this point, *I Want to Live!* resembles the film *Titanic*: The audience knows Graham will be executed, just as they know that the ship will sink. But a last-minute shift in fortune still seems possible. The ship will miss the iceberg; the phone will ring again with a reprieve.

But history stays on course. With a mask over her eyes, Graham walks slowly and regally to the gas chamber. Teets and Cates flank her, each holding one of her hands. She enters the gas chamber and is strapped in. The door closes and is locked from the outside—the wheel spins and clicks shut. Surely, viewers experienced a moment of panicked claustrophobia.

Outside the chamber, the executioner pulls the lever starting the process. It sounds like a toilet flushing, then like a radiator hissing. Graham's head is flung back, then forward. She dies with her head thrust forward onto her chest. Reporters rush to their cars with the story. Ed Montgomery, having waited in vain for Perkins to exonerate her, now walks to his own car. There he is met by Graham's attorney, Al Matthews, who hands Montgomery a letter from Graham thanking him for all of his help. Montgomery pulls out his hearing aid, and all is silent. There is no epilogue; the silence speaks for itself.

Reviews of *I Want to Live!* were almost uniformly ecstatic. Critics took particular note of the harrowing execution scene, and virtually all of them recognized the film as an indictment of capital punishment. Bosley Crowther of the *New York Times* called it "extraordinary. ... What could have been a hackneyed picture in less careful, adroit, and honest hands turns out a forthright drama that makes you feel and, in feeling, think. It is a grim invitation to reflection on capital punishment."

The "fist starts coming at you ... slowly at first," Crowther wrote, "as the genuine jeopardy of the woman begins to grow chokingly real. And then it comes sharp into the midriff as she is clamped into a cell in the death-house at San Quentin, and it pounds you unmercifully until she dies. This is probably the roughest death-house ordeal we've ever had on the screen."[28]

Philip K. Scheuer of the *Los Angeles Times* called the film

the most relentless indictment of capital punishment yet put on film ... and a terrific hunk of cinema in its own right. What it says or implies about the innocence or guilt of Barbara Graham may be open to question—and will be questioned. Nevertheless, what comes out on the screen is a progression of scenes, arguments and events that, intentionally or not (and one can scarcely believe they are unintentional) is loaded in favor of this woman.

Most significant of all is the manner in which—once she has reduced us to a mass of jangling nerve ends—the awfulness of the punishment to which she is to be subjected, the full horror of the death chamber in all its Inquisitional detail, is used to shatter whichever of our emotions are still unscathed.[29]

Motion Picture Daily declared: "By the very fact that [the filmmakers] have utilized as their 'innocent' victim of this practice such an amoral and anti-social character as Barbara Graham, they have stripped the issue of all false sentimentality and fuzzy romanticism.

They are saying, in effect, that all God's creatures, including the perjurers and prostitutes, deserve the same compassion."[30]

Time magazine took issue with the "far-out photography, real desperate sound track, and dragsville dialogue," but also dubbed *I Want to Live!* "a skillful screen version of the life and death of one of California's most celebrated criminals." *Time* took particular note of its depiction of the executioners as "friendly, ordinary, matter-of-fact men who look as though they had never dispatched anything more vital than a letter. Delicately they decant the sulfuric acid. Tidily they bundle the little white eggs of cyanide into a sack of gauze. Politely they unroll the carpet from the cell door to the gas chamber. And so it goes, on and on and on, for almost 40 minutes—right to the bitter end."[31]

Wanger also received congratulatory notes and letters from a number of esteemed writers, including playwright Arthur Miller, screenwriter Paddy Chayefsky, novelist Leon Uris and French writer Albert Camus, all of whom were ardent opponents of capital punishment.[32]

Filmgoers added their own voices and recognition of the film's power to shape public emotions and attitudes. However, not everyone held a positive view of this. S. A. Abbott of Beverly Hills, California, decried "the sensational barrage of publicity, for which one can only assume that producer Walter Wanger is ultimately responsible. . . . So it is pertinent to ask this question: Does Mr. Wanger or anyone associated with this production have any new evidence concerning this case? If the answer is yes, then it should be produced in the objective atmosphere of the courts of law and not in the emotions of the marketplace."[33]

Edward Grimm of New York City called *I Want to Live!* "a film of undeniable power, but it is not a pretty film. It seems to me that its harrowing nature can only be justified as a documentary case against either capital punishment or the practice of certain illegalities."

Grimm objected, however, to a certain publicity gimmick in which movie patrons emerging from theaters were handed cards asking them to weigh in on Graham's guilt or innocence. "It effectively strips the whole film of any high-minded motive," Grimm argued, and "at the same time, it clothes those involved with the gaudy rags of the pitchman."[34]

The paperback version of *I Want to Live!* also garnered a largely positive reception. It followed the film script in most respects, though it focused more attention on Graham's childhood and the circumstances that pushed her toward a life of crime. Robert Kirsch of the *Los Angeles Times* called it "an authentically powerful prose narrative based on a film script. There is a quality of [Theodore] Dreiser's *An American Tragedy* in the telling." (Dreiser's book, like *I Want to Live!* depicted the downward spiral and death sentence of a man whose guilt or innocence in a murder case is not entirely clear.) Most important for Wanger, the book version of *I Want to Live!* sold out its first printing.[35]

Wanger had expected hostile reactions from participants in Graham's case, but many of them had died by late 1958. They included superior court judge Charles Fricke; Los Angeles County district attorney Ernest Roll; San Quentin warden Harley Teets; the stool pigeon John True (killed in a boating accident), Mable Monahan's son-in-law, Tutor Scherer; as well as psychiatrist Carl Palmberg; her original attorney, Jack Hardy; and Polly Gould, the assistant to appellate attorney Al Matthews.[36]

Prosecutor Adolph Alexander had become a superior court judge and thus was expected to stay above the partisan fray. J. Miller Leavy was still a prosecutor, however, and officers involved in the case—including Sam Sirianni—were still working for the Los Angeles Police Department. Police condemned the film as "ridiculous" and "100 percent phony." Leavy plotted a counterattack.

Gene Blake, a *Los Angeles Times* reporter who covered Graham's trial and execution, acknowledged the "excellence" of the movie and acknowledged that filmmakers "are entitled to their opinions. Perhaps the death penalty should be abolished. And if the majority of the people of California or their elected representatives should decide to abolish it, I'll go along. But I would hate to see such a decision made on the basis of the half-truths and emotionalism presented in this picture, which I fear will be used as a vehicle in such a campaign. It has already started."[37]

Walter Wanger's decision to focus on Barbara Graham paid off handsomely. Critics tapped *I Want to Live!* as one of the ten best films of 1958. It earned Susan Hayward, on her fifth nomination, the Oscar for best actress. And it earned more than $3.5 million at the box office, taking in $1 million more than *The Defiant Ones*, the film United Artists had envisioned as its big winner for 1958. Wanger was immensely proud of his film, declaring it "the most exciting picture I have ever had anything to do with." Meanwhile, *I Want to Live!* ensured that Barbara Graham's story would remain in the public imagination, serving as a symbol for both sides in the debate over capital punishment in America.[38]

8

Due Process

ON MARCH 21, 1960, the California State Assembly's criminal procedures subcommittee convened a virtually unprecedented hearing. The nine lawmakers on the panel had only one item on their agenda: potential prosecutorial malfeasance in the trial of Barbara Graham. Specifically, they aimed to study prosecution witness John True's San Francisco confession to determine whether prosecutors had suppressed evidence that might have helped to exonerate Graham. It was rare for lawmakers to conduct hearings on behalf of one individual, but even rarer for them to go on record questioning the actions of powerful men like themselves.

With its strong implication that Graham had been framed, *I Want to Live!* served as a catalyst for the hearing, at least for liberal legislators. The film clearly had struck a nerve, despite taking liberties with some facts of the case. Nonetheless, it packed an emotional wallop, reminding people of the social costs of execution and suggesting that some executed individuals might actually be innocent. This image was reinforced in Tabor Rawson's book and in a 1959 song, "The Ballad of Barbara Graham," by Val Norman. Its refrain went, "Poor Barbara Graham was wild and couldn't be tied, but could she commit murder and should she really have died?"[1]

Graham's execution and the attendant publicity emerged at a propitious time for opponents of capital punishment. For decades they had tried, with little success, to convince Americans to oppose a practice they deemed arbitrary, capricious, and cruelly unjust. The post–World War II period seemed to herald enhanced opportunities. Recollections of Nazi death camps and the ever-present terror of nuclear annihilation made human life seem more precious and precarious. As the *Nation* magazine noted in 1956, "Capital punishment today faces fierce attack in many areas of a world in which the atom has posed a new threat and placed a new premium on human life."[2]

Declining numbers of executions reflected the changed atmosphere, from an average of 166 per year in the 1930s to an average of 71 in the 1950s. Graham was one of 76 people executed nationwide in 1955, and the only woman. By the end of the 1950s executions had dropped to fewer than 50 per year.[3]

Throughout the 1950s state legislatures—California among them—grappled with death-penalty laws, though only Delaware eliminated executions. Both Alaska and Hawaii entered the union in 1959 without capital punishment, bringing the total number of abolitionist states to nine.[4]

California abolitionists pressed lawmakers to enact anti-capital-punishment legislation throughout the 1950s but ramped up their efforts in the latter half of the decade following Graham's execution. Abolitionists included some of the state's most prominent figures: Edmund G. Brown, elected governor in 1958; Roger Traynor, state supreme court chief justice; Clinton Duffy, former San Quentin warden; and Erle Stanley Gardner, lawyer and author of the Perry Mason mystery series.

Liberal lawmakers introduced abolitionist legislation in every session starting in 1957, but the forces advocating for the death penalty prevailed each time. Bills passed the assembly, only to die in the state

Senate. Legislators did take one precedent-setting step, however. In 1957 California became the first state to mandate bifurcated trials in capital cases. This process separated trials into two parts, a guilt phase in which jurors acquitted or convicted defendants, and a penalty phase in which they condemned convicted defendants or sentenced them to life in prison.[5]

By 1960 most death penalty opponents in California and elsewhere recognized the futility of trying to attain outright abolition. A piecemeal approach, like the bifurcated trial legislation, would be more successful, liberals knew. Barbara Graham's case offered an opportunity to begin chipping away at some of the more egregious practices. If the majority Democrats on the criminal procedures subcommittee determined that evidence had been suppressed, they planned to introduce legislation limiting the kinds of evidence prosecutors could use at trial.

Conservative lawmakers adamantly opposed any challenges to death-penalty law. Governor Brown's election had put them on high alert. Twelve days before the subcommittee hearing on Barbara Graham, in fact, Brown had called an emergency session of the state senate judiciary committee, seeking a three-year moratorium on executions. The immediate catalyst for the March 9, 1960, hearing was Caryl Chessman, the so-called Red-Light Bandit," who was scheduled to die within a few weeks.

Condemned in 1948, Chessman had managed to evade execution for a dozen years. Brown wanted to commute Chessman's sentence to life in prison and viewed the hearing as a way to buy time. The emergency session was not about her, but the specter of Barbara Graham made a brief appearance, in the guise of Los Angeles prosecutor J. Miller Leavy.[6]

For obvious reasons, Leavy adamantly opposed efforts to revisit Graham's case. He had been enraged by Montgomery's work on her behalf and at *I Want to Live!* for sullying his previously sterling reputation. Soon after the film's debut, Leavy cast about for someone to produce a movie taking the prosecution's side. The proposed film, tentatively titled "Weep No More for Barbara," was never made. Leavy also recruited Hearst newspaper reporter Bill Walker to write magazine articles and a book. Walker had little success until *Cavalier* magazine, a downscale version of the men's magazine *Playboy*, purchased his article titled "Exposing the *I Want to Live!* Hoax."

Walker's piece appeared in the April 1959 issue of *Cavalier*. It took direct aim at *I Want to Live!* in general and at Ed Montgomery in particular. Montgomery had never attended a single session of Graham's trial and was merely a sob sister and a publicity seeker, Walker contended. A grisly photo of Mable Monahan lying dead in her hallway accompanied the article.

The article drew little attention, except from Montgomery, who filed a libel suit against *Cavalier* and its parent company, Fawcett Publications. Leavy was disappointed. Walter Wanger, on the other hand, viewed the article as good publicity for his movie and tried, without much success, to draw wider attention to it.[7]

The prospect of an entire legislative procedure devoted to Graham enraged Leavy even further. Since he also had prosecuted Caryl Chessman, he decided to place himself on the agenda at the March 9 senate hearing in hopes of derailing the March 21 meeting. Lawmakers had debated capital punishment for nearly twelve hours when Leavy arrived shortly before 9:00 p.m. and, without warning, dropped a bombshell. Barbara Graham had confessed to San Quentin warden Harley Teets just before she died, he told the packed room. The implication was clear: Why focus on suppressed evidence in the trial of a vicious, brutal woman who had admitted her involvement in murder? Stunned, Democratic senator Fred Farr asked Leavy: "Is this the first time this has been made public, here tonight?" "Yes, it is," Leavy acknowledged.

He had learned of the confession in 1959 at a district attorneys' convention in Fresno, Leavy told lawmakers. His source: Marin County district attorney William Weissich, who had gotten the information directly from Teets. San Quentin assistant warden Louis Nelson also knew of the confession, Leavy added.

Senator Farr, an abolitionist, asked Leavy why he had waited nearly a year, until a widely publicized state senate hearing, to reveal the information. Leavy offered a dissembling response. He was "waiting for the opportune moment. The damage had already been done in the Graham case through" *I Want to Live!* Leavy was certain, he added, that Teets himself "would have revealed the confession if he had known that a motion picture would leave the impression that Miss Graham died an innocent woman."[8]

Leavy did not succeed in derailing the March 21 hearing, but his revelation offered immediate dividends to pro-capital-punishment forces on the senate judiciary committee. They managed to beat back Brown's abolition effort by an eight-to-seven vote. Caryl Chessman would die on schedule. Leavy's declaration also ensured that the March 21 proceeding would focus on the alleged Graham confession as well as potential prosecutorial malfeasance.

Six Democrats and three Republicans sat on the assembly subcommittee. "This committee has learned of evidence in the possession of the prosecution, which was suppressed [and] not made available to Barbara Graham and her attorneys," said committee chair John O'Connell of San Francisco in his introductory remarks. If such allegations proved true, he added, lawmakers planned to adopt remedial legislation guaranteeing future capital defendants due process. He acknowledged, however, that the existence of a confession would render the effort "somewhat academic."[9]

Bruce Allen, a Republican lawmaker from Los Gatos, was a proponent of capital punishment. He also hoped to derail the investigation into suppression of evidence. "We are apparently trying [Graham prosecutors] on charges of unethical conduct and I'd like to know if we have afforded them the American right . . . to be heard." The committee had not invited Leavy to testify and this was unfair, Allen added. Leavy needed to be invited; otherwise the prosecutor was being denied his "basic right of due process."

Since Allen and the committee's other Republicans refused to back down, O'Connell agreed to postpone for a week any discussion of suppressed evidence. This would allow lawmakers to examine True's San Francisco statement in conjunction with his trial testimony to determine if there were enough discrepancies to warrant subpoenaing Leavy. The hearing had already convened, so subcommittee members would remain to discuss Graham's purported confession. Leavy, it appeared, had won the day, if not yet the battle.[10]

Alfred Arnaud, assistant deputy chief of the San Francisco Police Department, had brought to the hearing a copy of True's statement from June 4, 1953. It revealed that True did, in fact, change his story at trial. Moreover, a close examination of the confession illustrates why police and prosecutors might have felt pressured to lure Graham into a fake jailhouse alibi. True continually contradicted himself about dates, times, and meeting places. He also backtracked, corrected himself, and mangled his grammar and syntax.

Most of his inconsistencies were minor, but some were not. For example, at one point in San Francisco, he said he had met Graham for the first time the morning of the planned robbery at the motel where he was staying with John Santo. "I seen her. She was just a woman with Mr. Perkins," True said. Later in the same statement, he said he had met Graham the day of the murder at the diner where the group had gone to discuss plans for the robbery. On the witness stand, however, True said he had met Graham at the motel two days before the murder.

The most significant discrepancy had to do with the pillowcase covering Mable Monahan's head. At one point in San Francisco, True said that Monahan "fell to the floor and I grabbed her head in my lap. Perkins came in right behind me and ripped up some sheets and immediately tied her hands behind her and put a pillow case over her head." Later in the same statement, he placed Graham on the scene but was vague on the question of whether she did or did not have a pillowcase with her. During the trial, he testified that: "When [Mable Monahan] collapsed, I had her head—I went right down with her across my lap. Mrs. Graham came around the other way and put a pillow case over her head."[11]

True's San Francisco statement also revealed interesting details about the cozy relationship between Los Angeles police officers and some of their purported targets in the early 1950s. Perkins learned that police were looking for him almost immediately after Mable Monahan's murder, True said, because Perkins had an arrangement with unnamed officers. They allowed him to operate a gambling parlor in El Monte and warned him when vice-squad members seemed close to moving in on the operation. In exchange, he cut them in on the action.[12]

Following the March 9 hearing, assembly subcommittee members had subpoenaed Marin County district attorney William Weissich to appear March 21 to discuss Graham's purported confession. Specifically, they wanted to know how he learned of it and how he came to tell J. Miller Leavy—a man he had not previously known—about it. The story Weissich related was lengthy and somewhat convoluted.

In August 1957, Weissich said, he and Warden Teets had driven to San Francisco to meet with representatives of the state attorney general. The meeting concerned Caryl Chessman and a typewriter. During his dozen years on death row, Chessman had become a prolific writer, penning three nonfiction books and a novel. Following publication of the third book, Teets took away his typewriter. Prison regulations called for inmates to have typewriters only for personal use, yet Chessman had managed time and again to defy authorities. Since San Quentin is located in Marin County, Teets gave the typewriter to Weissich. Chessman demanded that Teets give it back. At the San Francisco meeting, a deputy attorney general told Teets to return Chessman's typewriter.

According to Weissich, Teets was furious at the media-addicted, arrogant Chessman, and he fumed at higher-ups who almost always gave into Chessman's demands. On the drive back from Marin County, Teets exploded and told Weissich about Graham's confession. Weissich was stunned and confused, and he asked Teets why he had never made this information public. Teets replied that "my job is to follow orders." Two days after the San Francisco meeting, Teets died of a heart attack at the age of fifty. Weissich blamed his friend's death on the constant stress of having to deal with Caryl Chessman.[13]

Weissich kept Teets's revelation to himself until he met Leavy eighteen months later, in February 1959 at a district attorneys' conference. *I Want to Live!* had been released four months earlier. Since Weissich had never met Leavy, he admitted to being somewhat surprised when Leavy sought him out. The two men had a "casual conversation" during which Leavy asked if he knew about Graham's purported confession. Left unexplained was why Leavy might think Weissich should be privy to this information.

Weissich was also somewhat taken aback, he told lawmakers, when Leavy asked him to talk to writer Bill Walker and to find out whether anyone else knew of the confession. "Frankly, I didn't do anything," Weissich said. Several months later, Leavy approached him at another professional conference: "He again asked me if I would try to find corroboration or something of this story and again I supposed I was derelict in my duties and forgot about it."[14]

By midsummer of 1959, Leavy clearly was getting anxious. On August 20, 1959, he traveled to San Quentin to witness the execution of Stephan Nash, a Southern California serial killer. According to Weissich, Leavy had stopped in to visit prison warden Fred Dickson and asked Dickson to peruse prison records to find any evidence of Graham's confession. Dickson looked through the files and came up with nothing.[15]

Then in September 1959 Leavy sent Bill Walker to Marin County to try to convince Weissich to go on the record with his information or, alternatively, to find another source willing to publicly corroborate it. As Weissich explained, in October 1959 he "drove down to San Quentin to speak with warden Dickson." Again, Dickson said he knew nothing about a confession. Then, according to Weissich, the warden paused. Perhaps associate warden Louis Nelson could prove more helpful, Dickson told him; Nelson had been at San Quentin for many years. Dickson "pressed a buzzer" to summon Nelson, who told Dickson and Weissich that he did, in fact, know about the confession. Teets had mentioned it to him at some point. Nelson admitted to being hazy about some of the particulars: "The details relative to the crime I do not remember."[16]

Leavy and Walker had asked both Weissich and Nelson to write formal letters recalling, as best they could, Teets's conversations about the confession. Both men had demurred. Teets had not wanted the information made public, they said. Furthermore, Nelson said he needed permission from department of corrections director Richard McGee before putting anything in writing. Leavy kept the pressure on Walker, who continued to lean on Nelson. He needed the information for his book, he said. Nelson agreed to seek permission, and McGee reluctantly agreed.

Nelson penned his letter in November 1959. It covered his conversation with Teets but offered few details of the crime, other than the claim that Barbara Graham allegedly had told Teets she "pistol-whipped [Mable] Monahan until she was dead." He sent copies of the letter to Leavy, Warden Dickson, and Richard McGee. Nelson also sent a copy of the letter to William Weissich. Once Nelson wrote his letter, Weissich felt free to do the same. In December 1959 he wrote to Bill Walker, relating his own story of the trip to San Francisco, Caryl Chessman, the typewriter, and the purported confession.[17]

Democratic assembly members expressed skepticism about Weissich's account. Jerome Waldie of Los Angeles asked how, in December 1959, he could recall explicit details of a conversation that took place more than two years before he wrote the letter. Weissich referred to *I Want to Live!* in his response: "It has been quite alive in my mind ever since I learned of it. This is especially so in view of [Tabor Rawson's] book and the motion picture. I have always felt it was unfortunate," Weissich acknowledged, "that the administration of justice in the state of California should be subjected to the false impression conveyed by the book and motion picture."[18]

Weissich was also asked whether Teets had provided him with details on the timing of Graham's confession. Was it during her seven-month stay at San Quentin in late 1953 and early 1954, or during the night before her execution? "I have been asked that question by dozens of newspaper people and I have no recollection as to whether Harley Teets told me when the confession took place or whether he didn't. My mind is a blank on the subject," he said.[19] Weissich did admit being somewhat surprised that Teets had failed to record the confession. The department of corrections is "very careful about recording things. . . . I think usually with about twenty copies."[20]

Three other witnesses also testified about Graham's reputed confession: California corrections director Richard McGee, nurse Barbara Cates, and Ed Montgomery. Montgomery had been subpoenaed to talk about discrepancies between True's statement and his trial testimony. When lawmakers postponed that discussion, he asked to remain so he could discuss Graham's reputed confession instead.

McGee said he had been "distressed" by Nelson's request that he be allowed to write a letter to Bill Walker. "This is, at this point, hearsay, something that went on between two people that are dead," he told Nelson. Teets's actions with regard to the alleged confession also seemed out of character, McGee added. The corrections department required wardens to "report any unusual incidents, particularly if they relate to condemned inmates." Teets had always been scrupulous about observing regulations. But, McGee concluded, if Nelson wanted to write a letter to Walker, it was "entirely up to him."[21]

McGee was reluctant to take either side of the confession argument. "I have no reason to believe that it didn't [occur] and no proof that it did," he explained, but he called the circumstances as related by both Weissich and Nelson "very unusual." Graham was appealing her death sentence during her initial stay at San Quentin and was hoping for a new trial or a gubernatorial reprieve. Confessing to murder would mean almost certain execution, since Graham had no reason to trust that Teets would not take the information to McGee or to then-governor Goodwin Knight.

Graham also had very few opportunities for one-on-one conversations with Teets, both during her earlier stay and the night leading up to her execution, according to McGee. During the initial stay, Graham "was confined to the hospital where we had a small section that was set aside and segregated from the men." Prison officials divided the space into four cells in advance of Graham's arrival from the California Institution for Women, Corona, in November 1953. Graham resided in one, a second was turned into a bathing facility a third was used for storage, and a female warden stayed in the fourth one.

Graham's status as the only female prisoner made it mandatory for a guard to keep watch over her twenty-four hours a day. Whenever anyone visited her, McGee said, "a nurse or the female attendant stood where she could see them and hear them talking."[22]

Teets took care to always have someone with him when he spoke with Graham, according to McGee. "We are particularly careful about [condemned] women because of the great public interest that attaches to them, and also [because of] accusations that might be made of irregularities and things of that sort," McGee noted. Finally, he went on to say, Teets's "failure to make this report is entirely out of character with my experience with him over [the] years".[23]

Nurse Barbara Cates was undoubtedly the most objective witness, since she was the only one with no personal or political stake in the outcome of the hearing. Her testimony also offered a window into the emotional cost of capital punishment for those whose jobs required them to interact with condemned individuals, particularly as they prepared for death. Cates no longer worked at San Quentin at the time of the assembly subcommittee hearing, having left that job in October 1956.

Teets had called Cates into his office a few days before Graham's scheduled execution to ask her to volunteer for the death watch, she recalled: "He said, 'I can't force you to accept . . . but would very much appreciate it if you would.' I told him that I would." Cates stayed with Graham from the moment she arrived "until her remains went out the gate" shortly after noon on June 3, 1955. The two women "seemed to hit it off and, I don't know, I was too upset to get any rest, and we got along fine. We both smoked and drank coffee all night." They also talked about their families. Cates said her husband had left her and she was raising two children on her own. Graham "worried about her youngsters, how the execution would affect them."

Cates was adamant that Graham had not confessed during that long night. "She did not make a confession. She could not have made a confession, and I think it's very unfair of them to say she did unless it was made to the Father—the two Catholic priests that visited her." The only time Cates left Graham alone, she said, was to wash her hands, "use the bathroom, or pour some coffee for the two of us." During her absence, the matron stepped in. Cates was also present for conversations between Teets and Graham. She was asked if she could hear every word: "Oh, very definitely," she replied.

Cates recalled only one conversation between the warden and the condemned woman. "[It] broke me up pretty much at the time, when [Teets] got the phone call that said he was to go ahead, to hurry up and execute her so the other two could get executed. He came over, patted her on the shoulder, and said, 'I'm sorry, Barbara.'"[24]

Ed Montgomery held the same agenda he had possessed since he became Graham's passionate partisan: to cast doubt on every aspect of the prosecution's case. He had been subpoenaed to talk about the discrepancies between True's statement and the trial record and had brought a dog-eared copy of the statement with him. Each page was marked up with doodles, underlined passages, and exclamation points. One page bore a drawing of bookended parentheses, with the face of a woman, her open mouth in an O shape, as if she were screaming, etched between the two semicircular lines.

As a condition of his testimony, Montgomery had agreed to focus only on Graham's purported confession. But he immediately segued to Bill Walker's *Cavalier* article, which he dubbed "a hatchet job." He had not previously known that Leavy collaborated on the article, he added, and was "glad to find that he was a part of it."

Walker's allegation that he had not attended the trial was "false," Montgomery added. He also took strong exception to being labeled a sob sister, since "I am generally found on the side of the prosecutor." As evidence, Montgomery offered up the Burton Abbott case, where his efforts to locate the body of the teenage victim, Stephanie Bryan, helped Bay Area prosecutors convict Abbott, who had been executed in 1957. Montgomery also had promoted Graham's guilt throughout her trial and for at least a year afterward, before changing his mind. And Montgomery would again take the side of law-and-order forces, during the free speech movement at the University of California, Berkeley, in 1964, when he railed against student protesters as Marxists.[25]

Asked if he had spent more time on Graham's story than on any other in his career, Montgomery acknowledged that he had. Then, turning to her alleged confession, he emphatically labeled it a "hoax" and said it was "entirely incompatible with statements that [Teets] made to me and to others as late as May of 1955." Montgomery had known the San Quentin warden well, he said. Teets was "my dinner guest at the [San Francisco] Press Club on occasions. I had lunch with him at San Quentin. We were fairly—I don't say intimate friends, but we were close friends."

Throughout the months that Montgomery in vain tried to stop Graham's execution, Teets mentioned nothing about a confession. "I think I knew Harley Teets well enough that if in fact Barbara Graham had confessed and he had knowledge of a confession, way back down along the line he would have said to me, 'Ed, you're wasting your time. I am satisfied that this woman is guilty.'"[26]

Montgomery said he and Teets did discuss the case on several occasions, particularly as the execution date neared. Montgomery always believed Emmett Perkins killed Mable Monahan and that Perkins and John Santo framed Graham in order to escape execution. On several occasions, he interviewed Perkins at San Quentin, and each time, "I had impressed upon him that if [Graham] was innocent, if she were not guilty of this crime, that he owed it to her to come forward. We left it on that basis, that if he decided he wanted to talk, he would send for me." On a Friday afternoon, in mid-May 1955, at nearly 5:00 p.m., Teets phoned Montgomery to tell him that Perkins wanted to talk.

The following Monday, Montgomery showed up at the prison to find Perkins "disturbed to the point of profanity over the fact that everyone in San Quentin knew that [Montgomery] was there and what he was there for." Over the weekend, Perkins said, he had gotten word from John Santo to "keep his mouth shut." Montgomery was, as he described it, livid. He had made the trip for nothing; Perkins was not going to exonerate Graham. Then, according to Montgomery, the condemned man "looked up at me with a sort of wide grin on his face and with considerable profanity, he finally got to the point, and he said, 'Montgomery, that old lady was never pistol-whipped, she was beat with her own cane.' I would like to have considered that a confession by Emmett Perkins, that he was responsible for the murder of Mable Monahan."

In a subsequent conversation with the San Quentin warden, Montgomery testified that Teets told him "he was satisfied it was Perkins who actually had killed Mabel Monahan, but he was not sure in his own mind but what [Graham] was present in Burbank the night of the murder." Associate warden Louis Nelson's contention that Teets said Graham "pistol-whipped Mabel [sic] Monahan until she was dead" was entirely false, Montgomery insisted. Monahan did not die from being beaten. The strip of cloth around her neck that held the pillowcase in place had strangled her.[27]

The subcommittee battle over Barbara Graham's confession essentially ended in a draw, with no conclusions and neither side landing a knockout punch. Depending on one's point of view on her guilt or innocence, Graham may or may not have confessed to murder. Nonetheless, the testimony had sucked much of the air out of the abolitionists' effort to enact remedial laws tightening rules on evidence, making Leavy's side the default winner.

The subcommittee's March 28 follow-up hearing on John True's statement was a subdued affair. Assembly members read over the document and compared it with his trial testimony, and both Republicans and Democrats agreed that discrepancies and contradictions did exist. J. Miller Leavy showed up with his former coprosecutor, Los Angeles Superior Court judge Adolph Alexander. Both men argued that the two accounts by True carried "no material discrepancies." Besides, Leavy said, Graham's attorney had never asked for a copy of True's San Francisco statement, and so the prosecution bore no obligation to provide the defense with this information. Thus, no suppression had occurred. Jack Hardy, Graham's original trial attorney, was not around to rebut this assertion; he had died of a heart attack on July 3, 1955, exactly a month after Graham's execution.[28]

Liberal lawmakers had to admit defeat. They announced their decision to abandon the effort for remedial legislation, since "the defense attorneys did have knowledge of the True confession in San Francisco and there was no apparent suppression of that document." Ed Montgomery, not surprisingly, saw the situation differently. "There was a gross miscarriage of justice in the Graham case," he said.[29] On May 2, 2960, less than six weeks after the March 28 assembly hearing, Caryl Chessman finally went to the gas chamber. Governor Brown again agonized about the decision but feared that reprieving Chessman would doom his political future. In the end, Chessman had managed to outlive his and Graham's trial judge, Charles Fricke, as well as San Quentin warden Harley Teets.

The following year, Ballantine published Bill Walker's *The Case of Barbara Graham*. Since Walker had collaborated with Leavy, the prosecution's version of the story stood front and center, as did Graham. According to Walker, Graham played the pivotal role in Monahan's death. She knocked on the door and asked to use Monahan's telephone. Brandishing a gun, she started beating Monahan about the head even before her male counterparts emerged from the darkness and pushed their way into the house. In an interesting deviation from John True's trial testimony, however, Graham appeared nowhere in Walker's rendition of the pillowcase incident. Instead, Perkins and Santo were responsible for this part of the crime.[30]

Walker piled on the details of Graham's sexual history and her life of small-time crime, including her efforts to steal items from various stores in Los Angeles prior to the Monahan arrest. His version of the May 4, 1953, arrest of Graham, Perkins, and Santo had police tailing Graham to a downtown Los Angeles park, where she purchased heroin and then injected herself in a park restroom. Police followed her to the trio's hideout. When they broke down the door of the makeshift apartment in Lynwood, Graham stood naked in the middle of one room while Santo lay seminude on a nearby bed. After the arrest, according to Walker's account, police offered Graham a lie detector test, but she replied, mockingly, "No thanks, that iron monster is not for me or my benefit." When police informed her of her status as a murder suspect, she growled, "You'll never prove it."[31]

Walker referenced the genre of the hard-boiled crime novel in his description of the atmosphere in Charles Fricke's courtroom during Graham's trial. It was "like a weird piece of fiction conjured out of the combined imagination of James M. Cain and Dashiell Hammett," with "threads of bizarre intrigues, incredible plots and counterplots, elaborate alibis, shadowy characters, threats and deadly reprisals, surprise witnesses, and explosive conflagration."[32]

Walker could not entirely ignore the police's and the prosecution's collaboration to snare Graham into a false alibi. He conceded that the tactic had been underhanded but argued that Graham had been complicit. Police did, after all, originally offer her immunity from prosecution in exchange for her testimony against Perkins, Santo, and True, but she had refused their offer.[33]

Walker's book, like his earlier *Cavalier* article, sold a few copies and then disappeared from view. In a *Los Angeles Times* review, Robert Kirsch lauded Walker for "balancing the ledgers of justice" and serving up *The Case of Barbara Graham* as an antidote to *I Want to Live!* "What you discover in this volume," Kirsch told readers, "is the day-to-day technique of investigation. The police were up against a difficult problem: there was no disinterested witness to this crime." Kirsch assured readers, however, that he did not condone the prosecution's "entrapment of Barbara Graham." In fact, he argued, "The whole episode offended propriety." In the end, Graham was "an interesting and pathetic example of womanhood. Perhaps there was room for mercy, certainly for compassion. But there is no real question of her guilt."[34]

By the time Walker's book appeared in 1961, Barbara Graham had been in the news for eight years and dead for six. Continuing debates over her guilt or innocence seemed to have little allure for members of the public, in California and elsewhere. It was a new decade and the world had moved on. But debates over capital punishment continued unabated. Graham's case had played a prominent role in keeping the issue alive in the media and political realms as abolitionists struggled to find a winning strategy. By the mid-1960s, they believed they had found one: challenging the death penalty on constitutional grounds.

9

Abolishing the Death Penalty

IN SEPTEMBER 1962 Edmund G. Brown and Richard M. Nixon were in the midst of a hard-fought gubernatorial campaign in California. Nixon hoped to revive his political fortunes following a narrow loss to John F. Kennedy in the 1960 presidential election, and Brown was fighting for a second term. Polls showed the two men locked in a tight race. Nixon struggled to gain traction via a number of issues. "He tried the old conservative broadsides—taxes too high, regulations too restrictive—but big government was not yet the enemy for Californians," noted Brown's biographer, Ethan Rarick. Nixon decided to bore in on the one issue he envisioned as Brown's main weakness: capital punishment.[1]

On September 19 Nixon appeared before a gathering of law enforcement officials in Los Angeles and announced his support for tougher death-penalty laws. Recidivist "dope peddlers" should be eligible for execution, he said: "To me, dope peddling is like kidnapping. Kidnapping has virtually been stopped by virtue of the death penalty—and my authority for that is J. Edgar Hoover. I have a basic disagreement with Brown.... We've heard too much about the rights of criminals and not enough about respecting the responsibility of the state to protect innocent people."[2]

In his public response, Brown mocked Nixon. "Maybe he'd like to have the death penalty for every crime, like they did in old England. It didn't do a bit of good," he said. But, privately, Brown took his Republican rival's words to heart. His long-stated opposition to capital punishment could, in fact, end his political career, he realized. California had its liberal tendencies, but the state was also home to the ultraconservative John Birch Society, which gained a following for its obsessive anti-Communism. As much as it pained him, Brown decided to neutralize the issue by allowing condemned inmates to die. In 1962 eleven people went to the gas chamber in California.[3]

They included one woman. Jurors in Santa Barbara County had condemned Elizabeth Duncan in 1959. Brown "felt a great repugnance about letting a woman die," he later wrote. The first week of August 1962 he presided over a clemency hearing for Duncan, but announced that he saw no grounds for a sentence commutation. If he feared a reprise of the controversy surrounding Barbara Graham's execution, he need not have worried. Duncan was no Graham. In her late fifties and matronly, journalists found her repulsive, due in part to the nature of her crime. Duncan was extraordinarily close to her son, Frank. Her possessiveness led Frank to keep his marriage secret. When Duncan discovered she had been duped, she decided to murder her pregnant daughter-in-law and hired two men to carry out the killing. In their effort to be cleverly ironic, reporters dubbed Duncan "Ma." On August 8, 1962, she became the fourth woman executed in California and the last woman executed in the United States for nearly a quarter century. Newspapers, radio, and television newscasters covered the event but then moved on to other stories. Duncan was soon forgotten.[4]

In November 1962 Brown won a second term. With the election behind him, he initiated a renewed effort to end the death penalty. The campaign continued virtually unabated until 1972, when first

California and then the United States Supreme Court ended executions. By the time abolitionists prevailed, Brown had left office and begun practicing law in Southern California, and former actor Ronald Reagan was governor. Many Californians only dimly recalled Barbara Graham, *I Want to Live!* and the rancorous arguments over her guilt or innocence. However, Graham had played an important role in keeping the issue of capital punishment alive until abolitionists could begin to close in on a winning strategy.

California's renewed abolition effort began in early 1963, when Brown initiated yet another legislative effort to end capital punishment, this time via a four-year moratorium that would substitute mandatory life imprisonment for execution in most cases. The murder of a police officer, a second conviction for murder, committing murder during a robbery or rape, and killing while incarcerated remained crimes that could still net individuals the death penalty.

Three hundred people packed the state capitol on April 9, 1963, to hear testimony on the proposed moratorium. California's attorney general, Stanley Mosk, soon to be named by Brown to the state supreme court, and Joseph Ball, Brown's future law partner, testified in favor of the bill. So did George Edwards, a former Michigan State Supreme Court justice. Michigan had abolished the death penalty in 1846. As a result, said Edwards, the state had never executed an innocent man or woman. He cited the case of three men convicted of murder and later determined to be innocent. If Michigan had retained capital punishment, all three might have been wrongly executed, Edwards argued.

Long Beach Republican assemblyman and later Republican governor George Deukmejian also testified. He was a relative newcomer to the death-penalty wars as well, but on the pro–capital punishment side. Some battle-scarred veterans also appeared at the hearing, including prosecutor J. Miller Leavy, still trying to resuscitate his reputation in the wake of *I Want to Live!* By 1963 Leavy, still obsessed with Barbara Graham, had elevated her to leadership of her own gang. He frequently referenced the "Barbara Graham gang who murdered an elderly Burbank widow."[5]

Predictably, the abolition bill passed the state assembly but failed passage in the state senate. Even senate Democrats proved reluctant to vote for it, out of concern, they said, "that it might damage President Kennedy's chances in California in 1964." Lawmakers debated the notion of putting an abolition initiative on the 1964 ballot to let voters decide the fate of capital punishment, but ultimately decided against this approach.[6]

With his legislative efforts stymied, Brown decided to adopt his own unofficial moratorium. Without fanfare, he began to commute to life in prison the death sentences of every condemned individual whose case reached the clemency-hearing phase. As a result, only one execution took place in California between January 1963 and the end of Brown's term four years later.[7]

Brown was not the only governor pressing for abolition in the 1960s. Ohio governor Michael DiSalle lobbied against the death penalty and even hired "convicted murderers for his household staff to demonstrate the possibility of rehabilitation." North Carolina governor Terry Stanford spoke out so frequently against executions that condemned prisoners "made a point of mentioning it in their clemency applications." Both states retained the death penalty.[8] So did Missouri, Indiana, and Texas. Even in states that allowed the death penalty, however, executions dropped into the single digits after 1964, and many states carried out no executions after that date.[9]

Five state legislatures abolished the death penalty in the 1960s. Voters in Oregon approved a November 1964 abolition referendum. Three men resided on Oregon's death row and Republican governor Mark Hatfield commuted their sentences to life in prison.[10] The following year, New York, Iowa, Vermont, and West Virginia all ended capital punishment.

In New York a bipartisan state commission recommended abolition. State lawmakers adopted the recommendation and governor Nelson Rockefeller—like Hatfield, a liberal Republican—signed the legislation. It provided for one exception: the murder of a police officer.

West Virginia, like California, debated capital punishment through the 1950s, introducing bill after bill, with Shirley Donnelly, a minister and journalist, as the major catalyst. Finally, in 1965, the legislature approved an abolition measure and governor Hulett Smith signed it.[11]

By the time governor Edmund G. Brown left office in January 1967, California, along with the rest of the country, stood on the cusp of abolition, largely as a result of shifting strategies by anti–capital punishment forces.[12] Lawmakers in many states had proved unwilling to risk alienating voters, so abolitionists turned to state and federal courts.

The timing seemed propitious. In 1963 Arthur Goldberg, an associate justice of the United States Supreme Court, had decried the death penalty as "the deliberate institutionalized taking of human life by the state." Previous courts had overturned individual death-penalty cases based on due process issues, but, as David Garland has noted, the court was now signaling its willingness to take on the constitutionality of the death penalty itself.[13]

Two national organizations—the NAACP and the American Civil Liberties Union (ACLU)—led the court-centered campaign. Both groups focused on two issues: unfettered jury discretion in sentencing and prosecutors' ability to exclude jurors who admitted to having qualms about capital punishment. Lawyers for both groups also pushed for bifurcated trials.

The NAACP's Legal Defense Fund focused on racial disparities in executions. The contention that African Americans were executed in numbers far exceeding their representation in the American population was not difficult to prove. Statistics from the U.S. Department of Prisons revealed that 53.5 percent of the 3,857 people executed in America between 1930 and 1966 had been black. In the south the percentage was even higher. In Texas fully 75 percent of people executed between 1924 and 1965 had been African American or Latino. African American women accounted for at least one-third of executed females nationally. None of the women executed between 1900 and the 1960s had been Latina, Native American, or Asian American.[14]

State courts laid the groundwork for capital cases that wound up in front of the U.S. Supreme Court. California's highest court was widely regarded by the legal community as "the nation's most aggressive and progressive," and thus it was destined to play an outsized role in abolitionists' national legal strategy during the 1960s.

Chief justice Roger Traynor led the court. He had been a law professor at the University of California, Berkeley, with no judicial experience when Democratic governor Culbert Olson appointed him as an associate justice in 1940. Traynor went on to become what the *New York Times* called "one of the finest jurists who never sat on the United States Supreme Court." His arrival on the California high court heralded a number of path-breaking rulings targeting practices long cited by civil libertarians as antithetical to fair and impartial jurisprudence.[15]

In 1948, in *Perez v. Sharp*, the court overturned the state's ban on interracial marriage. In *People v. Cahan* (1955), it barred prosecutors in criminal trials from using illegally obtained evidence, including information attained via wiretaps. In *People v. Morse* (1964), the court nullified a jury instruction notifying jurors that capital defendants could be "back on the streets in a few years" if given life sentences. In *People v. Dorado* (1965), the court ruled that police failure to advise a criminal suspect of the right to counsel automatically voided any confession he or she might have made.

Both the *Cahan* and *Dorado* rulings covered issues pertinent to Barbara Graham and many other condemned defendants. Graham's appellate attorney, Al Matthews had in fact cited *Cahan* in his last-minute appeal to the state supreme court on June 3, 1955. The *Dorado* decision focused on another pertinent issue for Graham: she had been lured into a confession without an attorney present.[16]

In 1964 Governor Brown elevated Traynor to chief justice. Under his leadership the *Wall Street Journal* deemed the California high court "perhaps the most innovative of the state judiciaries, setting precedents in areas of criminal justice, civil liberties, racial integration, and consumer protection that heavily influence other states and the federal bench." But conservatives railed against what they called its activist judges. On several occasions they tried unsuccessfully to have Traynor removed from the bench. He kept a desk drawer full of critical letters, one of which read, "You are a bunch of stupid idiots . . . stop coddling the criminal and do something for the victim."[17]

Roger Traynor never hid his abolitionist sentiments. Decisions such as *Cahan*, *Dorado*, and *Morse* provided him and other liberal justices with grounds to overturn death sentences and send cases back to trial courts for penalty phase rehearings. In April 1964 the high court vacated the death sentence, though not the conviction, of forty-five-year-old Iva Kroeger, the only condemned woman in California at the time.

Jurors in San Francisco had convicted Kroeger for the 1961 murders of a husband and wife. Kroeger had ingratiated herself with the wealthy couple, murdered them, and buried their bodies in the basement of her home. Afterward, she forged checks and used the money for a spending spree. Justices ruled that Kroeger's trial judge had prejudiced jurors by telling them that a life sentence might net her as few as seven years in prison.[18]

When Republican Ronald Reagan denied Edmund G. Brown a third gubernatorial term in November 1966, California had more than sixty men—though no women—awaiting execution. Reagan swept into office on a tide of voter antipathy toward civil rights activists and Vietnam War protesters on college campuses. Pro–capital punishment forces, hoping to see a quick return to executions, did not have long to wait. In April 1967 Reagan allowed the execution of Aaron Mitchell, condemned for murdering a Sacramento policeman.

Mitchell's was to be the last execution nationwide for a decade and California's last execution for a quarter century. By 1967 abolitionists at the state level had begun sifting through capital cases seeking those with potential grounds for federal appeal. One California case involved Emmett Thornton, a twenty-four-year-old aircraft worker condemned to die for raping and robbing three women in Los Angeles County. Prosecutors had described Thornton as "a man who would make the infamous Caryl Chessman . . . look like a choir boy."[19]

Superior court judge Herbert Walker was preparing to formally sentence Thornton when ACLU attorneys asked him to postpone the sentencing. The group hoped to use the case to challenge the constitutionality of the death penalty. Since he had not killed anyone, Thornton's punishment was too severe for the crime and thus amounted to cruel and unusual punishment, ACLU attorneys charged.

Prosecutors argued that Walker lacked standing to make such a significant decision. Only state legislators held "the power to decide what is a crime and what its penalty should be." A. L. Wirin, Southern California's chief ACLU counsel, disagreed. Lawmakers had relinquished their right to determine the legality of capital punishment, he said, when they refused to address constitutional issues in their many death-penalty debates.

Walker sided with the ACLU. He agreed to postpone sentencing Thornton until after a hearing into constitutional issues. "There is no question in this court's mind," he said, "that it has . . . the power to make its determination on the basis of evidence presented by either side."[20]

The hearing took place in November 1967 with six attorneys participating: two from the ACLU, two representing Thornton, and two from the district attorney's office. The last category included J. Miller Leavy. He had not been involved in Thornton's case, but he possessed more experience with capital cases than any other prosecutor in Los Angeles County. By 1967, in fact, journalists often referred to Leavy as "the doorman to hell." Barbara Graham had been dead a dozen years, but, as the hearing made clear, she still retained symbolic value for individuals on both sides of the capital-punishment question.

Participants ostensibly had gathered to address constitutional issues in Thornton's case, but instead, they mostly focused on the moral and social implications of capital punishment. Former San Quentin warden Clinton Duffy was an ardent abolitionist. He had spent years crisscrossing California, giving speeches and testifying at death-penalty hearings. He also had written a book, *88 Men and 2 Women*, detailing the executions he personally oversaw. "No killing can be decent," he testified in Walker's courtroom: "It is wrong for anyone to kill—condemned men, or the state."[21]

Former San Quentin chaplain Bryon Eschelman was also an abolitionist. During his sixteen years at the prison, he ministered to approximately 250 death row inmates. He also wrote *Death Row Chaplain*, a book that described his relationships with condemned prisoners. The book included Barbara Graham, whom Eschelman believed to be innocent. She had been a petty criminal who lacked good judgment, but also lacked the temperament to commit murder, he wrote. At the hearing Eschelman argued that capital punishment dehumanized condemned inmates. Aaron Mitchell, for example, "took off all his clothes the night before he died, cut his arm with a razor blade, and stood naked in a crucifix formation with blood running down his arms."[22]

San Quentin physician William Graves declared that "capital punishment violates all standards of decency and is far worse than any other kind of physical or mental punishment." Graves recalled, for example, how Barbara Graham "cried and was speechless because she couldn't see her infant son" before her execution.[23]

Prosecutors called police officers, a minister, and the wife of a potential murder victim to testify to the societal benefits of capital punishment. Thad Brown, chief of detectives on the Los Angeles Police Department, said, "Most people accused of homicide respect only their own lives, no one else's." The Reverend John Baird, a Presbyterian minister from Pasadena, had been a prison guard in an earlier career. The death penalty "does not harm society, it helps society," he said. Florence Diaz was married to a grocer. Two men had robbed his store, she testified. One threatened to kill him, before the second one said, "This ain't worth dying over." The pair ran out of the store, leaving her husband alive.[24]

Taking the stand himself, Leavy declared that "I could care less" about the anguish of condemned inmates. "They should have thought about that before they committed their offenses," he argued: "Wouldn't you say that the families of victims [have] the same anguish and tensions over the loss of loved ones as Barbara Graham? All punishment is cruel to some extent, but the death penalty is necessary because it serves as a deterrent to certain crimes, mostly murder."[25]

After twelve days and twenty-four witnesses, Judge Walker ruled that capital punishment "does not violate either the U.S. or California constitutions" and formally sentenced Thornton to death. Leavy cheered Walker's decision. "Any God-fearing man who knows he might go to his death for a crime will be deterred," he said. However, "many persons are not God-fearing."

Thornton's may not have passed muster as a test case, but within months of his hearing the U.S. Supreme Court began ruling on other appeals in death-penalty cases.[26] The first significant federal ruling came in the case of William Witherspoon, condemned in Illinois for murdering a Chicago policeman. Prosecutors had excused every potential juror who expressed doubts about the death penalty. NAACP attorneys claimed that this practice automatically skewed juries toward conviction and thus deprived defendants of fair trials. In early 1968 high-court justices agreed. The ruling held the potential to overturn sentences of hundreds of condemned inmates across the country sentenced by death-qualified juries.[27]

The NAACP focused on a different issue—unfettered jury discretion in the choice of verdicts—in the 1969 appeal of William Maxwell, an African American sentenced to die in Arkansas for raping a white woman. Maxwell, like Emmett Thornton, had not killed anyone. Thus abolitionists declared his sentence to be excessive and cruel. A majority of justices appeared to be leaning toward the NAACP argument. Before completing deliberations, however, associate justice Abe Fortas resigned from the court. Rather than risk a split decision, the remaining justices vacated Maxwell's death sentence and decided to await the appointment of a new colleague before tackling larger constitutional issues.[28]

In 1970 the U.S. Supreme Court accepted a death-penalty appeal from California. Dennis McGautha was an itinerant chauffeur who had once worked for actor Peter Lawford. Jurors in Los Angeles had sentenced him to die in September 1967 for killing a grocer during a robbery, but the jury had "no guiding standards to help them choose a verdict of life or death," his attorneys argued.[29] Justices were not sympathetic and ruled against McGautha. Abolitionists despaired, but they were heartened when justices announced they would hear four capital cases in their 1971 term, including one from California. Earnest Aikens had been condemned in Ventura County in 1966 for rape and murder.[30] The other three cases came from the south. All the southern defendants were black, but only one, William Henry Furman of Georgia, had been condemned for murder. Lucious

Jackson in Georgia and Elmer Branch in Texas had been condemned for rape.

In anticipation of the high-court arguments, nine current and former governors filed a friend-of-the-court brief urging the justices to abolish capital punishment. One of these former governors was Edmund G. Brown of California. The others were Milton Shapp of Pennsylvania, Michael DiSalle of Ohio, David Cargo of New Mexico, Elbert Carvel of Delaware, Philip Hoff of Vermont, Theodore McKeldin of Maryland, Endicott Peabody of Massachusetts, and Grant Sawyer of Nevada. All argued that the death penalty "does not deter murder." The governors cited Lee Harvey Oswald, who "killed President Kennedy, even though the assassins of Presidents Lincoln, Garfield, and McKinley were executed."[31]

The resignations of two justices pushed the death-penalty hearing's arguments to February 1972. In the meantime California justices had scheduled arguments to determine the constitutionality of capital punishment at the state level. The case before them involved Robert Page Anderson, a career criminal condemned in 1965 for murdering a San Diego pawnshop owner. Anderson's appeal had previously been argued before the state high court. In 1968 attorney Jerome Falk charged that jurors had too much discretion in capital cases and that condemned inmates were not guaranteed appellate attorneys. Three justices, including chief justice Roger Traynor, agreed with Falk. But four justices—a majority—disagreed. The court did vacate Anderson's death sentence, however, sending the case back for a penalty phase retrial.[32]

Jurors resentenced Anderson to death, and his case again went on appeal to the state supreme court. Roger Traynor had left the court in 1970 because of ill health, and it was now headed by Reagan appointee Donald Wright. This time attorneys argued on the grounds that Anderson's sentence was contrary to "evolving standards of decency," in addition to being cruel and unusual. The court's ruling would be based on California's state constitution, which differed only slightly, but significantly, from the federal Constitution. While the federal document's Eighth Amendment bars "cruel and unusual" punishment, California's constitution bars punishment that is "cruel or unusual."[33]

Two weeks after the California Supreme Court arguments in the Anderson case, the U.S. Supreme Court held hearings on the four combined capital cases. By that time California justices already were writing their opinions. On February 17, 1972, in a six-to-one ruling, the court declared the death penalty cruel, unusual, and thus unconstitutional.[34]

If Reagan viewed chief justice Donald Wright as a safe vote for capital punishment, the Anderson decision proved him wrong. Wright wrote the majority opinion. The death penalty "degrades and dehumanizes all who participate in its processes. It is unnecessary to any legitimate goal of the state and is incompatible with the dignity of man and the judicial process," Wright wrote. He insisted the ruling was "not grounded in sympathy for those who would commit crimes of violence, but in concern for the society that diminishes itself whenever it takes the life of one of its members."[35]

The decision commuted the death sentences of 102 condemned men and 5 women in California. All the sentences automatically reverted to life in prison. Among the reprieved were Emmett Thornton, Dennis McGautha, and Earnest Aikens. His vacated sentence rendered Aikens's further participation in the federal case moot.

Other reprieved California death-row inmates included some of the most notorious in the United States: Sirhan B. Sirhan, who had murdered New York Senator Robert F. Kennedy in Los Angeles in June 1968; Charles Manson, mastermind of a series of brutal slayings; and four of Manson's followers. Three of them were women—Susan Atkins, Leslie Van Houten, and Patricia Krenwinkel. In their twenties they had participated in two nights of butchery in August 1969 that left seven people dead, including actress Sharon Tate.[36]

Prison officials moved quickly to assure Californians that hardened criminals would not soon be freed to roam the streets. Few, if any, would ever see the outside world again. But not all condemned prisoners were anxious to join the general prison population, it seemed. Death row may have held some of California's most vicious slayers, but "you won't find no 'low riders'" there, San Rafael murderer Jack Gorman told a reporter soon after the Anderson decision, "and you don't have to worry about somebody sticking a shiv in you every time you turn a corner."

Former governor Edmund G. Brown lauded the outcome that had eluded him for so long. "It will do more to expedite criminal trials than anything in the last 100 years," he said: "The death penalty has never been a deterrent. In states where no death penalty is in force there are more murders than in states which have abolished it."[37] Governor Reagan expressed outrage at the ruling. "The court is setting itself up above the people and their legislators," he said. "In a time of increasing crime and increasing violence, capital punishment is needed."[38]

Opponents vowed to appeal the ruling to the U.S. Supreme Court, but it could not be appealed. The nation's highest court had "no power to tell a state court that it has misapplied its own constitution," wrote legal scholar Alan Dershowitz. For opponents of the ruling, only one possible avenue existed: new state statutes reinstating capital punishment. But it could not be applied retroactively.[39]

Four months later, California's ruling itself became moot. On June 29, 1972, the U.S. Supreme Court ruled five-to-four—in nine separate opinions—that capital punishment as it was then practiced, was unconstitutional under the Eighth and Fourteenth Amendments. Attorneys representing the three remaining condemned men had focused on the same issue that had long served as a linchpin of abolitionist strategy: a jury's discretion to give capital defendants any sentences they chose without regard to standards or guidelines.

To reinstate capital punishment, states had to draft new laws "designed to lead to less arbitrary, more consistent sentencing by giving juries less discretion in choosing a defendant's sentence." They also needed to utilize bifurcated trials.[40]

The federal court ruling invalidated the death sentences of more than 700 condemned inmates in 34 states: 697 men and 7 women. More than half were African American. Most had been convicted of murder, but 74 had been convicted of rape and 10 of other crimes, including robbery and kidnapping. Success proved fleeting, however, as legislatures in death-penalty states raced to rewrite laws.[41]

In December 1972 Florida became the first state to restore the death penalty, and by 1975 thirty-five states had new statutes in place. Some specifically enumerated offenses under which jurors could sentence defendants to death, but left it to a jury's discretion whether or not to impose death sentences. Other states imposed mandatory sentencing; if jurors convicted a defendant of a capital offense—virtually always murder, with one aggravating circumstance—they had to impose the death penalty. California's new death-penalty statutes went into effect in 1974. They followed the mandatory model.

By 1975 300 people across the country had been condemned, and polls showed support for capital punishment rising, from 54 percent in the mid-1960s to 68 percent of respondents in the mid-1970s. Abolitionist sentiment seemed to have run its course.[42]

However, continuing abolitionist challenges, specifically to mandatory death sentences, postponed executions. In 1976 the U.S. Supreme Court declared mandatory sentencing unconstitutional, but upheld the legality of capital punishment in general. A dozen states with mandatory sentencing—including California—had to rewrite their capital laws for a second time.[43]

Gary Gilmore's January 1977 firing-squad execution in Utah marked the resumption of capital punishment in the United States. Since then, more than 1,200 people have been put to death, nearly 90 percent of them in the south. All but 12 of the executed have been men.[44]

California enacted new capital statutes in 1978, but the state's first execution did not occur until April 1992. Robert Alton Harris spent fourteen years on San Quentin's death row following his conviction for murdering two teenage boys in San Diego. Harris had planned a robbery and arranged for a getaway car when he spied the boys at the drive-through window of a fast-food restaurant. Wielding a gun, Harris forced the boys to drive him to an isolated area, where he ordered them from the car and shot both in the back. Then he ate their hamburgers.[45]

As California officials readied the gas chamber for the first time in a quarter century, journalists around the state applied for credentials to cover the event. Two reporters who had covered earlier executions felt compelled to share their experiences—to tell what it had been like to watch the machinery of death up close. Independently, each man chose Barbara Graham's as the execution that had most affected him.

Gale Cook was in his sixties, retired from the San Francisco *Examiner* and working as a freelance writer. He described Graham as "fine-featured in a fragile, almost ethereal way . . . . In death she was to become a figure of tragedy and controversy." Cook had tried to remain detached during the execution, he said. As he began to write the story, however: "I realized that I was emotionally involved. And so I became undetached . . . . 'Barbara Graham was tortured to death by the sovereign state of California yesterday,' I wrote. That sentence lasted only through the first edition of the paper. Then a properly detached editor changed 'tortured to death' to 'put to death.'"[46]

Al Martinez had been a young reporter working for a small Bay Area newspaper when he covered Graham's execution. In 1992 he was a columnist for the *Los Angeles Times*. "The people have been crying for blood, almost as much as they cheered for their favorite movie to win an Oscar," he wrote in an early March 1992 column:

> The people are never at their best demanding blood. I don't like murder. I've seen too damn much of it in three decades as a reporter. But I don't like legal executions either. I've seen them too.
>
> I stood close to the window of the gas chamber and watched Barbara Graham die. She gasped and strangled and strained against the straps that bound her. Saliva sprayed the air like a fine mist. Foam bubbled at her mouth.
>
> I lack the capacity to distance myself from death. I can't cheer with the people. No more blood.

Seventeen years later Martinez said that Graham's execution "has haunted me all of my life."[47]

10

The Ultimate Penalty

CYNTHIA COFFMAN WAS living in Barstow, California, when she met James Marlow. It was May 1986, and her boyfriend was doing time for drug possession. Marlow, just released from the same jail, stopped by Coffman's apartment to inform her that the boyfriend had been moved to another facility. Within days, Coffman left Barstow with Marlow, "a Kentucky outlaw and speed addict who sported tattoos all over his body." The pair embarked on a cross-country trek that came to involve methamphetamines, robbery, and the murder of a drug dealer.

By fall, the pair had "drifted back to Southern California." Shortly after their return, young women started to disappear: two in Orange County, one in San Bernardino County, and one in the Mojave Desert town of Bullhead City, Arizona. Police arrested Coffman and Marlow after discovering one victim's checkbook in a bag that also contained the couple's personal papers, and the car of another missing woman near the couple's hideout.

The defendants stood trial in both San Bernardino and Orange Counties. Coffman provided grisly details of the slayings, which included robbery, rape, sodomy, and strangulation. She admitted to helping strangle one victim with a towel, but insisted that she had had no choice: Marlow beat and terrified her into helping him. Marlow claimed one of the murders had been Coffman's idea. San Bernardino prosecutor Raymond Haight characterized the duo as "two flaky sociopaths separately. But you put them together and it was like Bonnie and Clyde all the way."

Marlow earned death sentences in both trials. Coffman earned one sentence of life in prison and, in 1989, a death sentence, making her the first condemned woman in California in the so-called modern era. The state supreme court has upheld death sentences for both Marlow and Coffman, but neither has been executed. Marlow is in his early fifties; Coffman is nearing fifty.[1]

The experiences of Coffman and Marlow reflect California's changed environment with regard to capital punishment since Barbara Graham's time. Before court challenges slowed and then stopped executions in the 1960s and early 1970s, politicians touted the death penalty and then followed through by executing many, if not most, of the condemned inmates. Today's prosecutors still seek death sentences and jurors oblige them, but very few people are actually executed. Thirteen men—fewer than 2 percent of those condemned—have been executed since California resumed executions in 1992.

California currently has the largest death-row population in the country. San Quentin houses more than seven hundred condemned men on three separate death rows. As Coffman's case illustrates, women also receive death sentences in California. As of February 2012, twenty condemned female inmates resided at the Central California Women's Facility in the town of Chowchilla, but no woman has been executed in California since Elizabeth Duncan went to the gas chamber in 1962.

And no woman is likely to be executed anytime soon. Condemned females rank far down the list of inmates awaiting the ultimate penalty. The timing of their trials and death sentences offers some explanation for their status. The average time from condemnation to execution in California currently stands at about two decades. Only two condemned women, including Cynthia Coffman, have spent that much time on death row. The most recent female death sentence came in 2011. Some executed men spent much less than twenty years on death row. Three spent between fourteen and seventeen years there and one spent less than a decade.[2]

The political and legal establishment in California may be reluctant to execute men, but it has utterly lost its nerve when it comes to the prospect of executing women. No matter that many among the current crop of female death-row inmates committed crimes far worse than the one that earned Barbara Graham a one-way ticket to the gas chamber.

Three condemned women, including Coffman, committed sexual assaults and murders in concert with men. Janeen Snyder helped her partner kidnap, rape, and murder several female victims. Michelle Michaud helped her boyfriend kidnap, torture, and murder female victims inside a van specially equipped for the purpose. She committed some assaults herself and stood by as her partner raped her daughter. Michaud's partner also earned a death sentence.

Five killed their children. Susan Eubanks was divorced, broke, and unemployed when she shot her four sons to death. Sandi Nieves was involved in a custody dispute with her ex-husband when she asphyxiated her four daughters and then set the house on fire to cover her tracks. Dora Buenrosto stabbed her three children to death after a fight with her husband and then tried to frame him for the murders. Cora Socorro was the estranged wife of a doctor when she shot all four of her children as they lay sleeping in their beds. Three died, but a fourth survived. Manling Williams smothered her two sons.[3]

Five condemned women, including Williams, murdered other family members. In addition to her sons, Williams stabbed her husband to death with a ceremonial sword. Veronica Gonzalez starved and abused her four-year-old niece before scalding her to death in a bathtub. Gonzalez's husband also was sentenced to death for the crime. Mary Ellen Samuels hired a drug dealer to kill her estranged husband for his five-hundred-thousand-dollar estate. Then she hired two other people to murder the hit man.

Angelina Rodriguez poisoned her husband with oleander soup and Gatorade laced with massive quantities of antifreeze. An ex-husband suggested that Rodriguez earlier had killed their thirteen-month-old daughter by stuffing part of a pacifier down her throat in order to win a settlement from the manufacturer. Cathy Sarinana and her husband, Raul, brutally beat their nephew to death.[4]

Three women murdered acquaintances. Kerry Dalton tracked down a woman she believed had stolen her jewelry and tortured her victim to death with electrical wires, a cast-iron skillet, and injections of battery acid. Rosie Alfaro was high on drugs when she stabbed to death the nine-year-old daughter of friends. The girl, who sustained nearly sixty stab wounds, surprised Alfaro in the midst of a burglary. Maureen McDermott wanted to take sole possession of a home she owned with a friend, so she hired three men to murder the co-owner, who was stabbed forty-four times. According to the perpetrators, McDermott had ordered them to cut off the man's penis after he died to make the crime look like a homosexual slaying.[5]

Three women killed strangers. Celeste Carrington worked as a janitor, cleaning businesses in the San Francisco Bay area after hours. On several occasions, occupants surprised her in the process of burglarizing their offices. Carrington murdered two of them by forcing them to kneel. As they pleaded for their lives, she shot them in the back of their heads at close range. Brooke Rottiers was a prostitute who murdered two men she had lured to her hotel room on the pretext of having sex. Tanya Nelson robbed and murdered a fortune-teller and her daughter.[6]

Only one condemned woman committed a crime redolent of the kinds of murders that earned both men and women death sentences before the 1970s. She is African American, as is Celeste Carrington. Catherine Thompson hired a man to kill her husband for a four-hundred-thousand-dollar insurance payout.[7]

Some condemned men in California also languish for decades on death row, despite committing brutal murders. They include James Marlow and Richard Ramirez, the so-called Night Stalker, who was convicted of murdering fourteen people in Southern and Northern California during the 1980s. But some of these men have been executed. They include "Freeway Killer" William Bonin, who sexually assaulted and murdered more than a dozen teenage boys in the late 1970s and early 1980s; Kevin Cooper, who butchered a family in 1983; and David Mason, who robbed and beat four elderly victims to death, and also murdered a prison cellmate and a male lover.

Men can be executed in California without definitive proof that they perpetrated the crime in question. Thomas Thompson, a military veteran with no criminal record, was executed in 1998 for rape and murder. Rape provided the special circumstance enabling jurors to sentence him to death at his 1981 trial. The victim was an acquaintance of Thompson and the former lover of Thompson's friend. The friend blamed Thompson, and a jailhouse informant testified that Thompson had admitted the crime. Thompson vehemently denied the charges, but he admitted lying to police when they asked where he had been at the time of the killing.

In his appeal Thompson cited attorney incompetence and the false testimony of the jailhouse informant. It took seventeen years for his case to wind its way through the state and federal court systems. At one point, a federal appeals court overturned the rape conviction, thus invalidating Thompson's death sentence, but state and federal courts later reinstated it, making him again eligible for execution.[8] In July 1998 Thompson died in the gas chamber, still proclaiming his innocence.

Jurists may have been certain of his guilt, but not everyone shared their confidence. The *San Francisco Chronicle* later noted that "troubling questions remain about his crimes and the adequacy of his defense." Donald Heller, the author of California's current death-penalty law, cites Thompson's case as one reason why he now opposes capital punishment.[9]

California's differential treatment of men and women can best be seen, perhaps, in women who committed crimes equal in brutality or premeditation to those of condemned men and yet managed to evade death sentences. Dorothea Puente represents one example. Puente operated a boarding house for elderly pensioners in Sacramento. In late 1988, police responded to neighborhood complaints of strange nocturnal activities and bad smells.

A subsequent investigation unearthed seven bodies buried in the backyard. Puente poisoned her tenants, buried them and collected their pension checks as if they were still alive. Sensational pretrial publicity led prosecutors to seek a change of venue. Jurors in Monterey County deadlocked on whether to sentence Puente to death or to life in prison, before finally agreeing on a life sentence. Her age may have played a role in the dispensation of her case; she was in her sixties. As Puente's case illustrates, even serial killers can get a break if they are women.[10]

Female defendants nationally also experience differential treatment, both with regard to numbers of death sentences and of executions. Death rows across the country hold nearly 3,500 condemned inmates. Fewer than 60 are women. Twenty-six states have condemned women since the return of capital punishment in the late 1970s. Five states—Texas, California, Florida, North Carolina, and Ohio—account for nearly half the death sentences. More than 1,200 men have been executed nationally since 1977. As of March 2012, twelve women in eight states had met that fate.[11]

California's current contingent of condemned women clearly

committed more brutal crimes than their counterparts in the pre-Furman generations. The same can be said for some, though not all, of the women executed in other states since the resumption of capital punishment. A few of the modern executions involved high-profile women condemned for brutal crimes; Karla Faye Tucker was one of them. Tucker was high on drugs in 1983 when she helped to murder two people—one whom she stabbed to death with a pickaxe. Texas executed her in 1998. Her case gained widespread public attention after she became a born-again Christian in prison and ministered to other inmates. Aileen Wuornos, executed by Florida in 2002, seemingly had no redeeming qualities. She shot and killed six men at truck stops, though she claimed the first man had tried to rape her.[12]

But some modern executions featured women whose crimes seem only slightly more diabolical than those of their pre-Furman counterparts. For example, Anna Marie Hahn, executed by Ohio in 1938, had killed at least as many men as Wuornos shot, though poison was her method of choice. Poison also had been the method of Frances Creighton, executed by New York in 1938 for murdering her husband's lover. Judy Buenoano, executed by Florida in 1998 for killing her husband and son, also used poison, as did Velma Barfield of North Carolina, who poisoned several members of her family and blamed her actions on a longstanding Valium addiction.

Similarities can also be seen in the cases of Betty Lou Beets and Louise Peete. Texas executed Beets in 2000 for shooting two husbands to death, burying their bodies on her property, then collecting their insurance. Louise Peete, executed by California in 1947, also shot two people to death, buried their bodies, and spent their money.

Both Beets and Peete were in their sixties at the time of their executions and their crimes bore comparably colorful aspects. Peete buried her landlord in the basement after his 1920 murder, and then claimed he had fled with a "Spanish woman." Beets shot her husband, Jimmy Don, then buried him, placed his heart medicine in his fishing boat, and pushed it onto a lake to make it look like Jimmy Don had suffered a heart attack and fallen overboard.[13]

What accounts for the differences between California and other death-penalty states? Geography may provide one clue. All the executions of women in the modern era have occurred in the south, a region that executes more condemned inmates than any other. Oklahoma has executed three women; Florida and Texas have each executed two. North Carolina became the first state in the modern period to execute a woman when it electrocuted Velma Barfield in 1984.

Oklahoma executed two women—Marilyn Plantz and Lois Nadean Smith—in the same year, 2001. Plantz recruited her lover to murder her husband, who was shot to death soon after he returned home from his job as a newspaper pressman. The killers then drove his body to a deserted location and set it on fire.[14] Smith said she believed her son's former girlfriend planned to kill him, so she drove to a motel, confronted the victim, and then shot her nine times.[15]

Alabama executed Lynda Lyon Block and her common-law husband, George Sibley, in 2002, for killing a police officer. Block and Sibley were members of the Patriot Movement, an armed militia group that refuses to recognize any government authority. The duo fled Florida for Alabama after stabbing Block's ex-husband. They were stopped at a shopping center when an officer approached their car. Sibley claimed he thought the officer was going for his gun, so he pulled out his own. So did Block. At trial, both defendants argued that Alabama had no authority to try them since they did not recognize the state as a valid entity. Sibley was eventually put to death as well.[16]

Arkansas executed Christina Riggs in May 2000 for the poisoning deaths of her children. Riggs's case, though, had what seem to be extenuating circumstances. In 1995 she had worked in Oklahoma City and had helped remove bodies from the Alfred P. Murrah Federal Building debris after the 1995 blast. She relocated to Arkansas, but continued to suffer from post-traumatic stress disorder. In 1997 she poisoned her son and daughter and then tried unsuccessfully to kill herself.[17]

Some southern states seem to have actually loosened criteria for condemning and executing white women. Virginia executed Teresa Lewis in September 2010. Eight years earlier, Lewis had hired two men to murder her husband and her stepson in order to collect on an insurance policy. As part of the killers' payment, she offered both herself and her teenaged daughter as sexual partners. But Lewis was mentally handicapped, with an IQ of less than seventy-five.

Women of color are still executed by southern states under questionable circumstances with little outcry or media attention. Texas executed Frances Newton in 2005 for the murders of her husband and two children. Prosecutors claimed that Newton had killed her family for one hundred thousand dollars in insurance, but she maintained that drug dealers were the actual murderers. Newton's trial attorney never interviewed a single witness and was later disbarred.[18]

While Southern states do execute women, California still condemns them, thereby maintaining the largest female death row of any state in the country. What accounts for its reluctance to take the final step? It would be naive to give Barbara Graham either credit or blame for this circumstance, since so few people alive today have any memory of her trial and execution. Nonetheless, Graham's case retains its power as a cautionary tale.

When prosecutors decided in the summer of 1953 to seek the death penalty for Graham, they could never have imagined the consequences. They had carefully constructed a narrative that posited her as a woman devoid of morals or traditional values of any kind and they made certain that her trial followed this script. Her death sentence elicited no immediate controversy. How could such men have foreseen the possibility that respected members of the mainstream media—formerly staunch allies—would turn on them and hold them up to public ridicule, while suggesting that the object of their contempt might have been a victim, rather than the perpetrator of a vicious crime?

If such an unthinkable turn of events could happen in the tough-on-crime 1950s, when abolitionists had no means of proving the innocence of condemned individuals, surely it could happen sixty years later, with anti-death-penalty forces steeped in the notion of DNA and wrongful executions. As of October 2011 the Death Penalty Information Center listed 138 people exonerated and released from death rows across the country and 8 people executed despite "strong evidence of innocence."

Virtually all of the exonerated have been men—many of them African American—who drew much less media attention than women. But attention is being paid. Crime novelist and lawyer John Grisham featured the story of Ron Williamson, a former high school baseball star from Ada, Oklahoma, in his book *The Innocent Man*. Williamson was wrongly condemned in 1987 for rape and murder and ultimately exonerated by DNA. In an interview, Grisham admitted that he "had never spent much spent much time worrying about wrongful convictions. But, unfortunately, they happen all the time in this country, and with increasing frequency."[19]

In 2009 *New Yorker* writer David Grann detailed the case of Cameron Todd Willingham, executed for the 1991 arson deaths of his three small daughters. Toward the end of his thirteen-year appeals, arson investigators, using sophisticated technology, concluded that the fire probably had been accidental. Nonetheless, Texas governor Rick Perry refused to stop the execution.[20]

David Dow, a Texas law professor and death row lawyer, related the story of just one of dozens of possibly wrongly executed inmates in *The Autobiography of an Execution*. Dow detailed exhaustive efforts to win reprieves for clients represented by incompetent attorneys and victimized by a corrupt system in which prosecutors and police conspire with jailhouse snitches, and judges are "unprincipled and hostile to the rule of law."[21]

In 2012, Ray Bonner detailed South Carolina's specious 1982 murder case against Edward Elmore, an African American man railroaded into a death sentence by a judiciary that rushed to judgment and spent no time trying to find the actual killer of the well-to-do white woman found dead in her bed in the town of Greenwood.

One woman can be listed among the nearly executed. Florida condemned Sonia Jacobs in 1976. Jacobs, along with her common-law husband, Jesse Tafaro, and another man, Walter Rhodes, had parked their car alongside a Florida highway and fallen asleep. Police arrived to roust them. As the officers approached the vehicle, someone in the car drew a gun, shooting and killing both officers.

Although ballistics tests showed that Rhodes probably fired the fatal shots, prosecutors reduced his sentence in exchange for testimony against Tafaro and Jacobs. No physical evidence linked Jacobs to the killings, yet she was sentenced to die anyway, along with Tafaro. She was not executed, but instead served sixteen years in prison before her release in 1992. Tafaro was not so fortunate; he was executed in 1990.[22] Jacobs's ethnicity—she was white—may have been a key factor in sparing her life.

Currently, death-penalty opponents seem to again be making inroads in a number of states. Connecticut abolished capital punishment in April 2012, and in California an initiative to replace the death penalty with life in prison lost by a close vote on the November 2012 ballot. The latest efforts mostly emphasize the prohibitive cost of execution. But, should another defendant like Barbara Graham emerge, who can say whether it might shift the focus back to individual cases of equity and fairness, and whether this abolition strategy might again succeed?[23]

If all of the attention paid to one executed woman has any lesson to impart, it may be this: Narrative has the ability to shape public perception, and the possibility of executing a single innocent person is a risk not worth taking, for reasons both moral and political. Americans may happily declare themselves eager proponents of capital punishment, but they also believe in redemption. And they are suckers for good stories.

Notes

INTRODUCTION

1. Both Bernice Freeman Davis, in *The Desperate and the Damned*, and Byron Eschelman, in *Death Row Chaplain*, proclaimed Graham's innocence and protested her execution. Eschelman became so disillusioned that he left his job. Both, however, were avid opponents of capital punishment in general.

2. Fred J. Cook, "Capital Punishment: Does It Prevent Crime?" *Nation*, March 10, 1956, 191. The magazine also mentioned Caryl Chessman's case in connection with the movement to end capital punishment. It also got Graham's first name wrong, calling her Diane.

3. Dennis Bingham, "'I Do Want to Live!' Female Voices, Male Discourse, and Hollywood Biopics," *Cinema Journal* 38, no. 3 (Spring 1999): 4.

4. Shipman, *The Penalty Is Death*, 194.

5. Rapaport, "The Death Penalty," 377.

6. Bingham, "'I Do Want to Live!'" 7.

1. A MURDER IN BURBANK

1. "Quiz of Gambler Fails to Shed Light on Killing," *Los Angeles Times*, March 15, 1953.

2. Walker, *The Case of Barbara Graham*, 11.

3. Walker, *The Case of Barbara Graham*, 11; "Shoe and Hand Prints Burbank Murder Clues," *Los Angeles Times*, March 13, 1953. Monahan's given name was usually spelled Mabel in newspaper reports and trial coverage. However, other sources spelled her first name as Mable. Since it appears as Mable on

her gravestone, I am using that spelling. Newspapers and other sources cited various ages for Monahan, ranging from sixty-two to sixty-five. Her gravestone gives a birth year of 1888, and other sources cite her birthday as January 2. Therefore, she was sixty-five at the time of her death.

4. Barbara Graham trial transcripts, San Quentin Execution File, F3918, 410.

5. Barbara Graham trial transcripts, San Quentin Execution File, F3918, 16–17.

6. "Shoe and Hand Prints" *Los Angeles Times*, March 13, 1953.

7. "Quiz of Gambler," *Los Angeles Times*, March 15, 1953.

8. Buntin, *L.A. Noir*, 3.

9. Walker, *The Case of Barbara Graham*, 14–16.

10. Walker, *The Case of Barbara Graham*, 16–30. Walker's is the only account of Shorter's confession and description of the crime. He undoubtedly used the police report, since prosecutors in the case later recruited Walker to write a book from their viewpoint and gave him access to all of the records relating to Monahan's murder.

11. Buntin, *L.A. Noir*, 10.

12. "Defense to Open at Monahan Trial," *Los Angeles Times*, August 30, 1953.

13. Walker, *The Case of Barbara Graham*, 33–37; Stanford, *Lady of the House*, 105–9. Monroe and Sitler were convicted of attempted murder and sent to Folsom Prison. Graham later apologized to Stanford.

14. "Defense to Open," *Los Angeles Times*, August 30, 1953.

15. "Slaying Figure Victim of 'Last Ride' Kidnapping," *Los Angeles Times*, April 15, 1953.

16. "Slaying Figure Victim," *Los Angeles Times*, April 15, 1953.

17. "Murder Suspect Freed in Burbank," *Los Angeles Times*, April 17, 1953.

18. "Trap Nets Three Suspects in Slaying at Burbank," *Los Angeles Times*, May 5, 1953; "Girl, Two Men Seized as Murder Case Kidnap Suspects," *Los Angeles Examiner*, May 5, 1953.

19. "Trap Nets Three Suspects," *Los Angeles Times*, May 5, 1953.

20. "Girl, Two Men Seized," *Los Angeles Times*, May 5, 1953.

21. "Wife Picks Out Suspect as Kidnapper," *Los Angeles Times*, May 6, 1953.

22. "Shorter Case Suspects Will Be Arraigned," *Los Angeles Times*, May 6, 1953.

23. "Man Gives Self Up for Questioning in Shorter Case; New Clues Found," *Los Angeles Times*, May 14, 1953.

24. "Savagery of Monahan Murderers Disclosed," *Los Angeles Times*, June 16, 1953.

25. Stuart Palmer, "Barbara Graham in Her Own Words," *American Weekly*, April 4, 1954, 11–12.

26. Parrish, *For the People*, 46–49.

27. "Savagery of Monahan Murders," *Los Angeles Times*, June 16, 1953.

28. "Prosecutor Flies North in Monahan Inquiry," *Los Angeles Times*, June 5, 1953.

29. "Three Men, Woman Indicted in Burbank Widow's Slaying," *Los Angeles Times*, June 4, 1953.

30. Tom Cameron, "A Lawyer's Job as a Defender," *Los Angeles Times*, May 20, 1956.

31. O'Brien, *Hardboiled America*, 107.

2. A LIFE ON THE LAM

1. List of prior offenses, San Quentin Execution File, F3918, 409–10.

2. Stanford, *Lady of the House*, 105–9.

3. "For Wayward Girls," *Los Angeles Times*, March 13, 1914.

4. California Youth Authority, Ventura School, Admission Record for Hortense Ford, September, 4, 1925, F3738, 544, California State Archives.

5. Social history, San Quentin Execution File, F3918, 409.

6. Letter from Saint Mary's of the Palms, San Jose CA, social history, San Quentin Execution File. Graham also discussed her early life with Stuart Palmer in *American Weekly*, the Sunday supplement magazine for William Randolph Hearst's chain of newspapers, on April 4, 1954, 11–12, 22–23.

7. Graham, *American Weekly*, April 4, 1954, 11–12.

8. "Monahan Case Femme Fatale, Story of a Girl Who May Die for Killing," *San Francisco Chronicle*, September 20, 1953.

9. Gordon, *Dorothea Lange*, 108–9. Gordon discussed "placing out" children in a larger context, but also in connection with Lange and her husband, who placed out their own children.

10. Bess Wilson, "Rehabilitation of Girls Who Come Into Hands of Law Called Chief Aim of School" *Los Angeles Times*, February 25, 1939.

11. Admissions data from the Ventura School for Girls, San Quentin Execution File, F3918, 409.

12. Admissions data, July 24, 1937, San Quentin Execution File; "Must Eliminate Some Methods," *Los Angeles Times*, February 15, 1919.

13. Hortense Wood to Ventura authorities, n.d., San Quentin Execution File.

14. I have not been able to ascertain why Barbara's mother became a ward of the juvenile court at nineteen and why Barbara would have been eligible for release from supervision at the age of eighteen.

15. Ventura School for Girls parole report on Barbara Wood, July 1, 1939, to January 1, 1941, San Quentin Execution File, F3918, 409.

16. Ventura official M.G.M. to colleague L.S., July 1, 1939, San Quentin Execution File, F3918, 409.

17. "Death of a Seagull," *Time*, June 13, 1955, 26–27.

18. Notations from Ventura officials regarding Graham's whereabouts, July 1, 1939, to September 1, 1939, San Quentin Execution File.

19. San Quentin Execution File, October 1, 1939 to January 1, 1941.

20. Stuart Palmer, "Barbara Graham in Her Own Words," *American Weekly*, April 4, 1954, 11–12.

21. Eschelman, *Death Row Chaplain*, 173–79.

22. Eschelman, *Death Row Chaplain*, 173–79; Social history of Barbara Graham, list of prior offenses, San Quentin Execution File, F3918, 409. In a 1954 magazine story about her, Barbara said her second son's name was Darryl, but California birth records carry the name Michael. His family may have referred to him as Darryl, which might have been his middle name. By the time Graham awaited execution, his name apparently had been changed and he lived with friends in California. Graham's oldest son, William, remained in Washington.

23. Social history, Marital history, San Quentin Execution File.

24. Social history, San Quentin Execution File; John Kavanaugh of the San Francisco Adult Probation Department to Alma Holzschuh, superintendent of the California Institution for Women, November 16, 1953, San Quentin Execution File, F3918, 409.

25. Stanford, *Lady of the House*, 109.

26. Kavanaugh to Holzschuh, November 16, 1953.

27. Social history, San Quentin Execution File. Graham claimed to be confused about dates—"never very good" at them, was how she phrased it to lawyers and prison officials in 1953. She guessed she had married Newman in 1947 but said she had been in jail in San Francisco before the marriage. She left jail in early 1949, so her marriage could not have come before that time; Graham, *American Weekly*, April 4, 1954.

28. Social history, San Quentin Execution File; Graham, *American Weekly*, April 4, 1954, 11–12.

29. Discussion of Graham's children, San Quentin Execution File; Kavanaugh to Holzschuh, November 16, 1953.

30. Tom Caton, "Blonde Pleads With Eyes for Mate's Aid on Monahan Alibi," *Los Angeles Evening Herald and Express*, September 3, 1953.

31. Trial testimony of Barbara Graham, San Quentin Execution File, 2635.

32. Transcript on appeal, San Quentin Execution File, F3918, 410, 2620. Graham continually denied being a drug user, but evidence—including her 1951 arrest—points to the fact that she was. Graham also described her relationship with Henry Graham in *American Weekly*, April 11, 1954.

33. Walker, *Case of Barbara Graham*, 58.

34. Transcript on appeal, San Quentin Execution File, 886–93.

35. San Quentin Execution File, 2620–30.

3. A FEMME FATALE ON TRIAL

1. St. Joan and McElhiney, *Beyond Portia*, 22.

2. Among the many books that focus on how the attitudes, words, and behavior of female defendants have impacted their chances for acquittal or conviction are Carlson, *The Crimes of Womanhood*; Bakken and Farrington, *Women Who Kill Men*; Birch, *Moving Targets*; Gillespie, *Dancehall Ladies;* Victor Streib, *The Fairer Death*; and Neal, *Sex, Murder, and the Unwritten Law*. Marlin Shipman's *The Penalty is Death* focuses on how journalists cover women in capital cases from their trials to their executions. Some scholars also have argued that men and women killers differ with regard to victims and styles of murder. Men tend to kill strangers by shooting or stabbing them during the commission of other crimes or in an explosive rage. Women mostly kill family members after nurturing grudges or experiencing abuse. Though they also shoot or stab their victims, poisoning seems to be a particularly "feminine" method of murder. Condemned and executed women, however, are more likely to have committed predatory killings—in the style of men.

3. Bakken and Farrington, *Women Who Kill Men*, 152–59.

4. Among hard-boiled novels set in Southern California were *The Big Sleep*, *Lady in the Lake*, and *The Long Goodbye*, all by Raymond Chandler; and *The Postman Always Rings Twice* and *Double Indemnity* by James M. Cain. All of

them featured femme fatales who almost always were responsible for killings at the center of the novels' plots.

5. Courdileone, *Manhood and American Political Culture* discusses the masculine narrative that shaped post–World War II discourse. Dennis Bingham, "'I Do Want to Live!' Female Voices, Male Discourse, and Hollywood Biopics," *Cinema Journal* 38, no. 3 (Spring 1999): 3–26, examines how the film reflects cultural attitudes toward women.

6. Buntin, *L.A. Noir*, 191. The book presents the dual history of crime and the police force in Los Angeles through the careers of mob boss Mickey Cohen and police chief William Parker. James Ellroy's *L.A. Confidential* depicts police brutality and corruption in the early 1950s. Though it is fiction, it includes some real events, including the department's horrific treatment of ethnic minorities.

7. Among Judge Fricke's trials was that of Nellie May Madison, convicted in 1934 of murdering her husband. In addition to presiding in Madison's case, he took the stand to testify for prosecutors on a procedural matter. Fricke also presided in the 1948 trial of "Red-Light Bandit" Caryl Chessman and the 1942 Sleepy Lagoon case in which two-dozen Mexican Americans were convicted of murder despite a paucity of evidence. Their convictions were later overturned on appeal.

8. Joseph A. Spangler, "California's Death Row Dilemma," *Crime and Delinquency* 15, no. 1 (January 1969): 43–45. The entire volume of this journal was devoted to discussion of the death penalty.

9. "Death Penalty to Be Asked in Monahan Case," *Los Angeles Times*, August 14, 1953, 23; "Jury Selection Delays Monahan Case Argument," *Los Angeles Times*, August 18, 1953; Cairns, *Enigma Woman*, briefly discusses the cases of Eithel Spinelli and Louise Peete. Three other women received death sentences: Laura Fair in 1871, Emma Le Doux in 1906, and Nellie Madison in 1934. Fair was acquitted of murdering her lover at a second trial. Le Doux's death sentence for killing her husband was overturned because of court incompetence and Madison was reprieved with sixteen days to go until her execution. She had killed her abusive husband.

10. "Redhead Accused in Monahan Case," *Los Angeles Times*, August 19, 1953.

11. "Mrs. Graham Hurt; Death Case Delayed," *Los Angeles Times*, August 20, 1953.

12. "Witness Describes Monahan Slaying," *Los Angeles Times*, August 26, 1953.

13. Donna Prow was convicted of driving an automobile that struck another vehicle, killing the passenger in the other car.

14. "Monahan Case Alibi Plot Told," *Los Angeles Times*, August 28, 1953; "Monahan Case Figure Freed," *Los Angeles Times*, August 29, 1953.

15. Walker, *Case of Barbara Graham*, 116.

16. "Murder Case Alibi Recording Played," *Los Angeles Times*, September 1, 1953.

17. Gene Coughlin, "Graham Girl on Stand Has Unhappiest Day of Her Life, *Los Angeles Examiner*, September 1, 1953.

18. California Department of Corrections, appellate transcript of *People of the State of California vs. Emmett R. Perkins, John A. Santo, and Barbara Graham*, San Quentin Execution File, F3918, 410, 883–86.

19. San Quentin Execution File, F3918, 902.

20. San Quentin Execution File, F3918, 898–908.

21. "Blonde Answers Grilling in Low-Pitched Voice," *Los Angeles Examiner*, September 2, 1953; "Barbara Breaks in Monahan Death Case," *Los Angeles Examiner*, September 2, 1953; "Graham Girl on Stand Has Unhappiest Day of Her Life," *Los Angeles Examiner*, September 1, 1953.

22. "Barbara Graham Notes Tell of Sordid Jail Love," *Los Angeles Examiner*, September 3, 1953.

23. Transcript on appeal, San Quentin Execution File, 2693–705.

24. Barbara Graham Flares Up at Trial," *Los Angeles Times*, September 3, 1953.

25. Coughlin, "Graham Girl on Stand," September 1, 1953."

26. Transcript on appeal, San Quentin Execution File, 2474–75.

27. Tom Caton, "Blonde Pleads With Eyes for Mates Aid On Monahan Alibi," *Los Angeles Examiner*, September 3, 19531; "Mrs. Graham's Alibi Blasted by Mate," *Los Angeles Times*, September 4, 1953.

28. "Monahan Murder Witness Arrested," *Los Angeles Times*, September 5, 1953; "Graham Story Switched in Monahan Case," *Los Angeles Times*, September 9, 1953. Bernice Freeman discussed other Santo and Perkins murders in her book *The Desperate and the Damned*.

29. Transcript on appeal, San Quentin Execution File, 2426–30.

30. San Quentin Execution File, 2431–40.

31. "Death Asked for Monahan Case Trio," *Los Angeles Times*, September 16, 1953.

32. Transcript on appeal, San Quentin Execution File, 2605–6.

33. San Quentin Execution File, 2606, 2618, 2694.

34. "Prefers Death to Life Term, Says Barbara," *Los Angeles Times*, September 23, 1953.

35. "Death Decreed for Three In Monahan Slaying," *Los Angeles Times*, September 23, 1953.

4. CRIME DOESN'T PAY

1. Stuart Palmer to Richard McGee, November 16, 1953, San Quentin Execution File for Barbara Graham, F3918, 409–10; "Prefers Death to Life Term, Says Barbara," *Los Angeles Times*, September 23, 1953.

2. Palmer to McGee, December 4, 1953, San Quentin Execution File. William Randolph Hearst had been dead for two years by 1953, but his company owned two newspapers in Los Angeles, where Graham was tried, as well as papers in San Francisco, Chicago, Boston, Atlanta, and New York.

3. "Press Besieges Barbara Graham," *Los Angeles Times*, September 25, 1953.

4. "Press Besieges Barbara Graham," *Los Angeles Times*, September 25, 1953.

5. "Mrs. Graham Off for Corona; Guilt Denied," *Los Angeles Times*, October 15, 1953.

6. Social history of Barbara Graham, San Quentin Execution File, F3918, 409; John D. Kavanaugh to Alma Holzschuh, superintendent of the California Institution for Women, Corona, November 16, 1953, social history of Barbara Graham, San Quentin Execution File, F3918, 409.

7. Dilys Jones, "Barbara Graham Hopes to Escape Execution," *Examiner* (San Francisco), November 28, 1953.

8. "Mrs. Graham Off for Corona; Guilt Denied," *Los Angeles Times*, October 15, 1953; Jones, "Barbara Graham Hopes," *Examiner*, November 28, 1953.

9. The average time on death row for condemned men and women between 1943 and 1958 in California was 573 days, or approximately nineteen months. "Post-Conviction Remedies in California Death Penalty Cases," *Stanford Law Review* 11, no. 1 (December 1958): 94–135. The number included Caryl Chessman, however, who skewed the average upward.

10. George Draper, "Santo, Perkins Moved to Quentin Row," *Examiner* (San Francisco), October 13, 1953.

11. George Draper, "Santo's Mistress Says She Drove Getaway Car in Holdup Slaying," *Examiner* (San Francisco), December 4, 1953.

12. Jones, "Barbara Graham Hopes," *Examiner*, November 28, 1953.

13. Barbara Graham to California governor Goodwin Knight, February 16, 1954, San Quentin Execution File.

14. Eschelman, *Death Row Chaplain*, 176.

15. Jones, "Barbara Graham Hopes," *Examiner*, November 28, 1953.

16. Carolyn Anspacher, "Barbara Graham Secretly Taken to San Quentin for Her Safety," *San Francisco Chronicle*, November 26, 1953.

17. Davis, *The Desperate and the Damned*, 7–9.

18. Davis, *The Desperate and the Damned*, 81–83.

19. Davis, *The Desperate and the Damned*, 81–102.

20. Stuart Palmer to California corrections director Richard McGee, March 19, 1954, San Quentin Execution File.

21. "Roll Refuses Lie Test for Barbara Graham," *Los Angeles Times*, March 16, 1954.

22. Mickey Spillane's villains were almost always beautiful, seductive women, and he often killed them at the end, after they had tried diligently—but failed—to seduce him. Then he engaged in long, meandering discussions that justified their killings.

23. Palmer, "Barbara Graham in Her Own Words," 11–12.

24. Palmer, "Barbara Graham in Her Own Words," 11–12.

25. Palmer, "Barbara Graham in Her Own Words," 11–13.

26. Palmer, "Barbara Graham in Her Own Words," 11–13.

27. Palmer, "Barbara Graham in Her Own Words," 11–13.

28. Richard McGee to Alma Holzschuh, July 12, 1954, San Quentin Execution File.

5. AN EXECUTION IN CALIFORNIA

1. Edward S. Montgomery, first draft of screenplay for *I Want to Live!* April 9, 1957, folder 3, Walter Wanger Collection. The film originally was to be titled "The Barbara Graham Story."

2. Farrell, *Shallow Grave*, 86. Farrell's description of Montgomery is contained in his book recounting the 1955 kidnapping and murder of teenager Stephanie Bryan. Montgomery discovered the body near a remote cabin owned by the family of Burton Abbott, who was later executed for the killing.

3. Edward S. Montgomery, "Extortion Quiz in Income Tax Case Revealed," *Examiner* (San Francisco), August, 29, 1950. Information on Montgomery's salary comes from a letter he sent on March 19, 1957 to Hal Friedman, a lawyer

negotiating pay for Montgomery to write the initial outline for *I Want to Live!* folder 3, Walter Wanger Collection.

4. Obituary for Edward S. Montgomery, *San Francisco Chronicle*, April 8, 1992.

5. Edward S. Montgomery to Hal Friedman, March 19, 1957, folder 3, Walter Wanger Collection.

6. Rawson, *I Want to Live!* 117. Rawson was the pseudonym of Hollywood producer Irving Schulman, though the book was actually ghostwritten by Edward S. Montgomery. Both the film and book detailed his transformation from a reporter who believed Graham to be guilty of murder and deserving of execution to her strongest partisan in the effort to get her sentence commuted. The book was designed to coincide with the movie's opening.

7. Rawson, *I Want to Live!* 118–19.

8. Rawson, *I Want to Live!* 120.

9. Montgomery, outline of the screenplay for *I Want to Live!* April 9, 1957, folder 3, Walter Wanger Collection.

10. Rawson, *I Want to Live!* 118.

11. Rawson, *I Want to Live!* 120–21.

12. Telephone call from Edward S. Montgomery to Walter Wanger, February 5, 1958, folder 3, Walter Wanger Collection.

13. Barbara Graham to Al Matthews, February 10, 1955, folder 5, Walter Wanger Collection.

14. "Mrs. Graham Plea Denied," *Los Angeles Times*, September 9, 1954; "Justice Douglas Oks Monahan Case Trio Plea," *Los Angeles Times*, November 17, 1954; "Trio in Monahan Case File Writ in High Court," *Los Angeles Times*, January 6, 1955; "Monahan Case Trio Sentenced to Die June 3," *Los Angeles Times*, March 19, 1955.

15. Barbara Graham to Al Matthews, September 23, 1954 to March 8, 1955, folder 5, Walter Wanger Collection.

16. Information on Graham's middle son comes from her San Quentin execution file, F3918, 409, California State Archives, Sacramento. At the time of her death, he went by the name Lee Frazier and lived somewhere in California. (However, accounts differ. One had him in Redlands, another in Visalia). His new family brought him to visit his mother in December 1954, but she turned them away. Bernice Freeman discussed Graham's bleak mood in *The Desperate and the Damned*, 106.

17. Barbara Graham to Al Matthews, December 23, 1954, folder 5, Walter Wanger Collection.

18. Barbara Graham to Al Matthews, October 12, 1954, folder 5, Walter Wanger Collection.

19. "Doctor Urges Clemency for Barbara," *San Francisco Chronicle*, June 2, 1955.

20. "Doctor Urges Clemency for Barbara," *San Francisco Chronicle*, June 2, 1955.

21. Sherry Keyes to Barbara Graham, May 1955, San Quentin Execution File, F 3918, 409.

22. Barbara Graham to Al Matthews, October 15, 1954, folder 5, Walter Wanger Collection.

23. Edward S. Montgomery to Emmett Perkins, June 1, 1955, San Quentin Execution File.

24. Letter from anonymous corrections official, June 7, 1955, San Quentin Execution File.

25. "I'll Go With My Head Held High: Barbara," *Examiner* (San Francisco), May 28, 1955.

26. Note from the State of California to Alma Holzschuh, October 15, 1954, San Quentin Execution File.

27. Letter from unnamed San Quentin official regarding Henry Graham at San Quentin, June 2, 1955, San Quentin Execution File.

28. Wendy Lesser describes the gas chamber in *Pictures at an Execution*, 164–65. Until 1938 California hanged its condemned prisoners.

29. "Doctor Urges Clemency," *San Francisco Chronicle*, June 2, 1955.

30. Gene Blake, "Barbara Graham Dies in San Quentin Today," *Los Angeles Times*, June 3, 1955; Gale Cook, "Barbara, Pals in Quentin Death Cells; Still Hope for 11th Hour Stay," *Examiner* (San Francisco), June 3, 1955.

31. Blake, "Barbara Graham Dies," *Los Angeles Times*, June 3, 1955.

32. Cook, "Barbara, Pals in Quentin," *Examiner*, June 3, 1955.

33. Cook, "Barbara, Pals in Quentin," *Examiner*, June 3, 1955.

34. Cook, "Barbara, Pals in Quentin," *Examiner*, June 3, 1955.

35. Cook, "Barbara, Pals in Quentin," *Examiner*, June 3, 1955.

36. Rarick, *California Rising*, 76. Knight did plan to run in 1958 but decided instead to run for the United States Senate seat of Republican William Knowland, who in turn ran for governor. Both men lost their respective elections. Democrat Edmund G. Brown, a staunch opponent of capital punishment, defeated Knowland in the gubernatorial contest.

37. Douglas Barrett, "Governor's Office Under Goodwin Knight," interview by Sarah Sharp, 1979, Oral History Office, the Bancroft Library, University of California, Berkeley.

38. Blake, "Barbara Graham Dies," *Los Angeles Times*, June 3, 1955. Information on the offer to adopt Graham's son comes from Rawson, *I Want to Live!* 135. No other source reported this information, so its authenticity is uncertain.

39. "L.A. Police Chief Hits Evidence Ban As Crime Shield," *Examiner* (San Francisco), May 14, 1955.

40. Gene Blake, "Babs, Santo, Perkins Gassed After Delays," *Los Angeles Times*, June 4, 1955; Rawson, *I Want to Live!* 134.

41. "Timetable of Legal Moves on Executions," *Los Angeles Times*, June 4, 1955; Blake, "Babs, Santo, Perkins" *Los Angeles Times*, June 4, 1955.

42. Blake, "Babs, Santo, Perkins," *Los Angeles Times*, June 4, 1955.

43. Gale Cook, "Santo Murder Trio Executed; Delays Torture Barbara," *Examiner* (San Francisco), June 4, 1955.

44. Blake, "Babs, Santo, Perkins," *Los Angeles Times*, June 4, 1955.

45. Chester Hanson, "Confusion Reigns in Last Pleas," *Los Angeles Times*, June 4, 1955; "Shameful Bungling in California," *Los Angeles Times*, June 4, 1955; Rawson, *I Want to Live!* 12.

46. "Barbara's Family Just Wants to Be Left Alone," *Los Angeles Times*, June 4, 1955.

6. EXECUTING WOMEN IN AMERICA

1. Streib, *The Fairer Death*, 11.

2. Streib, *The Fairer Death*, 125.

3. Garland, *Peculiar Institution*, 124.

4. "Women Executed in the U.S., 1900–2002," The Death Penalty Information Center, http://www.deathpenaltyinfo.org/women-executed-us-1900. The website includes virtually all of the women executed in the United States, but it identifies one individual—Shellie McKeithen—as an "Oriental" woman. McKeithen probably was an African American man.

5. O'Shea, *Women and the Death Penalty*, 191. The book offers state-by-state information, including details of death penalty enactment and, when applicable, abolition dates for every state. It also lists all women executed, along with the circumstances of their crimes, if available.

6. Knox, *Murder*, places the Beck and Fernandez case into the larger context of sensational murder trials and executions, and she uses it to discuss themes of murder and execution in popular culture and the American imagination. Executions, she argues, enable an enthralled public to attain a kind of closure not available in most real life events.

7. Deakin, *A Grave for Bobby*, examines the Heady-Hall kidnapping of Bobby Greenlease, as does "Kidnapped," *New York Times*, October 11, 1953, p. E2.

8. Gillespie, *Dancehall Ladies*, 8; "Henry Woman Executed for 1940 Murder," *New York Times*, November 29, 1942. Norman German also wrote of Toni Jo Henry's life and execution in his book *A Savage Wisdom*. See also "Mrs. Creighton Dies for Poison Murder," *New York Times*, July 17, 1936.

9. "Mrs. Farmer Dies Praying in Chair," *New York Times*, March 29, 1909, 6.

10. O'Shea, *Women and the Death Penalty*, 312.

11. Franklin, *The Goodbye Door*; O'Shea, *Women and the Death Penalty*, 251–52.

12. "Louise Peete Dies Today in Gas Chamber; U.S. Supreme Court and Gov. Warren Spurn Final Pleas," *Los Angeles Times*, April 4, 1947.

13. O'Shea, *Women and the Death Penalty*, 54.

14. "Mrs. Coo, Scarnici Are Put to Death," *New York Times*, June 28, 1935; Gado, *Death Row Women*; O'Shea, *Women and the Death Penalty*, 252.

15. Watkins, *Chicago*.

16. William Marling, *American Roman Noir*, 149.

17. McKellar, "*Double Indemnity Murder*," traces Ruth Snyder's background, her unhappy marriage, her yen for a more exciting life, and the details of the plan to murder Albert Snyder. Judd Gray, a married man, was apparently a reluctant participant in the plot but was so smitten with Snyder that he went along.

18. In *The Postman Always Rings Twice*, female protagonist Cora Papadakis seduces drifter Frank Chambers into helping her kill her husband, Nick, for a fifty-thousand-dollar insurance policy. In *Double Indemnity*, Phyllis Nirdlinger lures her insurance agent into a scheme that entails taking out a life-insurance policy on her husband and then killing him. In both cases bad karma and the law catch up with the diabolical duos.

19. There are several books focused on the Logue-Timmerman feud and murder, as well as on Logue's relationship with Thurmond. They include Bass and Thompson, *Ol' Strom*; Flowers, *Wanton Woman*; and Dorn, *The Guns at Meeting Street*.

20. Shipman, *The Penalty is Death*, 6. The book examines how journalists construct personas for female capital defendants based on their physical appearances and clothing. He also discusses how such depictions soften as execution nears, at least for some condemned women, like Graham.

21. Knox, *Murder*, 88.

22. O'Shea, *Women and the Death Penalty*, 283.

23. Cairns, *Front-Page Women Journalists*, 73–103.

24. "Judge Charges Insult; Prosecutor Suspended From His $6000 Job," *Pittsburgh Post-Gazette*, December 3, 1944; "Second Death Trial Begun," *Pittsburgh Post-Gazette*, January 9, 1945.

25. O'Shea, *Women and the Death Penalty*, 192, 209–10.

26. Streib, *The Fairer Death*, 58.

27. Kathleen O'Shea lists Rosa Stinette's victim as her husband and maintains that insurance was the motive. It is unclear whether Stinette was white or black.

28. O'Shea, *Women and the Death Penalty*, 313.

29. O'Shea, *Women and the Death Penalty*, 253.

30. "Woman in Death House," *New York Times*, February 22, 1944.

31. Lela Phillips, *The Lena Baker Story*, discusses the circumstances of Baker's case, including the fact that her victim, Ernest Knight, had been sexually involved with Baker, information that probably angered the all-white jury.

32. Farrell, *Clarence Darrow*, discusses Darrow's lifelong opposition to the death penalty, though not in the Antonio case specifically.

33. Cairns, *The Enigma Woman*, 167.

34. Olmsted, *The Red Spy Queen*, 37, 164–65. Bentley walked into an FBI office in Connecticut in 1945, admitted being a spy, and elicited a promise to name names in exchange for not being charged or punished for her espionage activities.

35. There are many books that document the Rosenberg case. They include: Nizer, *The Implosion Conspiracy*; Radosh, *The Rosenberg File*; Scheir and Scheir, *Invitation to an Inquest*; Roberts, *The Brother*; and Schrecker, *Many are the Crimes*. The case has also garnered attention from playwrights and fiction writers, including E. L. Doctorow, who penned *The Book of Daniel* about the case. The Rosenbergs' sons, Michael and Robert Meeropol, also wrote a book, *We Are Your Sons*, based on prison letters from their parents. While scholars have unearthed evidence about Julius Rosenberg's involvement in low-level espionage, no such consensus exists about Ethel.

36. "Woman Fights Electric Chair," *Los Angeles Times*, July 2, 1934; "Woman Gets Stay After 2-Hour Wait at Execution Time," *New York Times*, June 29, 1934; "Mrs. Antonio Fails in New Trial Plea," *New York Times*, July 5, 1934; "Mrs. Antonio to Die in Chair Tonight," *New York Times*, August 9, 1934.

37. Roberts, *The Brother*, details Ethel Rosenberg's family background and the possible motives of judge Irving Kaufman, who subsequently worried that he would be remembered by history only for his role in the Rosenberg case. He was right.

38. Tony Kushner's play and miniseries focused on AIDS and its impact on a wide range of individuals, including Cohn, a closeted gay man who ultimately died of the disease. Cohn prosecuted the Rosenbergs and later claimed responsibility for recruiting judge Julius Kaufman to preside over their trial. Kaufman was deeply conservative and anti-Communist. He was also Jewish and labored diligently to avoid the appearance of favoring the Rosenbergs, who were also Jewish.

7. *I WANT TO LIVE!*

1. Walter Wanger to Edward S. Montgomery, December 7, 1956, folder 3, Walter Wanger Collection, Wisconsin Historical Society, Madison.

2. The quotes from Robert Wise are from Bernstein, *Walter Wanger*, xi. Information on Mankiewicz's original screenplay is from a letter written by Wanger to Edward S. Montgomery, July 23, 1957, folder 3, Walter Wanger Collection.

3. There are several biographies of Susan Hayward, born Edythe Marrener in Brooklyn, New York, in 1917. They include Kim R. Holston, *Susan Hayward, Her Films and Life*; Linet, *Susan Hayward*; and Robert LaGuardia and Gene Arceri, *Red: Tempestuous Life of Susan Hayward*.

4. Bernstein, *Walter Wanger*, 317.

5. Bernstein, *Walter Wanger*, 325–26.

6. Bernstein, *Walter Wanger*, 90–276.

7. Bernstein, *Walter Wanger*, 282.

8. Lesser, *Pictures at an Execution*, 50–51.

9. Bingham, "'I Do Want to Live!'" 7.

10. Nicole Rafter, "American Criminal Trial Films: An Overview of Their Development, 1930–2000," *Journal of Law and Society* 28, no. 1 (March 2001): 9–24.

11. Bingham, "'I Do Want to Live!'" 7; Marilyn Monroe played a murderous wife in *Niagara* (1952). Married to an emotionally troubled veteran, she and her lover plotted to kill her husband. He turned the tables on her, however, and killed her, but also ended up dead. Other female murderers in the 1950s included ten-year-old sociopath Rhoda Penmark in *The Bad Seed* (1956) and Cathy Ames, a bad-to-the-bone woman in John Steinbeck's *East of Eden* (1955). Ames killed her parents, tried to kill her husband, and murdered the madam who ran the house of prostitution where she worked.

12. Edward S. Montgomery to Walter Wanger, January 30 to March 19, 1957, folder 3, Walter Wanger Collection.

13. Montgomery to Wanger, January 18, 1957.

14. Montgomery to Wanger, June 5, 1957.

15. Wanger to Ed Rubin, January 20, 1958; Philip K. Scheuer, "Anxiety Jazz Killer-Diller," *Los Angeles Times*, April 14, 1958.

16. Montgomery to Wanger, December 10, 1957.

17. Montgomery to Wanger, May 7, 1957.

18. Montgomery to Wanger, May 18, 1957.

19. Montgomery to Wanger, September 4, 1957.

20. Montgomery to Wanger, June 25, 1957.

21. "To Whom It May Concern," affidavit signed by Edward S. Montgomery, June 18, 1958, folder 4, Walter Wanger Collection.

22. Bernstein, *Walter Wanger*, 330–38.

23. Montgomery to Wanger, February 5, 1958; Montgomery to Wanger, March 24, 1958, folder 3, Walter Wanger Collection. Though sources do not specify which execution Wise witnessed, Reese's is the only possibility since it occurred on February 14, 1958; the next execution did not occur until April 15, 1958. By that time, Wise was shooting *I Want to Live!*

24. Philip K. Scheuer, "Slayer Role Taxes Susan," *Los Angeles Times*, May 25, 1958. Beverly Linet also discusses Hayward's reaction to playing Graham in *Susan Hayward*, 225.

25. Bernstein, *Walter Wanger*, 334.

26. Bernstein, *Walter Wanger*, 327.

27. *I Want to Live!* directed by Robert Wise, produced by Walter Wanger, written by Don Mankiewicz and Nelson Giddings, United Artists Studio, 1958.

28. Bosley Crowther, "With Conviction, Film Drama of a Condemned Girl Makes its Points Plausibly," *New York Times*, November 23, 1958.

29. Philip K. Scheuer, "Taut 'I Want to Live!' Sets Nerves Aquiver," *Los Angeles Times*, November 16, 1958.

30. Bernstein, *Walter Wanger*, 338.

31. "The New Pictures," *Time*, November 24, 1958.

32. Bernstein, *Walter Wanger*, 338. In his 1942 novel, *The Stranger*, Albert Camus (offers a bleak view of human nature. His protagonist cannot manage any emotion—neither at his mother's funeral nor after killing a man who had threatened him earlier. In fact, the man's lack of appropriate emotion enables prosecutors to paint him as a sociopath and justify executing him. Unlike Barbara Graham, he did not seek solace in religion at the end of his life.

33. S. A. Abbott, "Upon the Law," *Los Angeles Times*, December 3, 1958.

34. Edward Grimm, "Readers Post Opinions on Four New Pictures," *New York Times*, November 30, 1958.

35. Correspondence between Wanger and Montgomery, December 1958 to January 1960, folder 3, Walter Wanger Collection.

36. Montgomery to Wanger, February 7, 1958.

37. Gene Blake, "Barbara Graham—Film and Fact," *Los Angeles Times*, November 28, 1958.

38. Philip K. Scheuer, "Times Critic Names Top Films of 1958," *Los Angeles Times*, January 4, 1959; Bosley Crowther, "The Best of 1958," *New York Times*, January 4, 1959; "City Film Critics Give Awards to 7," *New York Times*, January 25, 1959; "Gigi, Susan Hayward and Niven Win Oscars," *New York Times*, April 7, 1959; Bernstein, *Walter Wanger*, 338–41.

8. DUE PROCESS

1. Paul Coates, *Los Angeles Daily Mirror*, January 30, 1959. Conservative commentators declared "The Ballad of Barbara Graham" to be "out- and-out propaganda against capital punishment."

2. Fred Cook, "Capital Punishment: Does it Prevent Crime?" *Nation*, March 10, 1956, 194; Ethan Rarick also discusses the postwar climate on the death penalty in his book, *California Rising*, 163. Earlier periods of abolitionist activism included the reformist era of the 1830s and 1840s that also saw the emergence of the penitentiary system and the Progressive period, when reformers, including women, worked to ameliorate prison conditions and to establish separate prisons for women.

3. Bedau, *Death Penalty in America*, 25.

4. Theodore Hamm, *Rebel and a Cause*, 145.

5. John Poulos, "Capital Punishment, the Legal Process, and the Emergence of the Lucas Court in California," *University of California, Davis, Law Review* 23, no. 157 (1990); John H. Culver and Chantel Boyens, "Political Cycles of Life and Death: Capital Punishment as Public Policy in California," *Albany Law Review* 65, no. 4, (Summer 2002): 991–1012.

6. Brown and Adler, *Public Justice, Private Mercy*, 42–43. Ethan Rarick discusses the process by which Brown came to decide on the moratorium in his biography of the governor, *California Rising*, 160–69. Chessman's case was unusual for the time in that he was not condemned for murder, but for kidnapping. Additionally, his 1948 trial had been rife with problems. Most seriously, the court reporter died while transcribing the trial proceedings, leaving incomprehensible notes. Los Angeles Superior Court judge Charles Fricke refused a retrial, leaving Chessman grounds for appeal. While in prison, he authored four books.

7. Walter Wanger to Irwin Moskowitz, March 25, 1959, folder 4, Walter Wanger Collection. I have been unable to ascertain the outcome of Montgomery's lawsuit against *Cavalier* magazine and Fawcett Publications.

8. Walter Ames, "Three Tell Confession from Barbara Graham," *Los Angeles Times*, March 11, 1960, 10.

9. *Reporters' Transcript of Testimony*.

10. *Reporters' Transcript of Testimony*, 8–19.

11. *Reporters' Transcript of Testimony*. The statement by John True, which was taken in San Francisco on June 4, 1953, can also be found in the San Quentin Execution File for Barbara Graham, F3918, 409, 264.

12. Statement by John True, San Quentin Execution File. His allegations about the LAPD and criminals it purported to punish is reinforced by many other sources, both fiction and nonfiction. John Buntin, for example, most recently discussed police corruption in *L.A. Noir*. Fiction writer James Ellroy's best-known depictions of this cozy relationship can be found in his novels *L.A. Confidential* and *The Black Dahlia*.

13. *Reporters' Transcript of Testimony*, 72–78; Walter Ames, "Three Tell Confession from Barbara Graham," *Los Angeles Times*, March 11, 1960, 10.

14. *Reporters' Transcript of Testimony*, 52–77.

15. *Reporters' Transcript of Testimony*, 77.

16. *Reporters' Transcript of Testimony*, 72.

17. *Reporters' Transcript of Testimony*, 74.

18. *Reporters' Transcript of Testimony*, 54.

19. *Reporters' Transcript of Testimony*, 58–59.

20. *Reporters' Transcript of Testimony*, 59. Weissich spent another twenty-six years practicing law. After leaving the district attorney's office, he opened a private practice, but his earlier career came back to haunt him. A man he had successfully prosecuted for arson in 1955 was released from prison in 1986. The parolee came looking for Weissich and shot his former nemesis to death in his Marin County law office. Weissich was sixty-six when he died.

21. *Reporters' Transcript of Testimony*, 76.

22. *Reporters' Transcript of Testimony*, 89.

23. *Reporters' Transcript of Testimony*, 88.

24. *Reporters' Transcript of Testimony*, 40–48.

25. *Reporters' Transcript of Testimony*, 100.

26. *Reporters' Transcript of Testimony*, 98–101.

27. *Reporters' Transcript of Testimony*, 93–5.

28. "Jack Hardy, Attorney, Dies in Café," July 4, 1955.

29. "Confession Released in Barbara Graham Case," *Los Angeles Times*, March 29, 1960.

30. Walker, *The Case of Barbara Graham*, 78–81.

31. Walker, *The Case of Barbara Graham*, 53.

32. Walker, *The Case of Barbara Graham*, 86.

33. Walker, *The Case of Barbara Graham*, 125–30.

34. Robert R. Kirsch, "Barbara Graham Balances Justice," *Los Angeles Times*, July 14, 1961.

9. ABOLISHING THE DEATH PENALTY

1. Rarick, *California Rising*, 242. Rarick provides an extensive overview of the 1962 gubernatorial campaign, but focuses little attention on the issue of capital punishment. Theodore Hamm examines the death penalty and Brown's role in it, in *Rebel and a Cause*, 144–45.

2. Carl Greenberg, "Nixon for Death Penalty for Repeat Dope Sellers," *Los Angeles Times*, September 20, 1962.

3. Carl Greenberg, "Dope Death Penalty Proposal Hit by Brown," *Los Angeles Times*, October 13, 1962.

4. Jerry Gillam, "Duncan Case Hard One for Brown," *Los Angeles Times*, July 15, 1962. Brown also wrote of the Duncan case, among others, in his memoir, *Public Justice, Private Mercy*, 102–12.

5. Jerry Gillam, "Death Stay Bill Passes First Test," *Los Angeles Times*, April 10, 1963.

6. Daryl Lembke, "State to Consider Ban on Death Penalty Again," *Los Angeles Times*, June 3, 1963, p. D5.

7. Brown, *Public Justice, Private Mercy*, x–xiii. Information on the execution of Mitchell is from Joseph A. Spangler, "California's Death Row Dilemma," *Crime and Delinquency* 15, no. 1 (January 1969), 142–48.

8. Banner, *The Death Penalty*, 240–41.

9. Bedau, *Death Penalty in America*, 25.

10. R. W. Apple, "Zaretzki Pledges Vote," *New York Times*, February 25, 1965.

11. Apple, "Zaretzki Pledges Vote"; Hamm, *Rebel and a Cause*, 130–32. Information on states abolishing capital punishment is from Walter C. Reckless, "Use of the Death Penalty," *Crime and Delinquency* 15, no. 1 (January 1969), 49.

12. Reckless, "Use of the Death Penalty," 50.

13. Banner, *The Death Penalty*, 250; Garland, *Peculiar Institution*, 214–16. Most of the individual cases were from the south and involved African American defendants condemned by racist white juries. Garland wrote that such cases represented "a stinging insult to American law that, if left unanswered, threatened to bring the whole legal system into disrepute."

14. Jack Greenberg, "Variations of Attack on the Death Penalty," *Crime and Delinquency* 15, no 1. (January 1969), 112. Ethnic backgrounds of executed inmates in Texas comes from Rupert C. Koeninger, "Capital Punishment in Texas," *Crime and Delinquency* 15, no 1. (January 1969), 136.

15. "Chief Justice Traynor," *New York Times*, May 17, 1983.

16. Daryl Lembke, "Court Decision Keeps Gas Chamber Unused," *Los Angeles Times*, April 19, 1964.

17. "Trailblazing Bench: California High Court Often Points the Way for Judges Elsewhere," *Wall Street Journal*, July 20, 1972; Daryl Lembke, "State Supreme Court Faces New Barrage," *Los Angeles Times*, January 28. 1968.

18. Lembke, "Court Orders New Death Penalty Trials," *Los Angeles Times*, April 1, 1964.

19. Despite his harsh rhetoric, Reagan was not such a purist when it came to capital punishment. Just months after allowing the execution of Aaron

Mitchell, he commuted the death sentence of Calvin Thomas, a mentally ill man. He was not called on to make any other life or death decisions during his eight-year tenure.

20. Ron Einstoss, "Judge Refuses to Vacate Order on Death Penalty Testimony," *Los Angeles Times*, October 21, 1967.

21. Clinton Duffy's *88 Men and 2 Women* details the agonizing—for Duffy—experience of overseeing executions, even of individuals he disliked. This category included Caryl Chessman, whom Duffy described as arrogant and contemptible; and Louise Peete, who, Duffy maintained, concealed a black heart beneath a cheerful and grandmotherly demeanor.

22. Einstoss, "Any Killing Is Wrong, Duffy Tells Death Penalty Hearing," *Los Angeles Times*, November 3, 1967; Eschelman, *Death Row Chaplain*, 176.

23. Einstoss, "Former Prison Doctor Decries Death Penalty," *Los Angeles Times*, November 4, 1967.

24. Einstoss, "Fear of Death Penalty Saved Life in Robbery," *Los Angeles Times*, November 9, 1967.

25. Einstoss, "Former Prison Doctor Decries Death Penalty," *Los Angeles Times*, November 4, 1967.

26. Rarick, *California Rising*, 354–56.

27. Vila and Morris, *Capital Punishment*, 133; Ronald Ostrow, "Supreme Court Ruling Hits at Death Penalty," *Los Angeles Times*, June 4, 1968.

28. Banner, *The Death Penalty*, 255–57.

29. Ron Einstoss, "L.A. Killer's Plea Could End U.S. Death Penalty," *Los Angeles Times*, November 8, 1970; "The Law: Fatal Decision," *Time*, May 17, 1971, 46.

30. "Death Penalty to be Argued," *Times Daily*, July 29, 1971.

31. "Death Penalty to be Argued," *Times Daily*, July 29, 1971; "Shapp and Ex-Governors Call for End of Executions," *New York Times*, October 10, 1971.

32. Einstoss, "Judge Backs Constitutionality of Death Penalty in California," *Los Angeles Times*, November 28, 1967; Gene Blake, "Court Upholds Death Penalty," *Los Angeles Times*, November 19, 1968; Terry Robards, "Cost Suit Tests Cases on Death Row," *New York Times*, June 9, 1968.

33. California v. Anderson, 6 Cal. 3d 628. California's Constitution is one of the longest and most complex in the country. Ratified in 1879, it superseded the state's 1849 founding document. Many of its provisions reflect citizens' antipathy toward governmental overreach as a result of collusion between politicians and corporate behemoths, such as the Southern Pacific Railroad.

34. Richard Halloran, "Death Penalties Argued in Court," *New York Times*, January 18, 1972.

35. Earl Caldwell, "California Court, in 6–1 Vote, Bars Death Sentences," *New York Times*, February 19, 1972. Donald Wright proved reliably liberal throughout his tenure on the California Supreme Court, which enraged governor Ronald Reagan. In fact, just before Reagan left office, he tried to convince Wright—then in ill health—to resign, in order to give Reagan a high court appointment. By then, Wright had come to despise Reagan and refused. He waited to resign until Reagan's successor, Edmund G. Brown Jr., took office.

36. Sirhan B. Sirhan and all but one member of the Manson family remain in prison. The best book on the Manson family and murder of Sharon Tate and six other victims remains Vincent Bugliosi's *Helter Skelter: The True Story of the Manson Murders*. It tracks the background of the communal living arrangement that became the family, the murders and effort to find the killers, the trial of Manson and the three women—which became a media circus—and the death sentences. Patricia Krenwinkel and Leslie Van Houton remained in prison as of late 2011. Susan Atkins died in 2009 of brain cancer.

37. Bill Hazlett, "Waiting Isn't Over for Inmates of Death Row," *Los Angeles Times*, March 19, 1972.

38. Earl Caldwell, "California Court, in 6–1 vote, Bars Death Sentences," *New York Times*, February 19, 1972; Ed Meagher, "Death Penalty Ban Assailed by Reagan; State to Appeal," *Los Angeles Times*, February 19, 1972.

39. Alan M. Dershowitz, "A Decision That May Reach Far Beyond California," *New York Times*, February 20, 1972.

40. Vila and Morris, *Capital Punishment*, 140–41.

41. Banner, *The Death Penalty*, 267.

42. "Florida Restores the Death Penalty," *Los Angeles Times*, December 9, 1972; Vila and Morris, *Capital Punishment*, 148–49; Banner, *The Death Penalty*, 269–71.

43. Lesley Oelsner, "Decision is 7–2, Punishment is Ruled Acceptable, at Least in Murder Cases," *New York Times*, July 3, 1976.

44. Norman Mailer wrote of Gary Gilmore's life and death, as well as the media and politics of execution, in *The Executioner's Song*.

45. Much of the delay in executions in California can be attributed to governor Edmund G. Brown Jr. Like his father, "Jerry" Brown was an avid opponent of the death penalty. He had the opportunity in his two terms to appoint seven justices to the state supreme court. All were abolitionists. One

of them was Rose Elizabeth Bird, Brown's highly controversial chief justice appointee. The so-called Bird Court overturned all but two death sentences between 1977 and 1986.

46. Gale Cook, "A Penalty of Death; Barbara Graham's 1955 Execution has Eerie Echo in Robert Harris Case," *Montreal Gazette*, April 25, 1992.

47. Al Martinez, "When the People Cry for Blood," *Los Angeles Times*, March 31, 1990; Martinez, e-mail exchange with author, August 23, 2009.

10. THE ULTIMATE PENALTY

1. Nancy Wride, "Condemned and Waiting: Cynthia Coffman Came West for a New Life; Now She Faces 2nd Death Sentence," *Los Angeles Times*, April 26, 1992; Don Lasseter also writes of Coffman and Marlow in *Property of the Folsom Wolf: The Shocking True Story of Deviant Biker Couple Cynthia Coffman and Greg Marlow and their California Spree of Torture and Murder*.

2. Clarence Ray Allen spent the longest time on California's death row—twenty-six years—before his execution in 2006. At seventy-six, he was also the oldest man executed in California. David Mason, on the other hand, spent just under a decade there before his 1993 execution.

3. Caitlin Liu, "Execution of Women is Rare, Despite Sentencing," *Los Angeles Times*, August 10, 2000; Jose Arballo Jr., "Convicted Killer Lashes Out at Police, Attorneys," *Press-Enterprise* (Riverside CA), July 29, 1998; "Woman Gets Death for Three Sons' Murders," *San Diego Union-Tribune*, April 6, 2002; Sam Howe Verhovek, "Dead Women Waiting: Who's Who on Death Row," *New York Times*, February 8, 1998.

4. Ann O'Neill, "Woman Sentenced to Death in Paid Killings," *Los Angeles Times*, September 17, 1994; Gina Piccalo, "Fatal Lies, Angelina Rodriguez is Many Things—Wife, Mother, Sister, Daughter. She is Also a Convicted Killer," *Los Angeles Times*, March 9, 2005.

5. Howard Mintz, "Gender Complicates Debate Over Executions in California," *Knight Ridder Tribune News Service*, June 4, 2002.

6. Harriet Chiang, "Execution Debate: Should Women Die?" *San Francisco Chronicle*, January 31, 1998.

7. "Los Angeles Widow Sentenced to Death in Murder of her Husband," *Los Angeles Times*, June 11, 1993.

8. Calderon v. Thompson, Supreme Court of the United States, 97–215 120F–3d 1045.

9. "The Latest Execution Fails to End Doubts," *San Francisco Chronicle*, July 15, 1998, p; "Dead Sure," *Los Angeles Times*, July 16, 2011.

10. Maura Dolan, "Landlady Gets Life in Killings," *Los Angeles Times*, December 11, 1993. Dorothea Puente died in prison in early 2011.

11. Victor L. Streib, "Executing Women, Juveniles, and the Mentally Retarded: Second Class Citizens in Capital Punishment," in *America's Experiment with Capital Punishment*, eds. James R. Acker, Robert M. Bohm, and Charles S. Lanier, 304. According to Streib, 89 percent of condemned women had their sentences overturned between the 1970s and 2002. Since the late 1970s, 165 women have received death sentences. Twelve have been executed, and 53 remained on death row as of February 2012. Thus, more than 100 either had their sentences overturned or died in prison.

12. Aileen Wuornos, like Barbara Graham, captured the attention, though not the sympathy, of filmmakers. The 2002 film *Monster* depicted Wuornos as a victim of childhood abuse and neglect. She may have killed her first victim because he was trying to rape her, but filmmakers made it clear that she chose subsequent victims at random, with robbery as a motive, as well as a desire to impress her female lover. Charlize Theron, who played Wuornos, won a best actress Oscar for the role.

13. D.L. Stewart, "What's the Fuss over Granny?" *Daily News* (Dayton OH), February 27, 2000; Mary Alice Davis, "A Violent Life, Ended Violently," *Austin American Statesman*, March 3, 2000. Elizabeth Rapaport also discussed the cases of Karla Faye Tucker, Judy Buenoano, and Betty Lou Beets in "Equality of the Damned: The Execution of Women on the cusp of the Twenty-first Century," *Ohio Northern University Law Review* 26, no. 3 (2000): 581–600.

14. Ginnie Graham, "State Executes Woman; Marilyn Plantz Dies for Role in Murder of her Husband," *Tulsa World*, May 2, 2001.

15. Barbara Hoberock, "Woman Dies for Murder," *Tulsa World*, December 5, 2001.

16. "Alabama Executes First Woman in 40 Years," *Charleston Daily Mail*, May 10, 2002.

17. "Ruling Lets Execution Proceed Without Appeals," *Commercial Appeal* (Memphis TN), January 15, 2000.

18. Michael Graczyk, "Woman Executed for Slaying Husband, Kids," *Beaumont Enterprise*, September 15, 2005.

19. In *The Innocent Man*, John Grisham details the case of Ron Williamson and Dennis Fritz, both convicted of rape and murder in Ada, Oklahoma, in 1987, despite a paucity of evidence linking them to the crimes. Williamson was condemned to die, and Fritz received a life sentence. Both eventually were freed after police picked up the real killer. The interview with Grisham is featured on Amazon.com's page featuring Grisham's book. Writer Robert Mayer wrote of two earlier wrongful convictions in *The Dreams of Ada: A True Story of Murder, Obsession, and a Small Town*.

20. David Grann, "Trial by Fire: Did Texas Execute an Innocent Man?" *New Yorker*, September 7, 2009, 42–63. Grann's story suggests that Cameron Willingham was innocent and that Texas officials knew this to be true but executed him anyway. After the *New Yorker* article appeared, Willingham's former wife, Stacy, wrote an article for a Texas newspaper contending that her husband had confessed to her just before he died. Others suggested this would have been a foolish action, since Willingham was still appealing his death sentence.

21. Hollway and Gauthier, *Killing Time*; Dow, *Autobiography of an Execution*.

22. Cohen, *The Wrong Men*, 150–54.

23. Haines, *Against Capital Punishment*. Herbert Haines is one of many scholars who use the phrase "a mile wide and an inch deep" to describe today's support for capital punishment. Troy Davis's September 2011 execution in Georgia drew many protests and raised many issues about death-penalty politics. Convicted of murdering a policeman, many of the prosecution witnesses recanted their testimony and yet the state proceeded with Davis's execution.

Selected Bibliography

MANUSCRIPT COLLECTIONS

San Quentin Execution File for Barbara Graham, California Department of Corrections. California State Archives, Sacramento.

California State Legislature. *Reporters' Transcript of Testimony Before the Assembly Interim Committee on Criminal Procedure, Sub-committee Hearing Regarding Alleged Discrepancies and Suppression of Evidence: Re Barbara Graham*, March 21, 1960.

Walter Wanger Collection, Wisconsin Historical Society, Madison.

PUBLISHED WORKS

Acker, James R., Robert M. Bohm, and Charles S. Lanier. *America's Experiment with Capital Punishment: Reflections on the Past, Present, and Future of the Ultimate Penalty Sanction*. Durham NC: Carolina Academic Press, 2003.

Bakken, Gordon M., and Brenda Farrington. *Women Who Kill Men: California Courts, Gender, and the Law*. Lincoln: University of Nebraska Press, 2009.

Banner, Stuart. *The Death Penalty: An American History*. Cambridge MA: Harvard University Press, 2002.

Bass, Jack, and Marilyn Thompson. *Ol' Strom: An Unauthorized Biography of Strom Thurmond*. Columbia: University of South Carolina Press, 2003.

Bedau, Hugo Adam, ed. *The Death Penalty in America*, 3rd ed. New York: Oxford University Press, 1982.

Bedau, Hugo Adam, and Michael C. Radelet. "Miscarriages of Justice in Potentially Capital Cases." *Stanford Law Review* 40, no 1. (November 1987): 21–179.

Bernstein, Matthew. *Walter Wanger, Hollywood Independent*. Minneapolis: University of Minnesota Press, 2000.

Bessler, John D. *Kiss of Death: America's Love Affair with the Death Penalty*. Boston: Northeastern University Press, 2003.

Bingham, Dennis. "'I Do Want to Live!'": Female Voices, Male Discourse, and Hollywood Biopics." *Cinema Journal* 38, no. 3 (Spring 1999): 3–26.

Birch, Helen, ed. *Moving Targets: Women, Murder, and Representation*. Berkeley: University of California Press, 1994.

Blum, Howard. *American Lightning: Terror, Mystery, the Birth of Hollywood, and the Crime of the Century*. New York: Crown, 2008.

Bonner, Raymond. *Anatomy of Injustice: A Murder Case Gone Wrong*. New York: Knopf, 2012.

Brown, Edmund G., and Dick Adler. *Public Justice, Private Mercy: A Governor's Education on Death Row*. New York: Knightsbridge, 1990.

Bugliosi, Vincent, and Curt Gentry. *Helter Skelter: The True Story of the Manson Murders*. New York: W. W. Norton, 1974.

Buntin, John. *L.A. Noir: The Struggle for the Soul of America's Most Seductive City*. New York: Random House, 2009.

Cain, James M. *Double Indemnity*. New York: Vintage, 1989.

———. *The Postman Always Rings Twice*. New York: Vintage, 1989.

Cairns, Kathleen A. *The Enigma Woman: The Death Sentence of Nellie May Madison*. Lincoln: University of Nebraska Press, 2007.

———. *Front-Page Women Journalists, 1920–1950*. Lincoln: University of Nebraska Press, 2003.

———. *Hard Time at Tehachapi: California's First Women's Prison*. Albuquerque: University of New Mexico Press, 2009.

Carlson, A. Cheree, *The Crimes of Womanhood: Defining Femininity in a Court of Law*. Urbana: University of Illinois Press, 2009.

Cohen, Stanley. *The Wrong Men: America's Epidemic of Wrongful Death Row Convictions*. New York: Carroll & Graf, 2003.

Culver, John H., and Chantel Boyers, "Political Cycles of Life and Death: Capital Punishment as Public Policy in California." *Albany Law Review* 65, no. 4 (Summer 2002): 991–1012.

Cuordileone, K. A. *Manhood and American Political Culture in the Cold War*. New York: Routledge, 2006.

Davis, Bernice Freeman, and Al Hirshberg. *The Desperate and the Damned*. New York: Thomas Y. Crowell, 1961.

Deakin, James. *A Grave for Bobby: The Greenlease Slaying*. New York: Morrow, 1990.

Denton, Sally. *The Pink Lady: The Many Lives of Helen Gahagan Douglas*. New York: Bloomsbury, 2009.

Dorn, T. Felder. *The Guns at Meeting Street*. Columbia: University of South Carolina Press, 2006.

Dow, David R. *The Autobiography of an Execution*. New York: Twelve, 2010.

Duffy, Clinton T., and Al Hirshberg. *88 Men and 2 Women*. New York: Pocket, 1963.

Duffy, Clinton T. *The San Quentin Story*. Westport CT: Greenwood, 1968.

Eggers, Dave, and Lola Vollen, eds. *Surviving Justice: America's Wrongfully Convicted and Exonerated*. New York: McSweeney's, 2005.

Ehrenreich, Barbara. *The Hearts of Men: American Dreams and the Flight from Commitment*. New York: Random House, 1987.

Eschelman, Byron. *Death Row Chaplain*. New York: Prentice Hall, 1961.

Farrell, Harry. *Shallow Grave in Trinity County*. New York: St. Martins, 1999.

Farrell, John A. *Clarence Darrow: Attorney for the Damned*. New York: Doubleday, 2011.

Flowers, Anna. *Wanton Woman: Sue Logue, Strom Thurmond, and the Bloody Logue-Timmerman Feud*. iUniverse, 2007

Foster, Teree E. "I Want to Live! Federal Judicial Values in Death Penalty Cases: Preservation of Rights or Punctuality of Execution?" *Oklahoma City University Law Review* 22, no. 1 (1997): 63–95.

Franklin, Diana Britt. *The Goodbye Door: The Incredible True Story of America's First Female Serial Killer to Die in the Electric Chair*. Kent OH: Kent State University Press, 2006.

Gado, Mark. *Death Row Women: Murder, Justice and the New York Press*. Westport CT: Praeger, 2007.

Garland, David. *Peculiar Institution: America's Death Penalty in an Age of Abolition*. Cambridge MA: Harvard University Press, 2010.

Gillespie, L. Kay. *Dancehall Ladies: The Crimes and Executions of America's Condemned Women*. Lanham MD: University Press of America, 2000.

Gordon, Linda. *Dorothea Lange: A Life Beyond Limits*. New York: W. W. Norton, 2009.

Gray, Ian, and Moira Stanley. *A Punishment in Search of a Crime: Americans Speak Out Against the Death Penalty.* New York: Avon, 1989.

Grisham, John. *The Innocent Man: Murder and Injustice in a Small Town.* New York: Doubleday, 2006.

Gross, Samuel R. "Lost Lives: Miscarriages of Justice in Capital Cases." *Law and Contemporary Problems* 61, no. 4 (Autumn 1998): 125–52.

Haines, Herbert. *Against Capital Punishment: The Anti–Death Penalty Movement in America, 1972–94.* New York: Oxford University Press, 1996.

Hamm, Theodore. *Rebel and a Cause: Caryl Chessman and the Politics of the Death Penalty in Postwar California, 1948–1974.* Berkeley: University of California Press, 2000.

Hollway, John, and Ronald M. Gauthier, *Killing Time: An 18-Year Odyssey from Death Row to Freedom.* New York: Skyhorse, 2010.

Holston, Kim R. *Susan Hayward: Her Films and Life.* Jefferson NC McFarland, 2002.

Irwin, John. *Unless the Threat of Death is Behind Them: Hardboiled Fiction and Noir Film.* Baltimore MD: Johns Hopkins University Press, 2008.

Knox, Sara. *Murder: A Tale of Modern American Life.* Durham NC: Duke University Press, 1998.

LaGuardia, Robert, and Gene Arceri. *Red: The Tempestuous Life of Susan Hayward.* London: Robson, 1998.

Lesser, Wendy. *Pictures at an Execution.* Cambridge MA: Harvard University Press, 1998.

Linet, Beverly. *Susan Hayward: Portrait of a Survivor.* New York: Atheneum, 1980.

Malcolm, Janet. *The Journalist and the Murderer.* New York: Vintage, 1990.

Mailer, Norman. *The Executioner's Song.* New York: Little, Brown, 1979.

Marling, William. *The American Noir: Hammett, Cain, and Chandler.* Athens: University of Georgia Press, 1995.

McCann, Sean. *Gumshoe America: Hardboiled Fiction and the Rise and Fall of New Deal Liberalism.* Durham NC: Duke University Press, 2000.

McKellar, Landis. *The "Double Indemnity Murder": Ruth Snyder, Judd Gray, and New York's Trial of the Century.* Ithaca NY: Syracuse University Press, 2006.

Neal, Bill. *Sex, Murder, and the Unwritten Law: Courting Justice Texas Style.* Lubbock: Texas Tech University Press, 2009.

Nizer, Louis. *The Implosion Conspiracy.* New York: Doubleday, 1973.

O'Brien, Geoffrey. *Hardboiled America: Lurid Paperbacks and the Masters of Noir.* Cambridge MA: Da Capo, 1997.

Olmsted, Kathryn S. *The Red Spy Queen: A Biography of Elizabeth Bentley.* Chapel Hill: University of North Carolina Press, 2002.

———. *Real Enemies: Conspiracy Theories and American Democracy, World War I to 9/11.* New York: Oxford University Press, 2009.

O'Shea, Kathleen. *Women and the Death Penalty in the United States.* Westport CT: Praeger, 1998.

Parrish, Michael. *For the People: Inside the Los Angeles County District Attorney's Office, 1850–2000.* Los Angeles: Angel City, 2001.

Phillips, Gene.D. *Creatures of Darkness: Raymond Chandler, Detective Fiction, and Film Noir.* Lexington: University Press of Kentucky, 2000.

Phillips, Lela Bond. *The Lena Baker Story.* San Antonio TX: Wings, 2001.

Radosh, Ronald. *The Rosenberg File.* New Haven CT: Yale University Press, 1997.

Rafter, Nicole. "American Criminal Trial Films: An Overview of their Development, 1930–2000." *Journal of Law and Society* 28, no. 1 (March 2001): 9–24.

Rapaport, Elizabeth. "The Death Penalty and Gender Discrimination," *Law and Society Review* 25, no. 2 (1991): 367–82.

———. "Equality of the Damned: The Execution of Women on the Cusp of the Twenty-First Century," *Ohio Northern University Law Review* 26, no. 3 (2000) 581–600.

Rarick, Ethan. *California Rising: The Life and Times of Pat Brown.* Berkeley: University of California Press, 2005.

Rawson, Tabor. *I Want to Live! The Analysis of a Murder.* New York: Signet, 1959.

Roberts, Sam. *The Brother: The Untold Story of David Greenglass and How He Sent His Sister Ethel Rosenberg to the Electric Chair.* New York: Random House, 2001.

Rogin, Michael. *Ronald Reagan, the Movie, and Other Episodes in Political Demonology.* Berkeley: University of California Press, 1987.

Scheir, Walter, and Miriam Scheir. *Invitation to an Inquest.* New York: Pantheon, 1983.

Schrecker, Ellen. *Many Are the Crimes.* Princeton NJ: Princeton University Press, 1999.

Shipman, Marlin. *The Penalty is Death: U.S. Newspaper Coverage of Women's Executions.* Columbia: University of Missouri Press, 2002.

Slettedahl, Heidi MacPherson. "Spectacular Expectations: Women, Law, and Film." *Journal of American Studies* 41, no. 3 (October 2007), 641–58.

Spangler, Joseph A, ed. *Crime and Delinquency* 15, no. 1 (January 1969).

Spillane, Mickey. *I, the Jury*. New York: NAL, 2001.

Stanford, Sally. *Lady of the House*. New York: Ballantine, 1972.

St. Joan, Jacqueline, and Annette Bennington McElhiney. *Beyond Portia: Women, Law, and Literature in the United States*. Boston: Northeastern University Press, 1997.

Streib, Victor L., ed. *A Capital Punishment Anthology*. Cincinnati OH: Anderson, 1997.

———. *The Fairer Death: Executing Women in Ohio*. Athens: Ohio University Press, 2006.

Strunk, Mary Elizabeth. *Wanted Women: An American Obsession in the Reign of J. Edgar Hoover*. Lawrence: University of Kansas Press, 2010.

Vila, Bryan, and Cynthia Morris. *Capital Punishment in the U.S.: A Documentary History*. Westport CT: Greenwood, 1997.

Walker, Bill. *The Case of Barbara Graham*. New York: Ballantine, 1961.

Watkins, Maurine. *Chicago: The Story Behind the Broadway Smash Hit!* Carbondale: Southern Illinois University Press, 1997.